2nd Edition

TEACHING READING
COMPREHENSION PROCESSES

Judith Westphal Irwin
University of Connecticut

ALLYN AND BACON
Boston London Toronto Sydney Tokyo Singapore

Library of Congress Cataloging-in-Publication Data

Irwin, Judith Westphal.
    Teaching reading comprehension processes / Judith Westphal Irwin.
--2nd ed.
        p. cm.
    Includes bibliographical references.
    ISBN 0-13-892738-3
    1. Reading comprehension. 2. Reading. I. Title.
LB1050.45.I79 1991
428.4'3—dc20   90-35166
                                                         CIP

Copyright © 1991, 1986 by Allyn and Bacon
A Division of Simon & Schuster, Inc.
160 Gould Street
Needham Heights, MA 02194

Printed in the United States of America

10 9 8 7 6 5 4 3   96 95 94 93

ISBN 0-13-892738-3

CONTENTS

11   Informal Comprehension Assessment   194

12   Developmental and Remedial Applications: Some Examples   208

Index   225

PREFACE

This is a book about helping people understand what they read. The activities suggested are all based on the assumption that the students can already read the individual words: the purpose of this pedagogy is to help people who can already read words to better understand sentences, paragraphs, articles, chapters, books, and so on in ways that are useful to them.

Thus, this book is intended for all teachers. Elementary school teachers who overtly teach reading can use the material in this book to teach reading better. Secondary school and content-area teachers can use the suggestions in this book to help their students better understand the reading materials used in their courses.

This book is also intended for use as a college text for reading methods courses at both the undergraduate and graduate levels. For undergraduates preparing to be teachers, it will provide many useful ideas for their future teaching careers. For graduate students, reading researchers, and my colleagues who are training such, this book is intended to provide a review and synthesis of the current state of the art in comprehension research as well as a new application of theory to practice.

The title of this book, *Teaching Reading Comprehension Processes*, reflects the fact that the pedagogy suggested herein is based on recent discourse processing research in such fields as reading, cognitive psychology, and psycholinguistics. The premise is that now that we can describe some of the processes involved in comprehension, we can devise even more effective ways for helping students to use those processes. Thus, as the title suggests, this book is about teaching comprehension as a unified set of processes.

A second special feature of the pedagogy in this text is that it attempts to integrate discourse processing research with general principles of good teaching. Basic themes include the importance of providing each student with activities at his or her level of competence, using ongoing assessment for instructional choices, using instruction and modeling, teaching in a variety of meaningful contexts, integrating holistic and subskill approaches, and encouraging students to take an active role in their own learning.

Finally, the theory explained in this book represents an attempt to define comprehension in relation to all of the contexts that affect it. This is not an easy task! Comprehension involves a complex interplay of reader, text, and situational contexts that can be only partially specified.

Part I of this text presents a general model of the comprehension process that has emerged from recent research. This model is not the only one possible, nor is it final and complete; instead, I have tried to present a model that synthesizes current research in a way that is usable in the classroom. Thus, for each process described, specific teaching activities are suggested for both developmental and remedial situations. These suggestions are largely drawn from the plethora of recent articles presenting new and exciting ways to teach comprehension.

Chapter 2 of Part I provides an overview of the general teaching considerations on which the suggestions in this book are based. In particular, these include creating a literate environment, using various types of print, giving students ownership of their reading activities, making reading and writing connections, arranging discussions and collaborative learning activities, and using explicit instruction, process questions, and substantive feedback to focus discussion on the process on comprehension. All of these help to empower the learner to become actively involved in the process of comprehending.

Part II deals with the reader, text, and situational contexts each teacher must consider every time he or she teaches comprehension. A description of the importance of each context is followed by the implications for teaching. For instance, Chapter 7 presents ways for teachers to build background and increase motivation. Chapter 8 shows teachers how to examine reading materials critically, and Chapter 9 includes a demonstration of how to choose reading purposes and methods.

Part III extends the discussion of the general methodologies that can be used to teach reading comprehension. In Chapter 10, a new taxonomy for questions is presented along with the distinction between product and process questions. Chapter 11 describes an informal, multicontext approach to assessment, and Chapter 12 presents an overall structure for organizing lessons as well as fictional examples of teachers who are implementing comprehension process teaching into basal, whole-language, remedial, and content-area situations.

Those who have used this book before will notice that I have made some changes since the first edition. First, the general teaching suggestions that were in Chapter 12 have been moved to Chapter 2 in response to the large number of students who have said that understanding the pedagogic theory early in the text would help with interpreting subsequent chapters. Moreover, that pedagogic theory has been expanded to include procedures found to be useful by teachers who have implemented the suggestions in the first edition. In addition, I have attempted to update the theoretical and practical material with discussions of curriculum developments and research studies that have come to my attention since the submission of the first edition. Notable additions include reciprocal teaching, K–W–L, and reading response journals. Finally, I have attempted to make the applications to naturalistic, whole-language-based programs more explicit. My students have shown me that the material herein is useful to teachers with a wide range of philosophies, so I have extended the variety of my examples to encourage these adaptations.

As before, I have attempted to describe, synthesize, and apply everything I know about reading comprehension. I have tried to make new research theories and terminology understandable and usable without losing the complexity of the analysis. Above all, I have tried to write a book that will liberate teachers from being managers of meaningless activities and students from being passive recipients of meaningless drill. Much in current research can help with this, and I have attempted to communicate it here.

ACKNOWLEDGMENTS

I wish to thank my students for their numerous helpful suggestions, my reviewers at Prentice Hall, those who have kindly granted reprint permission for previously published material, and all the friends and colleagues who have contributed indirectly but substantially with their patient advice and support.

Judith Westphal Irwin

COMPREHENSION PROCESSES: AN OVERVIEW

All good reading instruction is based on an understanding of what is being taught. Thus, a book on teaching reading comprehension must include a description of the reading comprehension process itself. Indeed, one of the big problems in designing methods for teaching comprehension has been that comprehension is such a complex process that it has been difficult to understand fully.

In this chapter you will find an introduction to the description of reading comprehension on which this book is based. First, five types of processes that seem to occur during comprehension are briefly described. Following this is a discussion of the factors that influence what a reader understands when he or she reads. Finally, a definition of comprehension is presented.

Take some time to familiarize yourself with the new vocabulary introduced in this chapter, but do not be concerned if the new concepts are still a little unclear. This is just an introduction! All of these new terms will be discussed in more depth later in this book. In fact, you may wish to read this chapter again after you have finished reading all of Parts One and Two.

TRADITIONAL SUBSKILLS MODELS AND METHODS

If we were to begin with an examination of how comprehension has traditionally been taught, we would see that it is usually taught in the form of isolable subskills. Students are given worksheets or are asked questions that require them to make comparisons, find main ideas, recall sequences, and so forth. Recently, however, this subskill model of comprehension has received considerable criticism. Though, certainly, some of the activities have been worthwhile, some problems with this approach are worthy of note.

First, little research supports any one list of skills or, indeed, substantiates the theory that separable skills exist in the first place (see Rosenshine, 1980). As a result, lists of subskills vary considerably in terms of what skills they include. In a study of five commonly used lists, Rosenshine (1980) found that although several skills were found on all the lists, many more were unique to the separate lists. As a result, limited consistency exists in what has been taught as comprehension.

Another problem with the traditional subskills approach is the fact that the skill lists and the related activities tend to be based on the premise that comprehension is a passive, static process. Activities generally have a "one right answer" approach and are based on the assumption that the one right answer is to be found in the reading selection itself. There is little evidence of an awareness of the active nature of the reading process or of the facts that different people view situations differently and that reading strategies are related to purposes and situations. Thus, many of these instructional programs produce passive readers who cannot comprehend in realistic situations that require active inference and strategy selection.

COMPREHENSION PROCESSES[1]

Perhaps, instead of lists of isolable subskills, we need a model of what is actually happening when a reader comprehends. Perhaps, if we can understand how comprehension occurs, then we can teach students to do it. The model presented in this book, though not necessarily a perfect replica of the process, represents an attempt to model comprehension in a way that is instructionally useful. It is largely based on the models presented by cognitive psychologists (Just & Carpenter, 1980; Kintsch & van Dijk, 1978; Rumelhart, 1976), although it also integrates much of the recent research conducted by reading educators.

All of this research seems to indicate that at least five types of processes occur simultaneously during comprehension. Each of these involves various subprocesses. Let us look at each one of the basic processes separately before discussing how they fit together in one unitary act. (Remember, do not worry if you find these difficult to understand. Each will be discussed in more detail in future chapters.)

Microprocesses

The reader's first task is to derive meaning from the individual idea units in each sentence and to decide which of these ideas to remember. The initial chunking and selective recall of individual idea units within individual sentences can be called *microprocessing*.

[1]See Chapters Two through Six.

Assuming that the meanings of individual words are understood (see Chapter Seven), at least two subprocesses are required for understanding individual sentences. The first is the grouping of words into meaningful phrases. This is often called "chunking," and it requires a basic understanding of syntax and its use in written language. For instance, in sentence 1a, a reader would need to realize that "red" should be grouped with "balloon" because it tells what kind of balloon, that "slowly" similarly describes "disappeared" rather than "balloon," and so forth.

1a. The red balloon slowly disappeared into the blue sky.

A good reader would automatically "chunk" the sentence in this fashion while reading, and research indicates that good and poor comprehenders often differ in their responsiveness to these boundaries between meaningful phrases (Cohen & Freeman, 1978; Levin & Kaplan, 1970; and others).

A second major subprocess involved in microprocessing is the selection of idea units to remember. For example, when reading sentence 1a, a reader might choose to remember only that a balloon disappeared. If another idea, such as the fact that the balloon was red, was particularly important to the progress of the narrative that fact might also be remembered. As students mature, they are asked to read longer and longer passages. It is impossible to remember every detail (without extensive application of study strategies), and good readers select what is important in each sentence, retaining only that information in memory (Kintsch & van Dijk, 1978).

Integrative Processes

Readers can recall what they read only if the individual ideas are connected into a coherent whole (Kintsch & van Dijk, 1978; Thorndyke, 1976; and others). This means that the relationships between clauses and sentences must also be comprehended. The process of understanding and inferring the relationships between individual clauses and sentences can be called *integrative processing*.

Integrative processing requires the ability to identify pronoun referents, infer causation and sequence, and make other relevant inferences about the total situation being described. For instance, for sentences 1b and 1c, several inferences could be made to integrate these ideas.

1b. John went to the store.
1c. He was hungry.

First, one must infer that "he" refers to John. Second, one might infer that he went to the store *because* he was hungry. This would involve the added inferences that the store sold food and that he was going to buy some. (Note the amount of active inferring necessary to understand the relationships between two very simple sentences.)

Macroprocesses

Ideas are connected and retained in memory more effectively if they are organized around an overall organizational pattern. The main topics in an organized text make up a kind of summary. The process of synthesizing and organizing individual idea units into a summary or organized series of related general ideas can be called *macroprocessing*.

At least two subprocesses are necessary for macroprocessing. The first is summarizing the passage. This can also involve deleting unimportant information, and identifying or constructing general or main idea statements that summarize many details.

The second major macroprocessing strategy is using the author's general organizational pattern to organize one's own memory representation. Research has repeatedly shown that students who use the author's organizational pattern when they recall something they have read tend to recall more than those who do not (Meyer, Brandt, & Bluth, 1980).

Elaborative Processes

As we read, we often make inferences not necessarily intended by the author and not required for a literal interpretation. For instance, we may make a prediction about what might happen, we may form a vivid mental picture, or we may think about how the information relates to something similar we have experienced. The process of making inferences not necessarily intended by the author can be called *elaborative processing*.

Research indicates that elaborations help us to recall the text. In general, readers who make elaborations recall more than those who do not (see Reder, 1980). It is important to note, however, that elaborations must have some relationship to the text. Inappropriate elaborating may actually interfere with comprehension of the author's intended message.

Metacognitive Processes

Metacognition may be loosely defined as conscious awareness and control of one's own cognitive processes. This involves knowing when one does or does not understand something and knowing how to go about achieving a cognitive goal, such as successful comprehension or long-term recall. The process of selecting, evaluating, or regulating one's strategies to control comprehension and long-term recall can be called *metacognitive processing*.

Study strategies are the most common of the metacognitive processes. Rehearsing, reviewing, underlining, and note taking are all metacognitive processes that facilitate remembering. At a more basic level, checking an earlier part of the text to resolve an inconsistency, and even just being aware that something is unclear, are examples of ways that readers can have control over their own comprehension.

The Total Comprehension Process

All of the processes described earlier are included in Figure 1-1. Study this figure. It shows the five types of comprehension processes and their constituent subprocesses.

We are now ready to begin to define comprehension itself. On the basis of the previous discussion, we can define comprehension as

> [the] process in which a reader understands and selectively recalls ideas in individual sentences (microprocesses), understands and/or infers relationships between clauses and/or sentences (integrative processes), organizes and synthesizes the recalled ideas into general ideas (macroprocesses), and make inferences not necessarily intended by the author (elaborative processes). The reader controls and adjusts these processes according to the immediate goal (metacognitive processes). All these processes occur virtually simultaneously, constantly interacting with each other (interactive hypothesis).

The *interactive hypothesis* was added to this definition to stress that these processes do not occur separately. We must assume that they occur almost simultaneously in no prespecified order, and that they interact with each other. This is reflected in the fact that each process can, in some situations, contribute to the success of another. For instance, understanding the organization (macroprocess) can help a reader to infer intersentential relationships (integrative process). Elaborating on one detail (elaborative process) can lead to recalling other details selectively (microprocess). This *interactive hypothesis* has important implications for teaching.

Now we have a definition that seems to describe comprehension in terms of what is actually happening when a reader comprehends. Can we now teach students to comprehend everything, just by teaching these processes? Unfortunately, the answer is probably no. This definition still doesn't really explain why students who *can comprehend* in one situation *cannot comprehend* in another or why students with *similar* abilities often seem to perform *differently* at the same task. To understand these phenomena, we must understand how the comprehension process is influenced by the total context in which it occurs.

COMPREHENSION CONTEXTS

It is impossible to separate any act of comprehension from the contextual factors that influence it (see Spiro, 1980). The individual reader's characteristics (reader context), the specific text being read[2] (text context), and the total situation (situational context) all exert a strong influence on what is comprehended.

---

[2]Throughout this book, the term "text" will be used to refer to the written passage being read. It is not meant to refer to a textbook, which is only one kind of text. Magazine articles, newspapers, essays, and paragraphs are examples of other types of texts that might be read.

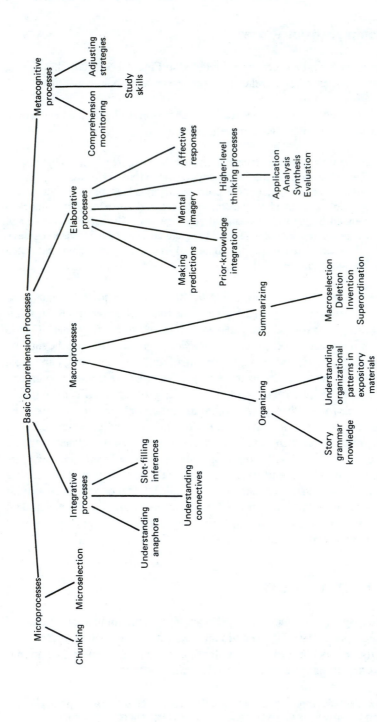

FIGURE 1-1   Basic Comprehension Processes

6

Comprehension is an active process to which each reader brings his or her individual attitudes, interests, expectations, skills, and prior knowledge (reader context). Because the writer's message can never be entirely explicit, the reader must actively infer and interpret what is on the page in the light of what he or she brings to the task. A good example of the effects of reader characteristics is provided by Anderson, Reynolds, Schallert, and Goetz (1977). They gave readers an ambiguous passage using words such as "play," "score," and "arrangement." Music students tended to interpret the passage as a discussion of a woodwind ensemble, whereas physical education students tended to interpret it as a card game. In addition, 62 percent of the students said that the other interpretation had never occurred to them.

Research has also provided many examples of how text characteristics can influence what is comprehended. Readability research has shown that word familiarity and sentence length can affect comprehensibility. More recent research has revealed that passage coherence and organization may also affect comprehensibility. Indeed, Chapter Eight in this text provides a checklist of thirty-five text factors that may influence the comprehension process.

Thus, we need a definition of comprehension that mentions both reader and text influences. One definition that does emphasize both of these has been suggested by Johnston (1981): "Reading comprehension is viewed as the process of using one's own prior knowledge and the writer's cues to infer the author's intended meaning" (p. 16). This definition stresses the fact that comprehension is affected by both the reader's background and the text characteristics. It also stresses the active role of the reader who can only infer the complete message from what is explicitly stated. One change in Johnston's wording that might be made is that changing "knowledge" to "experiences." This could be done to emphasize that *both cognitive* prior knowledge and *affective* attitudes and interests influence what is inferred.

On the basis of this definition, we can now predict that two readers will comprehend similarly only when they have very similar interests and backgrounds and are reading the same text; however, is it also possible for two similar readers reading the same passage to comprehend differently? The answer is definitely yes: a high school student reading a magazine article in the dentist's office is likely to comprehend differently from a similar student reading the same article to prepare for a debate. A sixth-grade student reading a book for a book-sharing club at the local library may comprehend differently from a similar student reading the same book for language arts class. You can probably think of other examples in which what is comprehended is affected by the total situation (situational context).

All of the factors influencing what is comprehended, the *comprehension contexts,* have been diagrammed as a "contexts pyramid" (see Figure 1-2) by Mosenthal (1984); this diagram emphasizes the fact that what is comprehended is influenced by the individual reader's characteristics, the text's characteristics, and the situation-related factors: the situation organizer, the task, and the total setting. In the classroom, the situation organizer is usually the teacher; the task usually consists of various instructions, questions, and/or activities provided in the teacher's manual

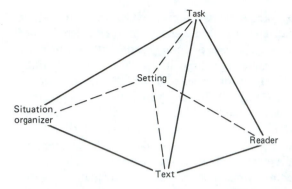

The Context Pyramid of reading comprehension. Following Jenkins (1979, p. 432), each vertex represents a cluster of variables of a given type shown to influence reading comprehension. Each degree represents a two-way interaction between Contexts; each plane calls attention to a three-way interaction, and the entire Figure represents the five-way interaction of all the variables that could possibly influence reading comprehension.

FIGURE 1-2   Context Pyramid of Reading Comprehension

Source: P. Mosenthal, "Reading Comprehension Research from a Classroom Perspective," in *Promoting Reading Comprehension,* ed. J. Flood. (Newark, Del.: International Reading Association, 1984), p. 18. Reprinted with the permission of Peter Mosenthal and the International Reading Association.

or workbook; and the setting is usually the classroom in an individual, small-group, or whole-class format.

DEFINITION OF COMPREHENSION

At this point, then, it may be useful to expand on Johnston's (1981) definition to include the situational contexts that influence comprehension. Perhaps the following expanded definition will suffice:

> Comprehension can be seen as the process of using one's own prior experiences and the writer's cues to infer the author's intended meaning. This process varies in ways designed to satisfy the requirements of the total situation in which it is taking place.

Is inferring the author's intended message, however, always the goal of comprehension? Can the author's intended message ever be fully known? Will two similar readers reading the same text in the same context always comprehend exactly alike? Probably not. Each act of comprehension seems to be a unique transaction. Research on the constructive aspects of the comprehension process has indicated that readers actually construct new meanings that have uses for them. Harste (1985) and others have referred to this as a *transactional model* of comprehension. Reading is a transaction between the reader and the text in a specific context that results in the creation of a new text in the mind of the reader. The goal of reading is not inferring the intended message of the author but, rather, creating a message that is useful to the reader:

> Comprehension can be seen as the process of using ones own prior experiences and the writer's cues to construct a set of meanings that are useful to the individual reader reading in a specific context.

How do readers "use" their prior experiences and the writer's cues to create this new set of meanings? They use the comprehension processes described earlier in this chapter! Moreover, if they consciously select those processes to achieve specific purposes, we can call those processes *strategies*. Indeed, throughout this book, the terms *processes* and *strategies* will be used virtually interchangeably, with the latter being used only to imply that the process is selected consciously to achieve a specific purpose.

Before reading any further, take out a sheet of paper and try to write out a definition of comprehension. Then try to expand this definition to include the five comprehension processes discussed earlier. Try to avoid using the new terminology. This will help you to check your comprehension of what you read in this chapter. You may wish to compare your definition with the one given here. The new terminology has been inserted to help you review.

> Comprehension can be seen as the process of using ones own prior experiences and the writer's cues to construct a set of meanings that are useful to the individual reader reading in a specific context. This process can involve understanding and selectively recalling ideas in individual sentences (microprocesses), inferring relationships between clauses and sentences (integrative processes), organizing ideas around summarizing ideas (macroprocesses), and making inferences not necessarily intended by the author (elaborative processes). These processes work together (interactive hypothesis) and can be controlled and adjusted by the reader as required by the reader's goals (metacognitive processes) and the total situation in which comprehension is occurring (situational context). When the reader consciously selects a process for a specific purpose, that process can be called a *reading strategy*.

WHEW!

AN EXAMPLE

Suppose that you are teaching current events to a class of fifth-grade students. You ask each student to read a newspaper article and tell the class what it said. Sally, an average reader with a generally good attitude, reads the following article.

> No issue has been more controversial in the political history of the United States than the right of "judicial review." Judicial review takes place when the federal courts decide

whether laws passed by Congress and signed by the president conform to the Constitution. This right is not a right at all, however, at least not like the first ten amendments to the Constitution, which establish a Bill of Rights for citizens of the United States. Rather, the right of judicial review is a long-honored tradition that began with the path-breaking decisions of the Marshall Court in the nation's early days.

The opponents of this tradition have been as loud as the tradition has been long. It is not surprising then that once again many wish to restrict or perhaps even abolish judicial review. Especially in the 1990s, after nearly two decades of "liberal" Warren Court decisions, this tradition is being challenged by conservatives who oppose the Supreme Court's decisions on school prayer, busing, abortion, and rights of accused criminals. In fact, Congress is presently considering nearly forty bills limiting the jurisdiction of the federal courts in such matters.

The alarming aspect of all this is that, beyond authorizing Congress to "ordain and establish" such courts as it chooses, the Constitution says nothing about what courts should exist, let alone what power they should have. It is unlikely but not impossible, therefore, that the current congressional attacks on judicial review could result in the complete elimination of the present federal court system. Some fiction of a court system might remain, but the remnants would be like the King's clothes.

In class, Sally says,

It talked about how the courts can say whether a law is OK, and some people don't like what the courts have done so the government might just get rid of the courts altogether. They are talking about passing forty laws to keep the courts from doing things about things like busing and school prayer like Sam talked about in his report last week. There was something about the King's clothes, but I didn't understand it. I didn't really care because I thought it was a dumb article anyway.

Now, let's look to see what processes Sally used to comprehend this article. Table 1-1 shows our best guess as to the processes evidenced in her recall. Study this chart. Note that even for this simple exercise, Sally seems to have used all five comprehension processes.

Sally's report also provides some examples of how the comprehension processes interact: Sally recalled the details surrounding the issue of school prayer because she elaborated in terms of Sam's report. She recalled the detail of "forty laws" because it was relevant to the main point of limiting the courts. Her summary did not include the point of the last sentence because she failed to understand it at the microlevel.

Moreover, Sally's report also provides us with some examples of the ways in which the text, the reader, and the situation can influence the five processes. For instance, the author's use of a literary reference limited Sally's microcomprehension (text effect). She might have been able to get the information she needed to figure it out, but her lack of interest caused her to choose not to try any metacognitive

TABLE 1-1   Comprehension Processes Evident in Sally's Report

RECALL	PROCESS
"It talked about how the courts can say whether a law is OK and some people don't like what the courts have done so the government might just get rid of the courts altogether."	Macroprocesses (She has reduced the article to a kind of summary statement.)
"They are talking about passing forty laws to keep the courts from doing things . . . "	Microprocesses (She has remembered specific details that she thought were important.)
" . . . about things like busing and school prayer . . . "	Integrative processes (She has integrated two sentences of the article.)
" . . . like Sam talked about in his report last week."	Elaborative processes (She has linked this article to something she heard before.)
"There was something about the King's clothes but I didn't understand it. I didn't really care because it was a dumb article anyway."	Metacognitive processes (She was aware of what she didn't understand and decided not to do anything about it.)

strategies (reader effect). Finally, it may be the case that her anxiety (reader effect) about the task of reporting to the class (situational effect) caused her poor attitude and somewhat low level of recall, or that knowing that she was going to report to the class (situational effect) caused her to focus on the part related to the other report she knew everyone in the class had heard. Indeed, it would be possible to speculate about how each of the comprehension contexts affected the way Sally used each of the five processes. (See Activity 5 at the end of this chapter.)

Finally, Sally's report shows how much active meaning construction is necessary for even such a simple task. For instance, "whether a law is OK" is what she constructed from "whether laws...conform to the Constitution." Even though the article said that it was unlikely, Sally said "the government might just get rid of the courts altogether" as if it were a likely possibility, probably because it was an intriguing notion to her. Finally, she constructed a set of meanings that were useful to her—that is, they were something that she could say in class that might interest her peers—and no more.

A FINAL NOTE

You may have noticed that "comprehension" often inherently implies recall, and it may sometimes seem that these words are being used interchangeably. Indeed, in practice, it is virtually impossible to separate them. We simply cannot tell what a student has comprehended without asking him or her to recognize or recall it in some way. Thus, in this text, if the terms "comprehension" and "recall" are separated, it will be only for the sake of emphasis. Usually this is done to distinguish between what the reader remembers soon after reading (comprehension) and what is remembered after a period of time (recall).

SELF-CHECK TEST

1. Define each of these terms in your own words (If you cannot, refer to the text and review:

   reader context   macroprocesses
   text context   elaborative processes
   situational context   metacognitive processes
   microprocesses   interactive hypothesis
   integrative processes   transactional model

2. Answer true or false.

   _____ (a) Everything to be comprehended is usually explicitly stated by the author.

   _____ (b) A reader's affective experiences affect what is comprehended.

   _____ (c) In practice, what a student comprehends and what that student recalls are difficult to separate.

   _____ (d) Macroprocesses always occur before elaborative processes.

   _____ (e) Inferring relationships between sentences is an elaborative process.

   _____ (f) Summarizing is classified here as a metacognitive process.

   _____ (g) Chunking is classified here as a macroprocess.

   _____ (h) Elaborations can affect microprocesses.

   _____ (i) Good readers remember everything they have read.

   _____ (j) Study skills such as note taking and underlining are classified here as integrative processes.

3. Fill in the blanks in the following passage.

   Comprehension can be seen as the process of using one's own prior _____ (reader context) and the writer's cues (_____ context) to _____ a set of meanings that are _____ to the individual reader reading in a specific context. This process can involve understanding and selectively recalling ideas in individual _____ (microprocesses), _____ relationships between clauses and sentences (_____ processes), organizing ideas around _____ ideas (macroprocesses), and making inferences not necessarily _____ by the author (_____ processes). These processes _____ (interactive hypothesis) and can be controlled and adjusted by the _____ as required by the reader's _____ (metacognitive processes) and the total _____ in which comprehension is taking place (_____ context). When the reader consciously selects a process for a specific purpose, that process can be called a reading _____.

SUGGESTED ACTIVITIES

1. Diagram your definition of comprehension.
2. Ask a student to read and recall a passage. Tape-record the recall and then write it out on paper. Try to mark each phrase or sentence as to the type of process he or she seems to have used. What were the contexts that caused the student to remember this way?
3. Read a magazine article and write down what you remember. What processes did you use? What contexts affected which processes you emphasized?
4. Begin a notebook or card file of teaching activities. Make a divider for each process and for the three major contexts (reader, text, situation). On each divider, define the process or context and explain why it is important. Add to this file as you read each chapter in this book.
5. Speculate on how each of the comprehension contexts affected the way Sally used each of the five processes (see page 11).

REFERENCES

Anderson, R. C., Reynolds, R. E., Schallert, D. L., & Goetz, E. T. (1977). Frameworks for comprehending discourse. *American Educational Research Journal, 14,* 367–381.

Cohen, G., & Freeman, R. (1978). Individual differences in reading strategies in relation to handedness and cerebral asymmetry. In J. Requin (Ed.), *Attention and performance* (Vol. 7). Hillsdale, N.J.: Lawrence Erlbaum.

Harste, J. (1985) Portrait of a new paradigm: Reading comprehension research. In A. Crismore, (Ed.), *Landscapes: A State of the Art Assessment of Reading Comprehension Research, 1974–1984* (pp. 12-1–24). Bloomington: Indiana University.

Jenkins, J. J. (1979). Four points to remember: A tetrahedral model of memory experiments. In L. S. Cermak & F. I. M. Craik (Eds.), *Levels of processing in human memory.* Hillsdale, N.J.: Lawrence Erlbaum.

Johnston, P. (1981). *Implications of basic research for the assessment of reading comprehension* (Technical Report. No 206). Urbana-Champaign: Center for the Study of Reading, University of Illinois.

Just, M. A., & Carpenter, P. A. (1980). A theory of reading: From eye fixations to comprehension. *Psychological Review, 87,* 329–354.

Kintsch, W., & van Dijk, T. A. (1978). Toward a model of text comprehension and production. *Psychological Review, 85,* 363–394.

Levin, H., & Kaplan, E. L. (1970). Grammatical structure and reading. In H. Levin & J. P. Williams (Eds.), *Basic studies in reading*. New York: Basic Books.

Meyer, B., Brandt, D., & Bluth, G. (1980). Use of top-level structure in text: Key for reading comprehension of ninth-grade students. *Reading Research Quarterly, 16*, 71–103.

Mosenthal, P. (1984). Reading comprehension research from a classroom prospective. In J. Flood (Ed.), *Promoting reading comprehension* (pp. 16–29). Newark, Del.: International Reading Association.

Reder, L. M. (1980). The role of elaboration in the comprehension and retention of prose: A critical review. *Review of Educational Research, 50*, 5–53.

Rosenshine, B. (1980). Skill hierarchies in reading comprehension. In R. J. Spiro, B. C. Bruce, & W. F. Brewer (Eds.), *Theoretical issues in reading comprehension*. Hillsdale, N.J.: Lawrence Erlbaum.

Rumelhart, D. E. (1976). *Toward an interactive model of reading* (Technical Report No. 56). San Diego: Center for Human Information Processing, University of California.

Spiro, R. J. (1980). Constructive processes in prose comprehension and recall. In R. J. Spiro, B. C. Bruce, & W. F. Brewer (Eds.), *Theoretical issues in reading comprehension*. Hillsdale, N.J.: Lawrence Erlbaum.

Thorndyke, P. (1976). The role of inference in discourse comprehension. *Journal of Verbal Learning and Verbal Behavior, 15*, 437–446.

OVERVIEW OF COMPREHENSION PROCESS TEACHING

In Chapter One, the constructive nature of comprehension was discussed. Reading was described as a transaction between the reader and the text in which the reader creates meanings that are useful to that reader. The reader creates those meanings by using the author's cues and the processes described in that chapter. Each of those processes requires that the reader be *actively* involved in *making meaning*.

Thus, if we are going to talk about teaching reading comprehension, then we are going to have to look for methods of teaching that create active rather than passive readers. (One of the problems with some methods of teaching is that they tend to result in passive learners who do not know how to direct their own learning and comprehension. Readers who are always told what to do and when to do it never learn to be actively involved.) Moreover, we need methods of teaching that involve learners in tasks that are meaningful to them, if we expect them to create meaning on their own. (Indeed, when reading is fragmented into the subskills lists discussed in chapter one, the reader is usually *not* engaged in making meaning. Instead, too often, the reader is filling in blanks or selecting answers in irrelevant, often meaningless materials.)

Thus, any approach to teaching reading comprehension processes must involve careful consideration of the teaching methods selected. Learners must be provided with materials that motivate them to become actively involved in constructing meaning, strategic guidance and support when their own repertoire of strategies is not adequate, a connection to writing as a similar meaning-making activity, questions and discussion that help them focus on both the content being created and the strategy being used, and meaningful interactions with other readers so that meanings and strategies can be shared. All of these learning experiences can be provided within the context of a variety of approaches, in basal, literature-based, integrated curriculum, content-area, or remedial situations.

MEANINGFUL READING TASKS

To involve students in comprehending, then, we must first create situations in which the material being read is meaningful. This means that the reason for reading and understanding the material must make sense to the students. They must be reading to get meanings that will be useful to them.

Another basic consideration in involving students in meaningful reading tasks is providing the students with what has come to be known as a *literate environment*. Students should be surrounded by all types of print including, but not limited to, trade books, literature, biographies, newspapers, magazines, pamphlets, and student writing so that they can use this material to find meanings that are useful to them. In the elementary school, this would include displaying books attractively in a reading corner or classroom library as well as in other displays. Exposing students to all types of print in secondary-level content classrooms would also enrich those students' ideas about reading in those content areas and, possibly, might involve them more deeply in the content.

For reading to be meaningful, it must be taught throughout the curriculum in real situations in which students are reading literature, content-area textbooks, and other materials to achieve meaningful goals. Indeed, strategies learned in one situation must often be transformed to apply in other situations. For instance, outlining a social studies chapter following a sequential organizational pattern involves a slightly different thinking process than does outlining a science chapter organized by classification. Herber (1970) has called the transformation of strategies across the content areas "horizontal transformation" (p. 225). Students will be unable to practice such *horizontal transformation* unless they are given opportunities to practice strategies in a variety of subject areas.

Another critical consideration in getting students actively involved in reading must be giving them some *ownership* of the activity (Langer & Applebee, 1986). Students must have some control over what they do. Hansen (1986) has talked about this in relationship to the concept of choice. Students must be able to choose as many aspects of the activity as possible if we expect them to become actively invested in its outcome. Choice can come in many forms though the degree of choice may be limited by the general philosophy of the specific teacher. Choice can be made available to students, in terms of what materials are read, when they are read, why they are read, how much time is taken for completion, when and with whom results are shared, what activities are related to the reading, what forms of evaluation are used, and so on. Indeed, it is difficult to imagine an activity being meaningful to the learner if he or she has no input in any of these areas.

Another requirement for ownership of reading tasks is what might be called the *multiple answer approach*. Students cannot learn to be actively involved in constructing meaning if they know that only one answer exists, and the teacher already knows what it is. Instead, students must know that their reasoning processes will be valued and their ideas respected. For many of the topics under discussion, students will have many good approaches and answers. The respect for alternative interpretations modeled by the teacher can be imitated by students in their responses to one another.

In summary, teaching comprehension processes must involve providing students with meaningful reading tasks. This is facilitated by providing a literate environment and opportunities for students to read material that they perceive to be useful, teaching reading throughout the curriculum whenever reading is being used for meaningful purposes, giving students ownership of the activity by providing for some student choice and control, and accepting each student's individual interpretation of print as a valid and important contribution to class interactions.

EXPLICIT PROCESS INSTRUCTION IN MEANINGFUL CONTEXTS

Another recent development in comprehension pedagogy is the direct, explicit teaching of reading strategies. This also follows from our new understandings about the comprehension process. If comprehension involves the active selection and use of strategies, then students should be told what those strategies are when they have a need for them.

Although this seems logical enough, research has indicated the students are seldom told how to comprehend. They are simply given worksheet after worksheet in the hopes that this "repeated exposure" will lead to independence (Duffy & Roehler, 1982). Durkin (1978–79), in an observation study of more than seven thousand minutes of reading instruction in twenty-four classrooms, found that less than 1 percent of the time could be construed as being used to tell the children "how to." The major forms of instruction were question asking after reading and workbook or worksheet activities.

After a review of the research on effective teaching, Baumann (1984) concluded that direct instruction was one of the factors consistently related to achievement. He says that research points to a five-step procedure involving (1) an introduction telling what they are to learn and why the skill is important, (2) an example of text on which it can be used, (3) direct instruction in which students are told and shown how to do the skill, (4) teacher-directed application of the skill, and (5) independent practice (Baumann, 1984).

Roehler and Duffy (1986) have begun to study the differences between teachers whose students do and do not benefit from such direct instruction. In a small study comparing two teachers, they found that the effective teacher had more emphasis on how and why the strategy is used and on how to decide when to use it.

In the effective teacher's classroom, the discussion of the mental processes used was carried throughout the lesson, the move toward asking the students to use the strategy independently was more gradual, the students were asked to explain their mental processes more often, and many concrete examples were used.

The *explicit process instruction* recommended in this book can be reduced to four steps as follows:

Explain: Explain the process to the students and tell them why it is important. Tell them how they can determine when to use the strategy and give concrete examples of situations in which it would be useful.

Examples

1. "While you read this passage, you will need to think about how it relates to what you already know about X. Good readers always stop and think about what else they know. This helps them to remember and understand the new information. This is especially important when you are reading in social studies and science in which there is a lot of new information to learn."
2. "When authors write, they often leave out information they think you can figure out for yourself. Therefore, it is important for you to actively infer aspects of the situation that are not necessarily stated outright. This is especially important when you are reading a good story."

Model: Model your own thinking processes as you use the strategy. Do this on a piece of reading material that is relevant to the students. Share your confusions.

Examples

1. "For instance, let's read the first paragraph silently. (Students read.) Now when I read this paragraph about the climate in Alaska, I thought about what it was like when it snowed here last year. When the author referred to "bitter" cold, I knew that she meant the kind of cold that makes you numb and tingly, like we get in January."
2. "Let me show you an example. (Teacher reads first part of story until coming to a required inference.) Now when I read that she stirred her coffee, I inferred that she probably did this with a spoon. I also inferred that it was sugar that she stirred in and that she was about to drink her coffee. That's why I was really surprised when she got up from the table instead!"

Question: Ask questions that provide opportunities for the students to model their thinking strategies to you. These questions will often focus on the process being used rather than on the answer being given.

Examples

1. "John, what do you already know that helps you to understand this paragraph?"

2. "Sally, what do the next two sentences have to do with each other? How do you know?"

Activity: When the students have modeled the process for you and for each other sufficiently, give them a chance to apply the strategy independently in meaningful reading tasks.

Examples

1. "Now, as you read about the way people live in Alaska, think about how it is like the way you live here."
2. "Now, as you finish reading this story, see how much you can figure out about what is going on that the author doesn't tell you directly."

The question of when to use such explicit instruction is also important. If the instruction is to be meaningful to the learner, then it seems that the best time is *when the need arises in meaningful situations.* For instance, suppose students were engaged in a book-sharing discussion and one student who read a book about turtles just said, "It said lots of things about turtles. I don't have time to tell you all of them. I don't know what to say." This might be a good time for the teacher to step in and ask if there is a need for a new strategy: "Yes, books like this that have many facts are difficult to discuss. Has this happened to anyone else? (Students nod.) Maybe I can help you by showing you how you can *summarize* a book like this one." An explicit process lesson (explain-model-question-activity [E-M-Q-A]) would follow.

Of course, some students will still have trouble with some activities even after E-M-Q-A. If students perform badly on an activity, try to assess the reason creatively. Problems with other processes can interfere: For example, if students cannot read the words, they cannot macroprocess; if they cannot chunk the words into meaningful phrases, they will not be able to elaborate; and so on. If you can determine that the problem is not interference from other processes, then you may wish to do more explication and modeling. If you can determine that a problem exists with another process, try to create a situation in which the other processes are easier: use simpler materials, give them necessary background, and so on.

Furthermore, you need not use all four steps of E-M-Q-A each time you teach. This E-M-Q-A model simply implies that comprehension instruction should include all these steps when the strategy is introduced and as many as are necessary thereafter.

To implement these E-M-Q-A steps, sometimes it will be necessary for you to conduct "group processing sessions." In a group processing session, you and the students read together, either silently or orally, discussing the reading after each section. This will result in constant interaction between you and the students during the reading. (The ReQuest activity suggested in Chapter Ten is an example of a group processing activity.) Discussion after every paragraph or section can focus on processes as well as content.

Table 2-1 shows how a fourth-grade teacher might teach causal inference to the middle-level reading group using an E-M-Q-A approach in a group processing lesson. The teacher has planned this session because the students have been having trouble with these questions in other lessons. Table 2-2 shows a seventh-grade teacher using E-M-Q-A to teach comprehension during a content-area lesson. This lesson was not planned but, rather, arose naturally because students needed to

TABLE 2-1   Teaching Comprehension: Fourth-Grade Reading Group

E-M-Q-A STEP	TEACHER	STUDENT RESPONSES
	Do you know why this author puts sentences in a certain order?	Because it sounds good.
	Yes! And why does it sound good?	Because it tells a story.
Explication	Yes! The sentences fit together. They are related to each other. Good readers read more than sentences. They figure out how the sentences fit together. To really understand this story, you will need to understand how the sentences fit together. Often, one sentence tells why something happened in another sentence.	
Modeling	Let me show you how I do this. Everyone read the first paragraph silently while I read it aloud [reads paragraph]. Now, let's see. The first sentence tells me that Janice loved the store. The second sentence tells me that it had a lot of pretty things. Now, I ask myself, how do these sentences fit together? Well, I know that most people love pretty things. So, she probably loved the store *because...*	It had pretty things!
	Good!	
Question	Now, let's read the next two sentences. Who can tell me how these fit together?	They sold the ribbon so they could get money.
	Good! One thing was the cause of the other. Now let's read on. [They read and discuss until another connective inference is needed.]	

TABLE 2-1   (cont.)

E-M-Q-A STEP	TEACHER	STUDENT RESPONSES
Question	Who can tell me why Janice didn't go home?	Because she wanted to buy a present.
Question	Right! But how did you get that answer? Show me where it says that.	[Student reads the next two sentences.] I just figured how they fit together, like you did.
Question	Right. You figured out that these two sentences fit together because one thing was the cause of the other.	
Activity	Now, read the next page. When you are finished I will ask you more questions about things that caused other things. Try to put sentences together as you read. You will understand the story better that way.	

understand the text. Note how E-M-Q-A provides an easy way to teach comprehension processes in the context of content-area and other meaningful reading situations.

A useful concept for helping the teacher with the questioning step of E-M-Q-A is that of *scaffolding*. Cazden (1988) provides the following picture to describe this sort of interaction: "Imagine a picture of an adult holding the hand of a very young toddler with the caption, 'Everyone needs a helping hand.' " She goes on to define this concept: "Exactly as Resnick (1985) says, the child does what he or she can and the adult does the rest; the child's practice occurs in the context of the full performance; and the adult's help is gradually withdrawn (from holding two hands to just one, then to offering only a finger, and then withdrawing a few inches and so on) as the child's competence grows" (p. 102). In the questioning stage, the child is reading a natural piece of reading material (context of full performance). The teacher will provide the student with answers and process advice when that student falters. For instance, suppose the student gives a good answer but cannot tell how he or she got it. Then the teacher can supply the description of the reasoning. Suppose that the student understands the process but cannot figure out how to apply it to the text. Then, the teacher can begin the thought process, pausing to let the student fill in the answers. This sort of scaffolding can continue until the students can apply the strategy on their own.

The major characteristic of such scaffolded instruction is, therefore, dialogue. The purpose of this dialogue is enabling the learner to complete a whole adult task. Langer and Applebee (1986) point out that it must involve reducing the size of the task to a manageable amount and controlling the frustration level of the learner.

To help students in this way, it is necessary to look at their reading abilities in terms of a *continuum of independence* (Herber, 1970). For every strategy, each

TABLE 2-2   Teaching Comprehension: Seventh-Grade Content-Area Class

E-M-Q-A STEP	TEACHER	STUDENT RESPONSES
	Why did the Americans move to Mexico?	[No answer.]
	Well, how could we find out the answer?	Reread that section and look for clues.
	Good—where does it say 'the Americans moved to Mexico'?	The first paragraph on page 251.
	OK. Good. Everyone read it silently. What clue do you see?	Well, it says that Mexico had slavery.
	Did Americans have slaves then?	Now, it was right after the war...so maybe they moved to Mexico so they could keep their slaves.
Explication	Good—there could really have been a "because" between those two sentences. Remember when we talked about how that happens a lot in this book?	
Modeling	If we were to read on, there would be other places just in this section. If I were to read on I would infer a "because" between the next two sentences: "Texas allowed slavery (because) Texas was a part of Mexico."	
Questioning	Read the rest of the page silently.	[Students read.]
	Who can find another place where we could insert a "because"?	The part about the Americans wanting more land. It was because of homesteading.
	Good. The author didn't use the word "because," but that was what he meant.	
Activity	As you read the rest of this chapter, try to find other places where the author could have said, "because." This should help you to understand it better.	

student can be placed on a continuum from being very dependent on the teacher or instructional materials for guidance to being capable of performing the strategy in a completely independent way. For instance, one student may be able to construct a chapter outline only if provided with a partial outline in which he or she is to fill in a few missing topics. In contrast, another student in the same class may be able to write the outline if given a blank sheet of paper. Both students can do some outlining, but one is more independent than the other. Thus, the question is not if a student can or cannot summarize, image, and so forth, but rather how much assistance is needed. Scaffolding is a form of assistance provided when students cannot use a strategy independently.

Similar to this concept of scaffolding full performance until students can work independently is the concept of *substantive feedback*. Weber and Shake (1988) have found that most teacher feedback, if given at all, takes the form of simple repetitions of student answers. This gives students little information about why an answer is good or poor, or how it was reached. Instead, as part of their scaffolding during the questioning stage, teachers can give students substantive feedback that first validates the appropriate strategies that the students have used and then, if appropriate, suggests another strategy. Examples of useful kinds of substantive feedback are provided in Table 2-3. Study this table. Do you think you will be able to give your students similar kinds of feedback? In a recent in-service program, Irwin (1989) found that teachers trained in a model of comprehension were able to begin to give substantive feedback related to comprehension processes.

You may have noticed that though direct, explicit process instruction (which may include scaffolding and substantive feedback) has sometimes been associated with teacher-directed subskills approaches, there is no logical reason for this to be so. If students are reading books of their choice, they may find that they are having a certain strategic problem. Then, the teacher can help them with some explicit strategy instruction. Goodman (1986) talks of the importance of "strategy lessons" in wholistic approaches (p. 52). Similarly, Hansen (1986) talks of the direct teaching of skills that students know they need in a literature-based approach. Others have also discussed the need for direct instruction within the context of a basal approach. Explicit process instruction is not, in and of itself, an approach or a philosophy. It is a technique that can be integrated into any reading pedagogy.

Finally, as with all the teaching suggestions provided in this chapter, explicit instruction will probably be more appropriate for some students than for others.

TABLE 2-3   Examples of Substantive Feedback

---

1. Student applies inappropriate background knowledge:

   "I see—you are using what you know about birds to understand this story about fish. It's good to try to use what you already know. But, since this is about fish, could you look at it again and use what you know about fish?"

2. Student selects unimportant detail for summary:

   "Yes, that certainly was interesting to some of us because we're going to be making costumes next week. But for summaries, it's good to try to pick out what's important for understanding the whole story."

3. Student makes appropriate inference:

   "Good—you have figured out that the Texans moved to Mexico *because* they had slaves and wanted to keep them. It's important to look for these cause-effect relationships when you are reading in your social studies textbook."

McFaul (1983) has reviewed research showing that although direct instruction is useful for some, it is the wrong approach for others. High-achieving task-oriented students, for instance, may do better with another approach (Peterson, 1979). Thus, although E-M-Q-A is being recommended as a general structure, its implementation must be varied according to the individual learning styles of the children in your classroom.

THE READING AND WRITING CONNECTION FOR MAKING MEANING

In a year-long in-service project conducted in the Archdiocese of Chicago Schools in 1985–86, teachers who were taught about the comprehension process made the decision to use extensive and sometimes lengthy writing experiences in the place of skills sheets (Irwin, 1989). What was clear to me in talking to these teachers was that they understood an important aspect of the connection between reading and writing: They are both processes for making meaning. Although many differences exist between these processes (see Langer, 1986), similarities also exist in how they develop. (See pages 48-49, for example.)

More importantly, many of the activities suggested in this book on teaching reading comprehension are actually writing activities. (See, for example, reading response journals in Chapter Five.) Writing is one of the most powerful tools for developing comprehension because it can "actively involve the reader in constructing a set of meanings that are useful to the individual reader." (See the definition of comprehension in Chapter One, p. 9) Moreover, if the writing process involves writing about reading, then the writer is "using ones own prior experiences and the author's cues" to construct that meaning. Finally, the writer is using various strategies, some of which are also used during reading—that is, summarizing, inferring, elaborating, and so on.

Perhaps an example will suffice. In Chapter One, the strategy of forming mental images was discussed as one possibly useful type of elaboration. Suppose a student (Johnny) was reading a fairy tale that took place in a distant land. He got so excited by the picture that he wanted to write about that fantasy land in his response to the book. He used his imagination while he was reading to create vivid details. While he was writing his response to the book, he often referred back to specific parts to remind him of the details he wanted to include. Is Johnny developing his reading or his writing abilities through this experience...or both?

Teachers who teach reading processes will find many opportunities to reinforce reading processes in writing lessons (and vice versa). For instance, suppose students are discussing a young adult novel in which an adolescent boy decides to leave home. The teacher can help students to see how the author prepared the reader for this decision by talking about stories that have written themselves: "Remember when Sam [student writer] had a difficult time showing us why his brother decided to sell his car? Well, this author has the same problem. He's trying to show us why

Slick would decide to run away. What did John do about his problem? What is this author doing about his?"

Returning to our example (p. 19) of the student who learned how to summarize his book on turtles, what if a student in his class were having trouble ending an essay he was writing about cars? A teacher could make the connection to the earlier lesson: "Remember when we were reading about turtles and there were so many facts that we decided to summarize? Could Sam [student writer] do something like that to help us remember what he knows about cars? How would he go about doing that?"

QUESTIONS ON CONTENT (MEANING) AND PROCESS (MAKING)

Chapter Ten in this text will deal with questions designed to encourage specific types of comprehension processes, but, because questioning interactions are such an integral part of comprehension experiences, a few general words are in order here. First, questions that engage students in an active process of making meaning will often focus on the meaning that the student is "comprehending." They will often encourage students to elaborate on an initial response. Gambrell (1987) found that most questions asked in the typical basal reading groups in her study required only one word for an answer. Questions in a process-oriented classroom will often encourage lengthy answers.

One type of question that can be used to help students elaborate on their answers can be called a *mirror question* (see Graves, 1983, p. 108). In these questions, a student's initial comment is mirrored back to him or her. For instance, suppose Sally was reading a novel and said, "I didn't like the way they treated the animals." The teacher might mirror this back: "Oh, you didn't like the way they treated the animals?" Then Sally would probably elaborate on her statement: "Yeah, and they weren't very nice to the children in the school or the forest or anything like that. I wonder what made those people so mean. Maybe it had something to do with…" Mirror responses communicate the message that the listener is interested without being as intimidating as "Can you elaborate on that?"

Moreover, because it is the students (readers) who are making the meaning, questions in a process-oriented classroom will often come from the students. Encouraging students to ask questions of the teacher and of each other will help them to become actively involved in comprehending. Research involving specific techniques for involving students in questioning has indicated that this can be a powerful teaching technique (Manzo, 1979; Palinscar & Brown, 1989). (See Chapter Ten for specific examples.)

Finally, questions in a comprehension process learning experience will often ask about processes. Throughout this text, these will be called *process questions*. Questions like "How did you decide that he felt that way?" or "What part made you feel frightened?" or "How did you figure out what that word meant?" are all asking students to talk about their comprehension processes. In the in-service program previously discussed, the teachers found that asking an average of one process question per lesson was sufficient for generating interesting process discussions (Irwin, 1989). Other examples of process questions are provided in Table 2-4. See if you can think of other examples.

Rekrut (personal communication, November, 1989) has suggested that process questions should always be used before explicit instruction. For instance, when Johnny was reporting on the turtle book, the teacher might have begun with "How might you go about summarizing this book?" to give Johnny a chance to explore what he already knows about the strategy first. This would also keep the responsibility for solving the problem in the hands of the learner.

DISCUSSION THAT PROMOTES MEANING MAKING

Finally, in classrooms in which students are actively comprehending, many lively discussions are likely to occur. The role of the teacher in such discussions may be different from the role of the teacher in traditional classrooms. Hansen (1986) talks about the teacher as a "responder" who teaches by responding to his or her students' reading responses. Langer and Applebee (1986) talk about the teacher as a "collaborator" in the group meaning-making process rather than an examiner who knows all the answers. Whatever the teacher's decision in this regard, the teacher must release enough control to allow students to become active rather than passive learners.

Alvermann, Dillon, and O'Brien (1987) have also stressed the importance of discussion for teaching comprehension. Moreover, they refer to Dillon's (1981) suggestion that to be a discussion, a group interaction must involve the students in doing the talking at least 40 percent of the time, and that the students must sometimes talk to each other rather than to the teacher. In such a discussion, students will be actively involved in creating their own interpretations. Alvermann, Dillon, and O'Brien (1987) also suggest that the group size used for discussion should be as small as possible to get the job done. This maximizes the input from each member.

Of course, the smallest-sized discussion is the one-to-one conference. Although conferences fit more directly into some general approaches than others, almost all teachers find the time to interact with some students on a one-to-one basis.

TABLE 2-4   Examples of Process Questions

---
1. How did you know what was the most important idea here?
2. What did you already know that led you to predict that this would happen?
3. What part made it difficult for you to understand?
4. How should we go about writing a summary of this article?
5. What words painted the picture in your mind?

These conferences can be used to promote active processing by encouraging the student to talk about what is being comprehended, and what strategies he or she is choosing to use. Ideally, the student should feel that he or she has some control over what happens in the conference, or what is decided as a result of it.

Various types of cooperative learning groups are also likely to lead to useful discussions. In cooperative learning, students "usually work together to complete tasks whereas students in other settings work at their seats or receive instruction in large groups" (Webb, 1982, p. 421). Cooperative learning groups provide settings in which students can discuss strategies and provide mutual assistance. Moreover, at least one study has examined the effects of combining cooperative learning with direct, explicit instruction. The Cooperative Integrated Reading and Composition Model (CIRC) combines explaining and modeling with practicing in cooperative groups. This combination of explicit instruction and cooperative groups is integrated into both reading and writing activities. Significant achievement gains were noted (Stevens, Madden, Slavin, & Farnish, 1987). Literature discussion groups provide another example of a cooperative discussion format in which the students do most of the talking (see Hansen, 1986, and others).

COMPREHENSION PROCESS TEACHING

The purpose of this chapter has not been to recommend a general approach or philosophy of teaching. Rather, this chapter has suggested some general considerations for teaching reading comprehension as an active process. These suggestions can be incorporated into various approaches and situations including basal, literature-based, content-area, and remedial programs. This discussion has been provided early in this text to provide a framework for the implementation of the activities that are suggested throughout the subsequent chapters.

To summarize, at least five characteristics of instruction can lead to active student involvement in comprehending. First, students are more likely to get actively involved if the materials are meaningful to them. They should be surrounded by all types of print, given choices about what to read whenever possible, encouraged to actively comprehend in different situations with various types of texts, and respected in their interpretations of print. Second, explicit process instruction involving explaining, modeling, questioning (scaffolding), and independently applying strategies can be provided when students need help with specific processes. Students can be provided with substantive feedback to their responses including validation of the strategies they have used and suggestions for other strategies if appropriate. Writing provides a way for students to get actively involved in making meaning as does questioning that focuses on both process and content. Students can get involved with asking questions and with large- and small-group discussions in which they do a large part of the talking. Conferences and cooperative learning groups are other examples of teaching methods that can be useful for stimulating interesting discussions.

SELF-CHECK TEST

1. Define each of the following, and tell why it is important for teaching comprehension as an active process:

   literate environment
   horizontal transformation
   ownership
   multiple-answer approach
   explicit process instruction
   explaining
   modeling
   questioning
   scaffolding
   continuum of independence
   substantive feedback
   reading and writing connection
   process questions
   discussion
   cooperative learning

2. Which of the following are examples of substantive feedback?

   (a) "Very good, Johnny. You always do so well."
   (b) "Sorry, Johnny. Good try, but I think you need to try again."
   (c) "Very good. You think that they moved to Mexico to get away from the people who were chasing them."
   (d) "Very good. You are trying to use what you know about Johnny to predict what his father would do. What do you know about his father that might also help you?"
   (e) "Good use of inference...but what is the author's purpose here? Could you use that information to guide your inferencing?"

3. Which of the following are examples of process questions?

   (a) "Who crossed the Delaware?"
   (b) "In your opinion, why did Johnny decide to do this?"
   (c) "How did you decide that Johnny felt that way?"
   (d) "How did you know what was the main point?"
   (e) "What will happen next?"

4. Which of the following is an example of a good strategy explanation (for explicit process teaching)?

   (a) "Today we are going to practice chunking. Chunking is grouping words into phrases. Good readers do this automatically...let me show you what I mean."
   (b) "When good readers read, they group words together so that they make sense. For instance, the word 'red' alone doesn't really tell you much, but 'the red ball' tells you about a specific thing. When people read aloud, they

often pause after groups of words that go together so the person listening can tell that they expressed an idea. When you read, you can do this for yourself, and it will help you to understand what you are reading...let me show you what I mean."

5. Which of the following is an example of a good strategy model (for explicit process teaching)?

   (a) "When I was reading this paragraph, I needed to know if the sentences went together. I could tell that 'he' in the second sentence referred to 'John' in the first...so both of these sentences were about the same person."

   (b) "When reading this paragraph you should make sure you know the antecedents for the referents."

6. In your own words, summarize this chapter.

SUGGESTED ACTIVITIES

1. For the major characteristics of comprehension process instruction discussed in this chapter that you think are important, tell how each is (or will be) reflected in your classroom.

2. What questions do you have after reading this chapter? What other suggestions could have been included in this chapter? If you do not agree with any suggestions in this chapter tell why you do not agree with them.

3. If you are not yet teaching, select a process you would like to teach. (See Chapter One for ideas.) Select a piece of reading material that you might imagine that your students are reading for a meaningful purpose. Write what you would say for the first two steps of explicit process instruction using this reading material and imagining a specific class.

4. If you are currently teaching, select a process that you have taught before (like finding the main idea, using context clues, and so forth), and write what you would say for the explaining and modeling stages of explicit process instruction. (*Note:* You will need a specific piece of meaningful reading material to do this activity.)

REFERENCES

Alvermann, D., Dillon, D., & O'Brien, D. (1987). *Using discussion to promote reading comprehension.* Newark, Del.: International Reading Association.

Baumann, J. (1984). Implications for reading instruction from research on teacher and school effectiveness. *Journal of Reading, 28,* 109–115.

Cazden, C. (1988). *Classroom discourse: The language of teaching and learning.* Portsmouth, N.H.: Heineman.

Dillon, J. T. (1981). Duration of response to teacher questions and statements. *Contemporary Educational Psychology, 6,* 1–11.

Duffy, G., & Roehler, L. (1982). The illusion of instruction. *Reading Research Quarterly, 17,* 438–445.

Durkin, D. (1978–79). What classroom observation reveals about reading comprehension instruction. *Reading Research Quarterly, 14,* 481–533.

Gambrell, L. (1987). Children's oral language during teacher-directed reading instruction. In J. Readance & R. Baldwin (Eds.), *Research in literacy: Merging perspectives* (36th Annual Yearbook, pp. 195–200). National Reading Conference.

Goodman, K. (1986). *What's whole in whole language?* Portsmouth, N.H.: Heineman.

Graves, D. (1983). *Writing: teachers and children at work.* Portsmouth, N.H.: Heineman.

Hansen, J. (1986). *When writers read.* Portsmouth, N.H.: Heineman.

Herber, H. (1970). *Teaching reading in the content areas.* Englewood Cliffs, N.J.: Prentice-Hall.

Irwin, J. W. (1989). Project ICARE: From theory to practice in comprehension instruction. Unpublished paper, University of Connecticut.

Langer, J. A. (1986). *Children reading and writing.* Norwood, N.J.: Ablex.

Langer, J. A., & Applebee, A. N. (1986). Reading and writing instruction: Toward a theory of teaching and learning. In E. Rothkopf (Ed.), *Review of research in education* (Vol. 13, pp. 171–194). Washington, D.C.: American Education Research Association.

Manzo, A. V. (1979). The ReQuest Procedure. In C. Pennock (Ed.), *Reading comprehension at four linguistic levels* (pp. 57–61). Newark, Del.: International Reading Association.

McFaul, A. (1983). An examination of direct instruction. *Educational Leadership, 40,* 67–69.

Palinscar, A., & Brown, A. (1989). Classroom dialogues to promote self-regulated comprehension. In J. Brophy (Ed.), *Teaching for understanding and self-regulated learning* (Vol. 1,). JAI Press.

Peterson, P. (1979). Direct instruction: Effective for what and for whom? *Educational Leadership, 37,* 46–48.

Resnick, L. B. (1985). Cognition and instruction: Recent theories of human competence and how it is acquired. In B. L. Hammond (Ed.), *Psychology and learning: The Masser Lecture Series* (Vol. 4). Washington, D.C.: American Psychological Association.

Roehler, L., & Duffy, G. (1986). Studying qualitative dimensions of instructional effectiveness. In J. Hoffman (Ed.), *Effective teaching of reading: Research and practice* (pp. 181–197). Newark, Del: International Reading Association.

Stevens, R. J., Madden, N. A., Slavin, R. E., & Farnish, A. M. (1987). Cooperative integrated reading and composition: Two field experiments. *Reading Research Quarterly, 22,* 433–454.

Webb, N. M. (1982). Students' interaction and learning in small groups. *Review of Educational Research, 52,* 421–445.

Weber, R., & Shake, M. (1988). Teachers' rejoinders to students' responses in reading lessons. *Journal of Reading Behavior, 20,* 285–300.

3

TEACHING MICROPROCESSES
AND INTEGRATIVE PROCESSES

Now we are ready to look at each of the comprehension subprocesses in more depth. How is the process used by good readers? What might be the best ways to encourage students to use these processes effectively?

From eye movement research, we have learned that readers often pause at the end of phrase boundaries (Just & Carpenter, 1980). Presumably, they are *chunking* words into meaningful phrases. Readers also pause at the end of each sentence. Research on what good readers recall has led many to speculate that several things occur during this pause (Just & Carpenter, 1980; Kintsch & van Dijk, 1978). Readers seem to select what was important from that sentence to keep in short-term memory for the interpretation of upcoming sentences (*microselection*). They then infer the relationships between the sentence just read and the sentences read previously—that is, they integrate text ideas already read before continuing (*integrative processing*).

For the purposes of this book, the processes that occur in relation to each individual sentence, chunking and microselection, are called **microprocesses**. The processes that the reader uses to integrate the information across sentence boundaries are called **integrative processes**.

MICROPROCESSES

The term, *microprocesses,* then can best be remembered by realizing that it refers to processes dealing with "micro" levels of information—individual phrases and sentences. This term, however, does not imply that they always occur first, in isolation. Remember that all processes interact. Successful use of elaboration, for instance, can help with microprocessing and vice versa. The two most important microprocesses are chunking and microselection.

CHUNKING

To comprehend, readers must be able to *chunk* words into meaningful syntactic units. Research continues to indicate that the clause is a basic processing unit for good readers (Hurtig, 1978). Because written syntax is somewhat different from that used in oral language (Leu, 1982) and because controlling eye movements is different from listening, the immediate transfer of this process from listening to reading cannot be assumed.

Researchers have found that poor readers sometimes benefit from chunking assistance. Cromer (1970) defined *difference readers* as those who had adequate word-level skills but inadequate comprehension skills. He found that these difference readers were aided by having the material divided into chunks for them. Mason and Kendall (1978) similarly found that poor readers' comprehension improved when sentences were segmented.

One possible cause of word-by-word, unchunked reading is the student's initial concept of the reading process itself. Research indicates that students learn what they are taught (Calfee & Piontkowski, 1981). If children are taught that reading is the decoding of individual words rather than the decoding of a meaningful message, they will concentrate their cognitive energies on simply decoding words. Goodman and Burke (1980) have reported that some beginning readers have said that the purpose of reading is "to learn to read words" and that authors write "to teach you letters and words." It can be predicted that these students may become word-by-word readers who do not chunk the words into meaningful phrases.

Another possible cause of chunking difficulty for some readers is word identification difficulty. If students are having trouble reading the individual words fluently, they may have difficulty with chunking. (See Chapter Seven for a discussion of decoding fluency.)

General Teaching Strategies

Chunking can be facilitated in classrooms at all grade levels and in all content areas. Students can be encouraged to view reading as a meaning-getting process and therefore to read individual words in the context of meaningful phrases: a third-grade student trying to understand a new word in a science class can be told to look at the whole phrase in which it is used; a fifth-grade student having trouble with an unreasonably long sentence in a social studies text can be shown how to break it into phrases and read it in shorter, meaningful parts first; a ninth-grade student reading Shakespeare for the first time can be shown how finding clause boundaries can make it more understandable and how the phrasal context often gives clues to unusual word meanings. In each of these situations, explicit instruction as described in Chapter Two can be used to explain, model, and practice chunking within the context of these meaningful reading assignments.

Moreover, chunking fluency probably develops best when students are given numerous opportunities to practice reading fluently. Because texts in different content areas tend to contain slightly different syntactic patterns, wide reading of easy materials in different subjects and genres would probably be useful. Stevens (1981) found that high school sophomores at all ability levels performed better on a standardized comprehension test when the passages had been chunked by drawing slashes between phrasal units. This seems to indicate that even students at the high school level are still developing in their ability to automatically chunk the kinds of language that they are encountering in their classes.

Remedial Chunking Instruction

In some remedial situations, it may be necessary to practice chunking intensively. Students who can read words, but read without intonation or in a jerky, word-by-word fashion may need to focus their attention on reading in meaningful phrases for an extended period. Although little research has shown the best way to remediate chunking problems, the following activities have been suggested.

Remember, however, that the best way to remediate chunking problems is to help students to view reading as meaning making rather than word identification. To some extent, anything the teacher does to emphasize the search for meaning rather than the identification of isolated words will help remedial readers to begin to chunk words into meaningful phrases. Thus, the exercises that follow should be used in moderation and connected to reading tasks that are meaningful to the learner.

Reading "chunked" material.   For students at the beginning stages of learning to chunk, passages can be rewritten in phrases for practice (see Figure 3-1). Reading "machines" can be made to help students to read in phrases (see Figure 3-2). Put comprehension questions at the beginning and end so that they will read the phrases as meaningful units. Students can practice rereading the same series of phrases until they can pull the paper through quickly and answer all the questions

FIGURE 3-1   Segment of Story Rewritten for Chunking Practice

One day	She wanted one
a little girl	that looked
decided	just like her.
that she wanted	
a new doll.	

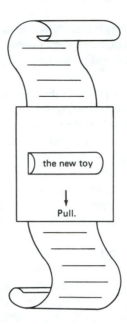

the new toy

Pull.

FIGURE 3-2   Reading "Machine" for Chunking Practice

completely. They can also time each other with stopwatches and, if appropriate, have contests for speed. (This is *not* speed-reading—it is not really even reading, at least, natural reading, at all. The main point is to show the students how the words fall into phrases, and the emphasis on rate may encourage them to process the information in phrasal chunks.) Finally, at a more independent level, students can make chunked material and reading "machines" for each other.

For older students, teachers can simply mark the phrasal boundaries with slashes on short passages that the students are reading. Eventually, these marks can be used only on the beginning sections of long passages and the students can be asked to try to continue "phrase reading" even after the marks stop. At a more independent level, students can divide passages into phrases themselves. Students can be asked to compare their markings so that they can clarify why they chunk words the way they do. Of course, being able to chunk in this fashion does not guarantee students' ability to chunk automatically as they read. Practice with reading simple but increasingly difficult material that can be processed fluently is still the final step in developing chunking automaticity.

Dramatic reading for chunking practice.   Another activity that may increase students' awareness of the syntactic patterns in written language is reading with expression. A story, play, or poem at the appropriate level and of an appropriate length can be selected on the basis of interest appeal and dramatic dialogue. Different levels of teacher support can be provided as needed. For instance, the teacher can model reading the selection sentence by sentence or section by section with the student imitating the intonation immediately afterward. Similarly, the teacher and student can mark the phrasal units together, and then the student can practice reading the phrases with the teacher or alone. Repeated readings of the same passage will be necessary, and this alone may increase fluency and self-confidence. The end result can be a tape recording for use by other students reading the story or a classroom dramatic presentation as well as an increased awareness of how written language can be divided into meaningful phrases.

Classroom and small-group activities can also be used to practice dramatic oral reading. Students can create a "Reader's Theater" for any story, poem, newspaper article, or play that they select (Pikulski, 1983). Have each student select a portion of the piece to prepare. The students should then take these sections home and practice reading them with expression. (This is a critical step to ensure that the reader be able to feel successful.) The next day, the students read their sections aloud, in order, with as much expression as possible. They can tape the final reading for a classroom oral library. A variation would be to change the oral readings in terms of the order, the number of people reading simultaneously, or the style of reading (Wood, 1983).

Another variation would be to have the students prepare to read together as a "verse choir" (Povenmire, 1977). The teacher could group them according to their voices (for example, boy-girl or light-dark) and have them read parts according to their grouping. Group reading is especially useful for students who are having trouble or who are shy about reading on their own. "Big books," those several feet high that have print large enough for a whole group of students to see, have been used successfully for encouraging shy students to read aloud with their peers.

Sentence organization instruction.   Practice in synthesizing sentences has been shown to be an effective instructional technique by Weaver (1979). Students can be taught to solve sentence anagrams (sentences in which the words have been scrambled) by using a "word-grouping strategy" (p. 135). In other words, they can be taught first to arrange the words into phrases and then to arrange the phrases into sentences. They should probably first identify the verb phrase and then ask "wh" questions to identify the other phrases. The strategy should be modeled first. Then, students can be given sentences of increasing length. Here is an example of a teacher modeling a sentence anagram task.

GIVEN: boy store the the was to going   [on cards]
TEACHER: Well, the verb is "going," so we'll start with that:

$\boxed{\text{GOING}}$ [placed on table]

Are there any helping verbs? Yes, "was" is a helping verb. Let's tape these together.

| WAS | = | GOING | [taped together]

Now, I can ask, *Who* was going? Well, it was either the boy or the store . . . probably BOY, and THE goes with it, so I'll tape THE to BOY and put it in front of my other phrase.

| THE | = | BOY | WAS | = | GOING | [two taped phrases placed next to each other]

Now, what words are left?

| STORE | THE | TO | [left on table]

Can I make a phrase from those? Yes, and I'll tape those together.

| TO | = | THE | = | STORE | [taped together]

Does this go with the rest? Yes, at the end:

| THE | = | BOY | WAS | = | GOING | TO | = | THE | = | STORE |

Result: three taped-together phrases placed in the correct order

Paraphrase instruction. One way to encourage students to focus on phrase meaning rather than on word identification is to provide tasks that require students to identify or supply a paraphrase of an original statement. Pearson and Johnson (1978) distinguish between semantic paraphrases as in 3a and 3b that follow and syntactic paraphrases as in 3c and 3d. Syntactic paraphrase tasks are probably more useful for chunking instruction than are semantic paraphrase tasks.

A semantic paraphrase is

3a. Jack jumped over the bushes.
3b. Jack leaped over the hedge.

A syntactic paraphrase is:

3c. Jack flew the kite.
3d. The kite was flown by Jack.

Note that the exact connotations of paraphrases are often somewhat different. For example, 3c emphasizes the person who is doing the action, whereas 3d emphasizes the object of the action. Thus, it would be better to ask students to select or write sentences whose meanings are "similar" rather than "the same."

Games in which students match pairs or triples of sentences with similar meanings can be used in the elementary grades. Also, team activities in which the person "up" must create a paraphrase in less time than the corresponding member of the other team can be used with older children. The purpose of these activities is to encourage word-by-word readers to focus on the meaning of the sentences. This requires them to chunk the individual words into meaningful phrases.

MICROSELECTION

As good readers read, they are constantly selecting what details to retain in their memories (see Kintsch & van Dijk, 1978). Even when reading individual sentences, students must be actively involved in selecting the most important ideas in each of those sentences. This can be called *microselection*. This is similar to the traditional skill of "finding the main idea of individual sentences," which has been suggested as a prerequisite skill for finding the central ideas in longer passages (Baumann, 1982).

Keeping the appropriate main idea of a sentence in mind helps the reader to connect that sentence to the next one. For instance, suppose the reader were reading sentences 3e and 3f.

   3e. New York is a very exciting place to visit.
   3f. It has lots of museums and fancy stores in which to shop.

If the reader chose to remember that visiting is exciting from sentence 3e, then the reference to "it" would make little sense, and the reader might then think that the point was that shopping is exciting. If, however, the reader remembered that New York is exciting, then "it" would make sense, and the reader would remember that museums and fancy stores were in New York.

There is much evidence that good readers are more likely to remember important rather than unimportant details (Meyer, 1977). As seen in the preceding example, "important details" are probably best defined as those details that are most highly related to the central idea of the passage or most necessary for the understanding of subsequent ideas. Thus, the ability to select important ideas from individual sentences successfully probably depends on the ability to summarize and use the author's organization, macroprocessing strategies which will be discussed later in Chapter Four. This is a good example of how various processes and strategies interact. Effective microselection leads to effective macroprocessing and vice versa.

General Microselection Instruction

Teachers at all levels can directly encourage students to select important details from sentences during class discussions. They can explain the concept of microselection so that students do not get bogged down in trying to remember every word. They can model the process themselves: "Now, what *I* want to remember from this sentence is…because…." Examples of teachers teaching microselection range from the kindergarten teacher who, when reading a story to the students, stops and asks, "What was the most important word in that sentence? Why?" to the high school chemistry teacher who, after students read a sentence with a long list of properties for a given substance says, "Which of these properties do you want to remember for our experiment?"

Activities for Microselection Instruction

Selective paraphrase.   Paraphrasing activities like those used to stress phrase meaning would probably be useful for teaching microselection. In this case, required or recognized paraphrases should be summary sentences that summarize the first sentence into its main point. For example, sentence 3h is a "selective paraphrase" of sentence 3g.

3g. The boy whom many of us called Gus was caught by the men in blue who had been chasing him.

3h. Gus was caught by the police.

Games in which students compete to supply the shortest selective paraphrase may also be useful. (Activities must reflect the students' level of independence. For students who are having trouble, selective paraphrases from which they can select the best should probably be supplied by the teacher. Students who already have some independence can be asked to supply their own.)

Writing your own test.   Students can get involved with meaningful selection by creating their own tests. To focus on microselection, give students worksheets containing important sentences about the material being studied. For each sentence, ask them to write a test question that reflects what is important in that sentence.

Selecting what to study.   Another meaningful selection task is involving students in deciding what to study. For microselection, the teacher can select or create sentences containing both important and unimportant details from the current unit. List them for the students on an initial study guide. Then, students can make up their own study sheets on which they list only one important detail from each of the sentences listed. They study and then are tested on the important details alone.

INTEGRATIVE PROCESSES

One of the most important words in the definition of comprehension that was stated in Chapter One is construct. Readers construct their comprehension of a passage by inferring ideas that are not directly stated by the author. The role of inference in comprehension cannot be overstressed. In fact, it could be said that little or no comprehension can occur without it.

Consider the following short passage. What inferences are you making as you try to comprehend the author's message?

> Sally rode her bike to the store. John followed her. He got a flat tire. He cried.

Well, the most obvious inferences are those involving the pronouns: "her" means "Sally's" and so forth. You also probably inferred that John rode a bike, that the flat tire was on his bike, and that the flat tire caused him to cry. Note that some of these inferences are necessary to understand the meanings of individual words, but, mostly, they are necessary for understanding how the sentences fit together.

Integrative processes can be defined as the processes involved in understanding and inferring the relationships between clauses and sentences. Three main types of integrative processes are understanding anaphora, understanding connective relationships, and making "slot-filling" inferences.

ANAPHORA

Anaphoric relations are associations between words in which one word or phrase is being used to replace another. For instance, in sentences 3i and 3j that follow, the pronoun "he" is being used to replace "John":

3i. John followed Sally.
3j. He got a flat tire.

The word being replaced, in this case, "John," is called the *antecedent*.

Anaphoric relations can be classified according to what is doing the replacing: Either a pronoun or a substituting word can replace the antecedent, as illustrated by the underlined words in examples 3k and 3l, respectively.

3k. *Jack* went to the store. *He* bought candy. (pronoun)
3l. He bought *candy*. The *sugary treats* delighted him. (substitution)

Also, remember that all kinds of pronomial terms can be used to replace antecedents: personal pronouns such as I, me, we, us, you, he, him, they; demonstrative pronouns such as this, that, these, those; proverbs such as so, does, can, will, and have; or locative pronouns such as here or there.

Anaphoric relations can also be viewed in terms of what is being replaced. Nouns, verbs, and clauses can all be replaced by pronomial or other substitutions.

Examples of each of these are provided in Table 3-1. Study this table. Research seems to indicate that relations in which the noun is replaced are easier to understand than relations in which an entire clause is replaced (Barnitz, 1980).

Finally, research also indicates that anaphoric relations are easier to understand when the antecedent and the replacement are in adjacent sentences or clauses. When the antecedent and the replacement are in sentences that are separated by other sentences, comprehension seems to be more difficult (Clark & Sengul, 1979; Moberly, 1978). The conceptual difficulty of the material, the clarity of the context, the prior knowledge of the students, and other textual factors will also affect the comprehensibility of anaphoric relations (Barnitz, 1986).

Incidental Teaching of Anaphoric Inference

Teachers at all grade levels and in all content areas should be alert to the use of anaphoric references in the materials students are reading. Are there any ambiguous referents? Ask questions that require students to understand referents in their readings. This will give you an idea of whether a process discussion about finding referents will be necessary (see Chapter Two). Here are some examples of teachers checking to see if their students are making anaphoric inferences. Note how this process is important at all grade levels.

EXAMPLE 1.   Third-Grade Average Reading Group

STUDENTS READ: John went home with Jack. He played his trumpet, and Jack played his drums. Their parents came by to listen. They were amazed by their music.

TEACHER ASKS: Who was amazed? [why?]

TABLE 3-1   Examples of Anaphoric Relations

	PRONOMIAL	SUBSTITUTION
Nominal	Jack went to the store.	He bought candy.
	He bought candy.	The sugary treats delighted him.
Verbal	Jack went to the store.	Jack ran to the store.
	So did Sally.	Sally dashed there, too.
Clausal	Jack went to the store that he always went to.	Jack looked as if he had lost his best friend.
	Sally went there, too.	Sally looked sad, too.

EXAMPLE 2.   Tenth-Grade Social Studies Class

STUDENTS READ: As part of the agreement, Americans gave up their claim to Texas. They were, however, already moving into the region. They were lured by the hope for practically free land.

TEACHER ASKS: To what region were the Americans moving?

Activities for Remedial Instruction in Anaphoric Inference

Many basal series already include some activities for teaching anaphoric inference, although basal activities differ significantly in amount and type. Generally, these activities usually involve students in filling in blanks with pronouns or referents, writing paraphrases, identifying referents for pronouns, or answering questions (Willekens, 1986).

No evidence exists however, that all students require or benefit from such artificial exercises. Thus, the use of these types of activities should be limited to situations in which you know that certain students need intensive training in this area.

In those situations, you may wish to explain and model this process using the following specific exercises. An excellent discussion of additional activities that can be used as supplements has been provided by Baumann and Stevenson (1986).

Anaphoric cloze.   Activities in which students must supply the pronoun or referent can be called *anaphoric cloze* activities. At the most dependent level, students can be given several choices from which they must select the correct word for the blank space in the passage. At a more independent level, students can be asked to supply the correct word themselves. A similar activity might involve students in replacing all pronouns with referents, or vice versa.

"Tying it together."   Students can be shown how sentences are linked by anaphoric reference. Then they can be asked to mark pairs of sentences as follows:

(Jack) went to the store. He bought some candy.

Pairs of sentences can be constructed to give systematic practice with different types of relations. In the beginning, each activity should emphasize one type and direction. As students mature, types, directions, and distances between referents can be mixed. Then, students can work on similarly marking whole passages. Here is an example of a passage from a social studies assignment that students could have marked together using an overhead projector:

By 1859, 100,000 *Easterners* had headed toward *Pikes Peak* in the Rockies. Find (this mountain) on the map at the right. (Many) had left (their) families and (their) sweethearts at home. (Some) wanted to get rich. (Others) just wanted enough money to make a new start in life for (their) families.

"Make it shorter."   Students can also be given pairs of sentences in which anaphoric substitution could be used to shorten one of the sentences. For instance, students could be asked to make one of these sentences shorter:

3m.   Jack, Sally, and Sue went to the store.

3n.   Jack, Sally, and Sue bought some candy.

This is a good example of an exercise in which reading and writing instruction can overlap.

Indeed, there are many opportunities for discussing the use of pronominal terms and interesting substitutions when students are actively involved in meaningful writing assignments. Students writing stories may notice that they use the character's name too often and therefore need to use a pronoun instead. Students may notice that they use the same term repeatedly and may then decide to look for substitutions. Discussions about these issues can lead back to discussions about how these techniques apply to reading processes as well.

Finally, probably the best time to schedule activities like *anaphoric cloze, tying it together*, and *make it shorter* is when students are having trouble with meaningful reading assignments and realize that they need to learn how to go about understanding them. You can then use these activities to introduce the process and follow them with applications to the reading materials that created the need for the discussion in the first place.

CONNECTIVES

Anaphoric relations tie separate clauses and sentences together because the antecedent and the replacing term refer to the same thing. Clauses and sentences can also be tied together through *connective concepts*. Connective concepts are the concepts that relate two events to each other. For instance, in sentence 3o one event caused another (a causal connective); in sentence 3p one event happened before another (a time sequence connective).

3o.   The blossom opened <u>because</u> the sun was shining.

3p.   I went to the store, <u>and then</u> I went to the park.

Table 3-2 shows some possible types of connective concepts and the explicit cues often used to express them. Study this table.

Connectives can be expressed explicitly with the use of specific words, as exemplified in Table 3-2, or they can be implicit—that is, implied by the author but not directly stated. For instance, sentences 3q and 3r are related by means of an implicit causal connective—that is, a causal relationship that is *not* directly stated:

3q.   Mary had a stomachache.

3r.   She ate too much.

TABLE 3-2   Some Common Types of Connective Concepts

TYPES	CUES USED		EXAMPLE
Conjunction	and in addition to also along with		Jack went to the store. Sally went also.
Disjunction	or either . . . or . . .		Either Jack went to the store, or he went home.
Causality	because so consequently		Jack went home because he was sick.
Purpose	in order to for the purpose of so that		Jack went home in order to get his money.
Concession	but although however yet		Jack left for home, but he hasn't gotten there yet.
Contrast	in contrast similarly (also comparative and superlative forms of adjectives)		Jack was very sick. In contrast, I feel better!
Condition	If . . . then . . . unless except		If Jack is sick, then he can't play ball.
Time	before after when	always while from now on	Before Jack got sick, he went to the store.
Location	there where		Jack is at home where, he will be able to rest.
Manner	in a similar manner like as		Jack was blue and feverish, as Sally was yesterday.

Source: The list of connectives is derived from a taxonomy presented by Turner, A. & Greene, E. *The construction and ease of a propositional test base.* (Technical report no. 63, Institute for the Study of Intellectual Behavior, University of Colorado, Boulder, 1977).

A recent study of implicit connectives in children's social studies texts has indicated that these are as common in primary-level texts as they are in high school texts; the two types most often stated implicitly are causal and time sequence connectives (Irwin, 1982). Moreover, research also indicates that implicitly stated connectives are more difficult to comprehend than are explicitly stated ones (Irwin, 1980; Irwin & Pulver, 1984). Further examples of implicit causal and time sequence relations are provided in Table 3-3. Look through the materials your students read. Can you find other examples of implicit connectives?

TABLE 3-3   Typical Implicit Connectives

	CAUSAL	TIME SEQUENCE
Fiction	Johnny loved playing the trumpet. He loved being good at something.	Johnny got first place at the country fair. He got first place at the state fair. He flew to Washington to compete against all the other state fair winners.
Content area	It was easy to go into making iron. Only one machine was needed.	Several Northern recruits overpowered the watchman. They ordered the telegraph wires cut. They freed the slaves. They escaped while it was still dark.

Like so many comprehension tasks, inferring implicit connective concepts almost always requires that the reader have specific kinds of prior knowledge. In sentence 3s, students who know that they are reading about a time in history in which many Americans owned slaves will be more likely to make the correct inference than will students who do not know this. Thus, teaching connective inference will often involve a review of students' prior knowledge (see Chapter Seven for methods).

3s.   Mexico allowed slavery. Many Americans moved to Mexico.

Finally, before you teach students to understand either explicit or implicit connective relations, you must be able to identify them. In Passage 3-1, the connective concepts are marked and available cue words are underlined. Each connective has also been classified according to the following abbreviated key:

C   =   causality
T   =   time sequence
P   =   purpose
Cn   =   concession
Ct   =   contrast

Study this passage. How many of these connectives are only implicitly stated? What types are they? Mark Passage 3-2 in a similar fashion. The answers can be found at the end of this chapter.

(Clue: There are five connective concepts. Two are only implicitly stated.)

PASSAGE 3-1

                                          C   C

People were building homes and stores.   They bought more and more wood.   The
                         Cn   C

sawmills were very busy. But soon there was no wood left to cut down.   One after another,
         C   C

the sawmills closed.   Workers had to find something else to do.   They began to plant
    P   C   T

wheat so they could sell it. Thus, farming became important after all the trees had been cut
   C   Ct

down. Now, more people were farmers than builders.

Source: E. A. Anderson, *Communities and Their Needs* (Morristown, N.J.: Silver Burdett, 1972), p. 62. Reprinted by permission.

PASSAGE 3-2

Only a few people in the Denver area became rich from mining gold and silver. But many stayed anyway. There were many opportunities to become rich by farming. Many of the wealthy people built large homes in order to show how rich they were.

But Denver needed a railroad. Denver's citizens organized their own railroad company.

Adapted from J. H. Dempsey *This Is Man* (Morristown, N.J.: Silver Burdett, 1972), p. 185. Reprinted by permission.

Incidental Teaching of Connective Inference

As with anaphoric relations, teachers in all grade levels and content areas can promote connective inference by asking relevant questions. If they find that students have failed to make the appropriate inferences, they can direct students to the appropriate sentences. They might then discover that the problem involved a lack of background knowledge. Then, students can simply be given the important background information. If the problem seems to be a lack of awareness of the importance of looking for implicit relationships, this can be discussed directly using the teaching methods introduced in Chapter Two.

Remedial Connective Instruction

As with some other processes discussed in this book, little research has demonstrated what activities best teach this process. The following activities have been suggested, however, for introducing this process to students who are having trouble. As with the anaphora activities, it is important to tie these exercises to the students' regular reading and writing activities. Show them how using connectives can improve their writing. Wait until the students need to learn to infer implicit connectives to understand a book or content-area article and then demonstrate the process using these activities. Use process questions and activities in which they use connective inference with the original reading materials.

Connective cloze.   Pulver (1986) has recommended that after students have had some practice with identifying and interpreting explicit connectives, they can be given sentence sets in which the connectives have been deleted. Begin with easy sentences involving common events, as in sentence 3t, but eventually you can ask students to supply connectives deleted from content-area sentences, as in sentence 3u. Students can be given connectives from which to choose, or, at a more independent level, they can choose their own.

  3t. Susie wanted to go to the party, _____ she was too sick.
  3u. The homesteaders often wanted Indian land, _____ it was good for raising cattle.

The final step would involve asking students to supply implicit connectives deleted from whole passages they are reading in class.

Sentence combining.   Activities involving sentence combining effectively integrate the teaching of reading and writing processes. Younger students can be given cards with main clauses and cards with a variety of connective cue words. They can then work to see how many ways the clauses can be put together. This would be a good follow-up activity for the sentence anagram task described in Chapter One. Older students can be asked to fill in missing connectives from a suggested list to match clauses that can be connected with "because" and so on. One more difficult variation for older students would be to ask them to reverse the order of the clauses by changing the connective. For instance, in the sentences that follow, 3v can be rewritten as 3w, and 3x can be rewritten as 3y.

  3v. The batter was old, so the cake did not rise.
  3w. The cake did not rise because the batter was old.
  3x. It was raining, but John went to the game.
  3y. John went to the game, although it was raining.

A final step here might be to try to insert connectives into their own or a friend's writing project.

Finding implicit connectives.   Students who are at a more independent level for this strategy can be asked to find the explicit and implicit connectives in their reading assignments. Because they are often implicit, this could probably involve causal and time sequence connectives only. Pulver (1986) has suggested that students be taught the following four-step procedure (p. 77):

1. Look at where the sentences come together.
2. Think about how they might be related.
3. Use what you already know about the topic to determine if your guess made sense.
4. Try to insert a connective between the two sentences. Does this new sentence make sense?

SLOT-FILLING INFERENCES

Let us look again at the inference example given in the introduction to this chapter. This time some of the required inferences have been marked (A = anaphora, C = connective).

A   A   A   CA

Sally rode <u>her</u> bike to the store. John followed <u>her</u>. <u>He</u> got a flat tire. <u>He</u> cried.

We can now see at least four uses of pronominal anaphora and one implicit causal relation. You will remember, however, that you also inferred that John rode a bike, and that the flat tire was on this bike.

These are called *slot-filling inferences* (Trabasso, 1981). Slot-filling inferences are inferences that fill in important missing aspects of the given situation. In general, the relevant missing "slots" are determined by the situation and may involve answering the following questions (based on Fillmore, 1968, and Kintsch, 1974):

Agent	=	Who did it?
Object	=	To whom or what was it done?
Instrument	=	What was used to do it?
Experiencer	=	Who experienced the feeling or thought?
Source	=	Where did it (or they) come from?
Goal	=	What was the result or goal?

In the example, it can be inferred that the bike was the instrument of travel and the object of the broken tire.

Other slot-filling inferences might involve character motivation, other psychological and physical causes, enabling circumstances, and spatiotemporal relationships (adapted from Warren, Nicholas, & Trabasso, 1979). For instance, in the example, the story content might have resulted in an inference that John followed

Sally because he liked her (character motivation), or that he no longer had a broken leg (enabling circumstance). If the reader knew nails were in the road, he or she might infer that they caused the flat tire (physical cause). If the reader knew that the store was at the corner of the block on which they both lived, he or she might infer that the flat-tire incident occurred somewhere on the block (spatiotemporal relationship). Notice how such inferences work to connect the ideas and create a much richer interpretation of the events in the story than one lacking in such inferences. Readers who use such inferences are much more likely to remember what they read as a coherent whole.

Finally, our prior knowledge of the situation also determines what might be inferred. For instance, for sentences 3z and 3aa, potential slot-filling inferences are given in parentheses. Can you tell what slot-filling inferences might be made for sentences 3bb and 3cc? What kind of prior knowledge is necessary to make these inferences?

3z. She stirred the coffee. [She used a spoon.] (instrument)

3aa. They moved to the South. [They moved from the North.] (source)

3bb. She dropped the china plate.[1]

3cc. The rain quickly turned to ice on the streets.[2]

In example 3bb, a reader would need to know the characteristics of a material called "china." Students who eat primarily from plastic dinnerware might not automatically make the inference. In example 3cc, the reader would need to know that rain turns to ice when it gets cold. One can imagine young children in warm climates not necessarily making this inference.

Instructional methodology for slot-filling inference will probably be similar to that used for anaphora and connective inference. Students can be asked questions about the slot-filling inferences required in their reading assignments. Prior knowledge should be checked when it is found that students have not made the necessary inferences. Students can discuss the reasoning processes used to make various inferences, and, if necessary, the teacher can model these processes. Activities that require students to combine sentences with slot-filling inferences can be used to supplement more natural reading tasks when serious problems are noticed.

A FINAL LOOK AT INTEGRATIVE PROCESSES

When we look at passage coherence in a general way, we can see that two kinds of relationships tie sentences and clauses together: (1) "local" connections, or those that link individual sentences and clauses to each other; and (2) "global" connections, or

[1][The plate broke.] (goal)
[2][It was cold outside.] (enabling circumstance)

those that link each individual clause and sentence to the main idea or focal event of the passage. In this text, the term "integrative processes" is used to refer to the processes involved in comprehending local connections only. Global connections are understood through macroprocesses, which will be discussed in Chapter Four.

Recent research on the integrative processes used by children in their reading and writing activities suggests that this distinction between local and global connections may have important developmental and instructional implications. Scardamalia and Bereiter (1983) found evidence that elementary school children, when reading for comprehension, tend to rely on global connections rather than on local ones more than did the adults in their study—that is, they tied each idea to a general topic, but they did not connect individual ideas to each other. McCutchen (1982) similarly found that, when writing, older (sixth- and eighth-grade) students used a higher proportion of local connections than did younger (second- and fourth-grade) students. Thus, it may be that explicit instruction in integrative processes can improve both the reading and writing skills of students who do not use these local connections, and that this instruction can begin in the intermediate grades in meaningful reading and writing situations.

Indeed, the meaningful integration of reading and writing process discussion and instruction can easily be demonstrated in the area of integrative processes. When students are reading their writing to others in writing group discussions, some students might suggest that they do not understand who is doing the action (pronoun reference) or how one section led to another (slot-filling or connective inference). These discussions can be related to situations in which students note similar problems when they are reading: "Remember how John made us understand his story better by showing that Sally loved animals and that was why she was upset about Susie's attitude? Well, this author wants you to think about what you know about Jack to determine why he is reacting this way."

SUMMARY

To comprehend even the simplest passage, readers use many active reading strategies. First, they actively *chunk* the sentences into meaningful phrases. Then they *select* from those phrases the important ideas that they want to keep in mind as they read the upcoming information. These sentence-level comprehension processes can be called *microprocesses*.

Readers also pause at the end of each sentence to tie the selected ideas together. Many inferences are necessary to integrate clauses and sentences conceptually. Inferences and direct interpretations that are necessary for such integration are the result of *integrative processes*.

Three main types of integrative processes are understanding anaphoric references, understanding explicit and implicit connectives, and making other necessary "slot-filling" inferences. In *anaphoric relations,* one word or phrase is being used to replace another. Anaphoric terms can replace nouns, verbs, or whole clauses. The substituting term can be a pronoun or a synonym (substitution).

Connectives are concepts that connect events. There are at least ten kinds of connectives. Examples include conjunction, causality, concession, and time sequence. Many different cue words can be used to state these relationships explicitly, or they can simply be implied by the author. Causal and time sequence relationships are the types most frequently stated implicitly. Implicitly stated connectives are probably more difficult to comprehend than are explicitly stated ones.

Finally, many other types of inferences are required to integrate sentences. These include filling in necessary information about agents, objects, instruments, character motivation, and enabling factors. They are therefore called *slot-filling inferences.*

When working with students in the area of integrative processes, it is important to assess the students' prior knowledge of the passage topic. Integrative inferences usually require some background information. Activities can be designed to show students the various ways in which sentences can be connected and to give them practice with the various integrative processes. It must be stressed, however, that isolated drill with artificial activities will have only limited utility. Probably the best instructional activity is the natural discussion that precedes and follows meaningful reading tasks. During this time, teachers of all grade levels and content areas can encourage, model, and explain integrative processes.

SELF-CHECK TEST

1. Define the following terms.

   chunking
   difference readers
   "reading machine"
   Reader's Theater
   verse choir
   sentence anagram task
   syntactic paraphrase
   microselection
   selective paraphrase

   anaphora
   locative pronoun
   demonstrative pronoun
   verbal substitution
   concession connective
   causal connective
   implicit connective
   slot-filling inference
   local connection
   global connection

2. Answer true or false.

   ____ (a) A student's intonation often gives a clue about his or her chunking ability.

   ____ (b) Microprocesses should be taught only in the elementary schools.

   ____ (c) If students can read the individual words, they can chunk appropriately.

_____ (d) A difference reader is one who cannot select what to remember.

_____ (e) Word identification tasks are useful for teaching chunking.

3. For each of the following anaphoric relations, tell whether it is pronomial or substitution.

(a) I returned six library books yesterday. I forgot to return these.

(b) Jack chased the spider. The insect was afraid.

4. For each of the following pairs of sentences, tell what kind of connective could be inferred to connect them.

(a) It never rains here. It is raining now.

(b) Jack was nervous. He had to give a speech.

(c) He went to the store. He went to the party.

(d) The dog was small. The cat was smaller.

5. Here are a reading passage and a series of questions asked by Ms. Jones, a remedial reading teacher at John Doe High School. The answers are those given by Jack, a tenth-grade student diagnosed as reading at somewhere around the third-grade level. What can Ms. Jones guess about Jack's ability to integrate sentences in various ways? Be specific.

It was Bob's first day of school, though it was already December. He was very excited. He did not know which pair of shoes to wear. Getting dressed always confused him, and choosing footwear was especially puzzling. He had such big feet. He looked outside to check the weather. He wore his boots.

Q: What happened in the story?
A: Someone wore boots.
Q: What day was it?
A: Bob's first day of school in December.
Q: Was someone excited?
A: Yes.
Q: Who?
A: I'm not sure.
Q: What was puzzling?
A: Choosing footwear.
Q: Why was choosing footwear a problem?
A: I don't know.
Q: What was the weather like?
A: It did not say.

SUGGESTED ACTIVITIES

1. If appropriate for your students, create a lesson that encourages the students to chunk words into meaningful phrases. Be sure to tell how you would explain

and model this process. If possible, try your lesson with an appropriate student. Evaluate its success.

2. Create a lesson that encourages students to select what is important in sentences from a typical reading assignment in your class. Be sure, again, to tell how you would explain and model this strategy. If possible, try the lesson and evaluate its effectiveness.

3. Look through a textbook you do or would use in your teaching. Find several kinds of anaphoric relations. What kinds are generally used? What kinds of explicit connectives are used? Do you see any implicit connectives? Read through a typical chapter or story. What kinds of slot-filling inferences are required? Write a short description of the integrative processes necessary for comprehending this textbook.

4. Copy a page from a textbook you do or would use in your teaching. Mark all the intersentential connections. Are they implicit or explicit?

5. For the grade level and content area you do or will teach, design an instructional activity to teach a specific type of integrative process. Try to make it as meaningful as possible by using materials the students will be reading for other purposes and by focusing on something with which they usually have difficulty.

PASSAGE 3-2 (Answer)

$$\text{Cn}$$
Only a few people in the Denver area became rich from mining gold and silver. But many stayed
$$\text{C}$$
anyway.   There were many opportunities to become rich from farming. Many of the wealthy
$$\text{P}\qquad\qquad\qquad\qquad\text{Cn}$$
people built large homes in order to show how rich they were. But Denver needed a railroad.
$$\text{C}$$
Denver's citizens organized their own railroad company.

REFERENCES

Barnitz, J. (1986). The anaphoric jigsaw puzzle in psycholinguistic and reading research. In J. W. Irwin (Ed.), *Understanding and teaching cohesion comprehension* (pp. 45–56). Newark, Del.: International Reading Association.

Barnitz, J. (1980). Syntactic effects on the reading comprehension of pronoun-referent structures by children in grades two, four and six. *Reading Research Quarterly, 15,* 268–289.

Baumann, J. (1982, December). Teaching children to comprehend main ideas. Paper presented at the annual meeting of the National Reading Conference, Clearwater, Fla.

Baumann, J., & Stevenson, J. (1986). Teaching students to comprehend anaphoric relations. In J. W. Irwin (Ed.), *Understanding and teaching cohesion comprehension* (pp. 95–124). Newark, Del.: International Reading Association.

Calfee, R. C., & Piontkowski, P. C. (1981). The reading diary: Acquisition of decoding. *Reading Research Quarterly, 16,* 346–373.

Clark, H. H., & Sengul, C. J. (1979). In search of referents for nouns and pronouns. *Memory and Cognition, 7,* 35–41.

Cromer, W. (1970). The difference model: A new explanation for some reading difficulties. *Journal of Educational Psychology, 61,* 471–483.

Fillmore, C. J. (1968). The case for case. In E. Bach & R. T. Horms (Eds.), *Universals in linguistic theory.* New York: Holt, Rinehart and Winston.

Goodman, V., & Burke, C. (1980). *Reading Strategies: Focus on comprehension.* New York: Holt, Rinehart and Winston.

Halliday, M. A. K., & Hasan, R. (1976). *Cohesion in English.* London: Longman Group.

Hurtig, R. (1978). The validity of clausal processing strategies at the discourse level. *Discourse Processes, 1,* 195–202.

Irwin, J. W. (1980). The effects of explicitness and clause order on the comprehension of reversible causal relationships. *Reading Research Quarterly, 15,* 477–488.

Irwin, J. W. (1982). Coherence factors in children's textbooks. *Reading Psychology, 4,* 11–23.

Irwin, J. W., & Pulver, C. (1984). The effects of explicitness, clause order, and reversibility on children's comprehension of causal relationships. *Journal of Educational Psychology, 76,* 399–407.

Just, M. A., & Carpenter, P. A. (1980). A theory of reading: From eye fixations to comprehension. *Psychological Review, 87,* 329–354.

Kintsch, W. (1974). *The representation of meaning in memory.* Hillsdale, N.J.: Lawrence Erlbaum.

Kintsch, W., & van Dijk, T. A. (1978). Toward a model of text comprehension and production. *Psychological Review, 85,* 363–394.

Leu, D. J. (1982, May). Written text and oral expectations: Discourse conflicts for beginning readers. Paper presented at the annual meeting of the International Reading Association, Chicago.

Mason, J., & Kendall, J. (1978). *Facilitating reading comprehension through text-structure manipulation* (Technical Report No. 92). Urbana-Champaign: Center for the Study of Reading, University of Illinois.

McCutchen, D. (1982). Development of local coherence in children's writing. Unpublished manuscript, University of Pittsburgh.

Meyer, B. J. F. (1977). What is remembered from prose: A function of passage structure. In R. O. Freedle (Ed.), *Discourse production and comprehension* (Vol. I). Norwood, N.J.: Ablex.

Moberly, P. (1978). *Elementary children's understanding of anaphoric relationships in connected discourse.* Unpublished doctoral dissertation, Northwestern University, Evanston, Illinois.

Pearson, P. D., & Johnson, D. D. (1978) *Teaching reading comprehension*. New York: Holt, Rinehart and Winston.

Pikulski, J. (1983). Reader's Theater. *Reading Teacher, 37*, 223–224.

Povenmire, E. K. (1977). Using multipaired simultaneous oral reading. *Reading Teacher, 40*, 239–240.

Pulver, C. (1986). Teaching students to understand explicit and implicit connectives. In J. W. Irwin (Ed.), *Understanding and teaching cohesion comprehension*. Newark, Del.: International Reading Association.

Scardemalia, M., & Bereiter, C. (1983). Topical versus propositional approaches to text processing. In H. Mandl, N. Stein, & T. Trabasso (Eds.), *Learning and comprehension of texts*. Hillsdale, N.J.: Lawrence Erlbaum.

Stevens, K. (1981). Chunking material as an aid to reading comprehension. *Journal of Reading, 25*, 126–129.

Trabasso, T. (1981). The making of inferences during reading and their assessment. In J. T. Guthrie (Ed.), *Comprehension and teaching*. Newark, Del.: International Reading Association.

Turner, A., & Greene, E. (1977). *The construction and use of a propositional text base*. (Technical Report No. 63.) Boulder, Colo.: Institute for the Study of Intellectual Behavior, University of Colorado.

Warren, W. H., Nicholas, D. W., & Trabasso, T. (1979). Event chains and inferences in understanding narratives. In R. O. Freedle (Ed.), *New directions in discourse processing* (Vol. 2). Hillsdale, N.J.: Lawrence Erlbaum.

Weaver, P. A. (1979). Improving reading instruction: Effects of sentence organization instruction. *Reading Research Quarterly, 15*, 129–146.

Willekens, A. (1986). Anaphoric reference instruction: Current instructional practices. In J. W. Irwin (Ed.), *Understanding and teaching cohesion comprehension* (pp. 83–94). Newark, Del.: International Reading Association.

Wood, K. D. (1983). A variation on an old theme: 4 way oral reading. *Reading Teacher, 37*, 38–41.

4

TEACHING MACROPROCESSES

You may remember that in Chapter Three it was pointed out that readers cannot usually remember every single idea in a passage. Rather, even at the level of individual sentences (during microprocessing), they are selective about what to remember. *Macroprocessing* is the ongoing process of creating or selecting an organized set of summary ideas, presumably for the purpose of organizing recall and reducing the number of ideas to be remembered. Macroprocessing aids in the recall of details by providing "hooks" or general ideas to which those details can be linked. It requires the ability to select what is important and the ability to summarize details. Both of these require an awareness of the overall organizational structure of the passage. Thus, in this chapter, teaching students about general organizational patterns will be discussed first. This will be followed by some ideas about teaching students how to use the organization and other clues to select the most important ideas from whole passages (macroselection), and how to use the organization and the selected important information to summarize effectively.

Macroprocessing interacts with microprocessing in that it helps students decide which individual idea units to remember (microselection). It can also be related to integrative processing: just as integrative processes enable readers to see relationships between sentences (local connections) so that they can be remembered as a unified whole, macroprocesses enable readers to tie ideas together by means of an overall summary structure to which every individual idea is related (global connections). Macro- and integrative processes interact in that local connections provide cues as to the global connections, and vice versa. For instance, if a reader decides that the overall structure of the passage is going to be a chronological description of a historical event, then that reader will be likely to look for time-sequence connectives at the local level. Similarly, a predominance of local time-sequence relations will lead a good reader to see that the global organizational structure is probably a chronological one.

The way each of these processes is used varies according to the reader's purpose. When reading for a test in physics, a student will generally spend a great deal of time understanding and reviewing individual, specific details. When reading several editorials for preparation for a classroom discussion, a student may decide simply to summarize each author's position into one general statement. Similarly, a reader can probably control the amount of material summarized during macroprocessing: Finding the main idea is one degree of specificity in which each paragraph is reduced to one summary idea. Other levels are also possible. An entire chapter can be summarized into two or three statements, for instance.

STORY GRAMMARS

Good readers remember stories better when they are organized like other stories (Mandler & DeForest, 1979; Stein & Nezworski, 1978). Moreover, children's knowledge of story structure seems to become more elaborate as they grow older (Fitzgerald, 1989). Researchers have tried to characterize a typical story structure, although much disagreement exists as to which characterization is most accurate (see Fitzgerald, 1989, p. 15). One such *story grammar* has been provided by Stein and Glenn (1977). According to their grammar, the information in a well-formed narrative can be broken into six categories (see Table 4-1). The last five categories form a group called an "episode" and occur in the specified temporal sequence. Sometimes parts of episodes are signaled by words such as "suddenly" or "finally," but usually the division is based on the content. Sometimes the information required by a given category is not stated explicitly but, rather, is to be inferred by the reader. Finally, many stories have several episodes, and these episodes are connected by means of time sequence (*then...*), causal (*because...*), and simple conjunctive (*and...*) relations. Table 4-1 also includes a typical story that has been divided into story grammar categories according to the Stein and Glenn grammar. Study this example.

Figure 4-1 presents another story for you to label. Note that it has more than one episode. Answers can be found at the end of this chapter. (If you are an elementary teacher or a literature teacher, you will also wish to complete Activity 1 at the end of this chapter.) Of course, every story does not fit this grammar exactly, so do not worry if you find some variations. The point is to identify the important categories of information in the story so that you can help children to see how the story is organized around these categories.

It is probably clear how story structure relates to summarizing. When readers select or construct ideas that represent the "gist" of a story, they often use the ideas

TABLE 4-1   Categories Included in a Simple Story

1.	Setting	Introduction of the protagonist; can contain information about physical, social, or temporal context in which the remainder of the story occurs.
2.	Initiating event	An action, an internal event, or a natural occurrence which serves to initiate or to cause a response in the protagonist.
3.	Internal response	An emotion, cognition, or goal of the protagonist.
4.	Attempt	An overt attempt to obtain the protagonist's goal.
5.	Consequence	An event, action, or end state which marks the attainment or nonattainment of the protagonist's goal.
6.	Reaction	An emotion, a cognition, an action, or an end state expressing the protagonist's feelings about his or her goal attainment or relating the broader consequential realm of the protagonist's goal attainment.

A Well-Formed Story

1.	Setting	a.	Once there was a big gray fish named Albert.
		b.	He lived in a big icy pond near the edge of the forest.
2.	Initiating event	c.	One day, Albert was swimming around the pond.
		d.	Then he spotted a big juicy worm on top of the water.
3.	Internal response	e.	Albert knew how delicious worms tasted.
		f.	He wanted to eat that one for his dinner.
4.	Attempt	g.	So he swam very close to the worm.
		h.	Then he bit into him.
5.	Consequence	i.	Suddenly, Albert was pulled through the water into a boat.
		j.	He had been caught by a fisherman.
6.	Reaction	k.	Albert felt sad.
		l.	He wished he had been more careful.

Source: N. L. Stein, "How Children Understand Stories: A Developmental Analysis," in *Current Topics in Early Childhood Education,* Vol. 2, ed. L. Katz (Hillsdale, N.J.: Ablex, 1979), p. 265. Reprinted by permission.

FIGURE 4-1   A Simple Exercise in Analyzing Story Structure

Once there was a very tall girl named Alice. Alice was the tallest girl in her class. All of her classmates made fun of her. This made her feel very bad. She even tried walking with her knees bent. That just made her look funny. Looking funny made her feel even worse.

One day Alice's teacher said that they were going to have a guest speaker, and in walked the tallest woman Alice had ever seen. She was the star of the local women's basketball team. She talked to the students about the new league, the games that had been played, and what it was like to be a professional athlete. Everyone admired her. Alice was very excited. She asked if she could, maybe, be a player someday. The woman replied that because she was so tall, she would have a better chance than many. For the first time, Alice was proud of being tall.

that summarize the major informational categories. Thus, a sensitivity to typical story structures probably enables students to summarize the information in a story more efficiently (see Kintsch & Greene, 1978). (See also p. 78 and Figure 4-16.)

Instructional Procedures for Story Grammar Awareness

If you teach with fiction, you may wish to investigate the possibility of improving your students' awareness of story structure. This does not mean that you must teach them an elaborate system for parsing stories. Instead, activities like the following have been suggested by Whaley (1981). They can be used as either reading or listening activities and may involve writing responses.

1. *Prediction task*. Have students tell what comes next in an unfinished story. Using a variety of choices, discuss how the same sort of thing tends to come at this point in the story. In this manner, you can gradually call attention to various categories in the story structure.
2. *Macrocloze task*. Have students fill in information omitted from the middle of the story by giving them the story with blank space where a given category of information had been. Discuss why one kind of information is usually supplied. An interesting variation is to have different groups completing this task for different portions of the story. Then, a new story can be created by putting all the new portions together.
3. *Scrambled stories*. Separate the story into categories and then scramble the order of the categories. Students decide on the best order. (If the story categories are on different strips of paper, this would be a useful extension of the sentence anagram and sentence-combining exercises recommended in Chapters Two and Three, respectively.)

Rubin and Gentner (1979) have developed an instructional technique called "story maker." Students are given choices on cards for each stage of the development of the story. Each choice leads to another specific set of choices. Figure 4-2 diagrams such a story-maker tree. In this case, the setting and the initiating event have been combined on card set 1. Card set 2 contains possible internal responses. Card set 3 contains possible attempts. Card set 4 contains consequences and reactions combined. Combining categories is not necessary and can be done in other ways, or students can write endings themselves. Cards can be hung on hooks on a pegboard or presented to the class by the teacher. Students may even progress to the level of story-maker creator. That is, in groups, they can make up their own story-maker trees; then, they can "write" stories using each other's story makers. (This is another good example of combining reading and writing instruction.)

With young children, you may wish to use pictures to depict the major events of a story. Smith and Bean (1983) have suggested dividing large butcher paper into six squares representing the major story categories: one to three for the setting in terms of who, what, and where; four and five for the initiating events; and six for the outcome. Figure 4-3 presents a sample for "Little Miss Muffet." After the teacher demonstrates the procedure, the children can try it with their own stories.

FIGURE 4-2   Simple Story-maker Tree

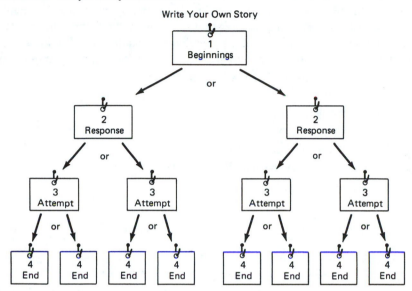

FIGURE 4-3   Picture Sample for "Little Miss Muffet"

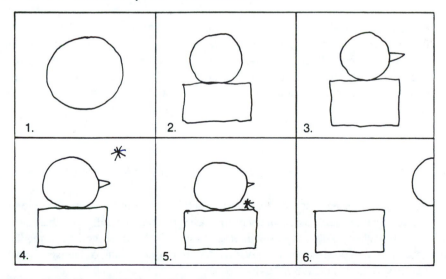

Source: M. Smith and T. W. Bean, "Four Strategies that Develop Children's Story Comprehension and Writing," *Reading Teacher,* 37 (1983), 295–301. Reprinted with permission of Marilyn Smith and the International Reading Association.

Morrow (1986) has found that story retelling with structural guidance when needed improved kindergarten students' sense of story structure as evidenced in their inclusion of important story elements in original stories. She recommends that teachers involve students in retelling stories that they have read or heard to get them involved in constructing meaning on their own (Morrow, 1989). Before reading the teacher should tell the students that retelling will be going on. Modeling retelling should also precede asking the students to do it on their own. When students have trouble, prompts that direct them to critical elements can be used. For instance, to begin, the teacher might say, "Once upon a time..." Other questions that might come later include the following (see Morrow, 1989, p. 43):

1. Who was the story about?
2. Where did the story happen?
3. What was the main character's problem?
4. How did he or she try to solve the problem?
5. How did the story end?

Repetitive books and books with a clear plot structure will probably work best for retellings.

Finally, the connection between reading and writing can be used to develop story structure awareness. The macrocloze task described earlier is really a reading and writing task. Morrow (1986) found that retelling of stories helped in the generation of original stories. Irwin and Baker (1989) have suggested that students be given a "Story Recipe" form to complete before writing a story (see Figure 4-4). Students can use this form to brainstorm a story as a class, or they can use it for individual planning. It could also be used after reading to help a class or small group to summarize a story. Gordon (1989) has suggested that teachers use direct, explicit instruction in story structure, modeling through thinking aloud while reading, and then having students, either independently or collaboratively, write an alternative setting, episode, outcome, and so forth for the story, depending on which story element was being taught.

ORGANIZATIONAL PATTERNS IN EXPOSITORY MATERIALS

Research has repeatedly shown that readers who use the author's organizational pattern to organize their own memory of the passage actually recall more than those who do not (Elliot, 1980; Meyer, Brandt, & Bluth, 1980). Moreover, good readers are more likely to do this than are poor readers (Gabriel, Braun, & Neilsen, 1980; Meyer, Brandt, & Bluth, 1980; Taylor, 1980).

For instance, Example A shows what two students recalled after reading a passage from a sixth-grade science book.

FIGURE 4-4 Recipe for a Story

Directions: Fill in the blanks with the ingredients of a _____ story.

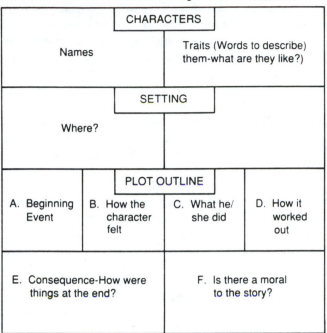

CHARACTERS	
Names	Traits (Words to describe) them-what are they like?)

SETTING

Where?

PLOT OUTLINE

A. Beginning Event | B. How the character felt | C. What he/she did | D. How it worked out

E. Consequence-How were things at the end? | F. Is there a moral to the story?

Source: J. W. Irwin, and I. Baker, *Promoting Active Reading Comprehension Strategies* (Englewood Cliffs, N.J.: Prentice Hall, 1989), p. 153.

EXAMPLE A

The atmosphere is made up of gases, liquids, and solids. The atmosphere is like all matter. It has mass and takes up space. It is held around the earth by gravity. You know that gravity is the force of attraction between objects.

You live in the layer of air that is at the bottom of the atmosphere. This layer contains dust, smoke, clouds, and invisible gases. Because of this, the lowest layer of the atmosphere often looks hazy. The upper layers of the atmosphere contain mostly invisible gases. There are few solids or liquids in those layers. They look perfectly clear.[1]

Here is what Johnny said when asked about what he read:

It said about gravity being a force and about atmosphere being matter. It also said that there are invisible gases in the atmosphere.

In contrast, let us look at Sally's recall:

It was about how the atmosphere is made out of matter like gases and solids and, like matter, is held down by gravity. The lower layer has things like smoke that make it hazy, but the upper layer is clear.

[1]*Source:* G. G. Mallinson, and others, *Understanding Your Environment,* Book 6 (Morristown, N.J.: Silver Burdett, 1981), p. 201.

Johnny has recalled little and has failed to grasp the main points in the passage. In contrast, Sally has recognized that the first paragraph was a description of the characteristics of the atmosphere and the second paragraph was based on a comparison of the clarity of the lower and upper layers. Probably because she was sensitive to these organizational patterns, she remembered more, and what she remembered was the more general and, therefore, in this case the most important information.

To illustrate further the importance of organizational awareness, Example B shows the recall of a fourth-grade student who does not know what to remember on social studies materials but can easily summarize stories in basal readers. In this case, we might speculate that this student did not grasp the definition-example pattern in the social studies selection but did understand the basic categories to be expected in a well-formed story.

This example is not really unusual. It seems that awareness of organizational patterns in expository materials develops much later than does an awareness of story structure. In the research of Stein and Glenn (1977), even seven-year-old children showed an awareness of story structures. In contrast, Meyer, Brandt, and Bluth (1980) studied the recall protocols of ninth-graders and found that only the good readers in this high school sample used the organizational structure to organize their recall. Thus, although many teachers will find that their students have an awareness of the story structures found in basal readers and literature, fewer will find that their students have mastered the organizational patterns in their content-area materials.

Several categorization systems are available to classify the organizational patterns used in expository materials (see Armbruster & Anderson, 1982; Calfee & Curly, 1984; and others). It is probable that none is complete, and that authors may use variations and combinations; however, it is useful to be aware of typical patterns. Table 4-2 shows the classification system given by Armbruster and Anderson (1981) along with the authors' purposes and questions addressed by each. According to this system of classification, content-area materials usually use one of the following organizational patterns: *description, temporal sequence, explanation, comparison-contrast, definitions-examples,* and *problem-solution.* (Note that *cause-effect* is included in *explanation; process descriptions* are included in *temporal sequence;* and *classification* is probably a kind of *definition* pattern.) Study Table 4-2 and then try to fill in Table 4-3. (Answers can be found on page 84.)

Clue words also provide information about what organizational pattern to expect. Table 4-4 lists some of these words. You may be able to think of others that are commonly used in your students' reading materials. Indeed, if you teach in one of the content areas, you will also want to complete Activity 2 at the end of this chapter, which asks you to identify the patterns used in your textbook. This can provide much useful information for guiding students' recall (see following section on instructional procedures).

EXAMPLE B

SOCIAL STUDIES PASSAGE[2]

One of the most important parts of the Hindu religion was the caste system. This was a way of organizing people into separate groups.

There was a separate caste for almost every occupation. There was a caste for farmers and one for carpenters. There was a caste for leatherworkers, a caste for sweepers, and castes for many others. People in the lower castes were not allowed to be educated. Nor could they take part in religious services. And the poorest people, who did the dirtiest work, were called the untouchables. They did not even dare to let their shadows fall on people of the highest castes.

RECALL

There were farmers and carpenters and people that worked with leather. You couldn't touch some people.

PASSAGE FROM STORY[3]

Wendall lived with Mother, Father, William, Alice, and the baby, Anthony.

Everybody was happy—most of the time. There was always work to do.

"William," Mother would say, "would you please put these newspapers outside?"

"I have to play ball," William would say.

"Send Wendall."

Or Father might ask Alice to go to the store. "I have to do my homework," Alice would answer. "Send Wendall."

Wendall loved his mother and father very much. He liked to help them. But sometimes he wished—just a little—that William and Alice liked to help as much as he did.

RECALL

It was about a boy named Wendall who lived with his family. Whenever there were chores to do, his brother and sister were busy with things like playing ball and doing homework, so he had to do them.

[2] *Source: This Is Man* J.H. Dempsey, (Morristown, N.J.: Silver Burdett, 1972), pp. 102–103.

[3] *Source:* Genevieve Gray, *Send Wendall* (New York: McGraw-Hill, 1974), p. 244.

Finally, another way to characterize the organization of content-area texts is through the main idea–detail structure. Research indicates that the presence of main ideas seems to facilitate recall (Christie & Schumacher, 1978; Fishman, 1978; and others). Certainly, students who have mentally arranged ideas according to main topics have organized those ideas in terms of global connections, and thus their recall will be better than that of students who have not mentally organized the material around main topics. Thus, this skill is critical for reading and remembering expository material.

TABLE 4-2   Types of General Author Purposes and the Corresponding Text Structures

IMPERATIVE FORM	INTERROGATIVE FORM	STRUCTURE
Define A.	What is A?	
Describe A.	Who is A?	Description
List the features (characteristics, traits) of A.	Where is A?	
Trace the development of A.	When did A occur (in relationship to other events?)	Temporal sequences
Give the steps in A.		
Explain A.	Why did A happen?	
Explain the cause(s) of A.	How did A happen?	
Explain the effect(s) of A.	What are the causes of, reasons for (effects, outcomes, results of) A?	Explanation
Draw a conclusion about A.		
Predict what will happen to A.	What will be the effects, outcomes, results of A?	
Hypothesize about the cause of A.		
Compare and contrast A and B.	How are A and B alike? different?	Comparison-contrast
List the similarities and differences between A and B.		
Define and give examples of A.	What is A, and what are some examples of A?	Definitions-examples
Explain the development of a problem and the solution(s) to the problem.	How did A get to be a problem, and what is (are) its solution(s)?	Problem-solution

Source: B. Armbruster, and T. Anderson. "Content Area Textbooks" (Reading Education Report No. 23. Center for the Study of Reading, University of Illinois at Urbana-Champaign, 1981.) pp. 5 and 6. Reprinted by permission.

Instructional Procedures

Explicit instruction. McGee and Richgels (1985) have recommended a seven-step procedure for teaching expository text structure to elementary students. First, find a textbook passage that is a good example of the structure you want to teach. Prepare a "graphic organizer" showing the key ideas and how they are related. Figure 4-5 shows a graphic organizer for a chapter on the War of 1812. Note that the important information is at the top. Introduce the students to the idea of text structure and show them the organizer. Have the students write a passage based on the organizer. Encourage them to include key words that show relationships among

TABLE 4-3   Simple Exercise in Identifying Organizational Patterns

SIMPLE PARAGRAPH	PATTERN USED?
The two groups used different approaches. One group tried to solve the problem alone, whereas the other group immediately began to look for someone to ask. One group divided the tasks among the individuals, and the other group did everything as a whole.	
Many reasons existed for the move from country to city. More jobs were in the city. More cultural events, shops, and educational opportunities were also in the city.	
A chemical change is a process by which new substances are created. Burning and rusting are examples of chemical changes.	
So many people were moving into the cities that many had trouble finding places to live. New homes were built at an amazing rate.	

TABLE 4-4   Common Structure Words

ORGANIZATIONAL PATTERN	STRUCTURE WORDS
Spatial description	across, over, at, from, into, between, beyond, outside, near, down, far, up, within
Temporal sequence	next, first, second, then, originally, finally, before, earlier, later, after, following, then, while, meanwhile, soon, until, since, beginning, during, still, eventually
Explanation	because, so, thus, consequently, therefore, for this reason, as a result
Comparison-contrast	by comparison, similarly, but, yet, although, as well as, unlike, on the other hand, in spite of, on the contrary, nevertheless, whereas
Definition-example	for example, such as, that is, namely, to illustrate, for instance

Source: J. W. Irwin, and I. Baker, *Promoting Active Reading Comprehension Strategies* (Englewood Cliffs, N.J.: Prentice Hall, 1989), p. 149.

ideas. Then have the students read the text and compare it with what they wrote. You may wish to put up a large poster illustrating the structure studied (see Figure 4-6). Finally, you may eventually be able to extend this sort of activity into work with long passages that consist of several types of structures.

Pattern guides. Pattern guides (graphic organizers completed during reading) can be used to focus the students' attention on the appropriate organizational

FIGURE 4-5   Graphic Organizer from the War of 1812 Passage

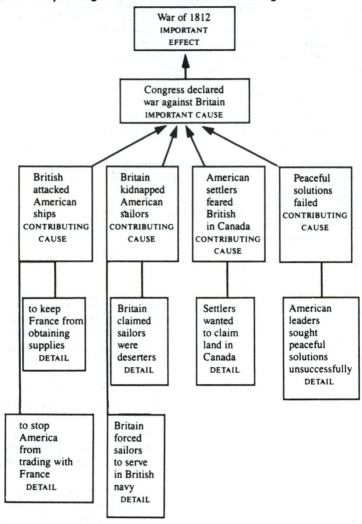

Source: D. G., Richgels, L. M. McGee, and E. A. Slaton, "Teaching Expository Text Structure in Reading and Writing," in *Children's Comprehension of Text,* ed. K. D. Muth. (Newark, Del.: International Reading Association, 1989), p. 177. Reprinted with permission of Donald J. Richgels and the International Reading Association.

patterns. Tables, charts, and diagrams that students complete while they are reading are especially effective, because they help the students to visualize the organizational patterns. Examples include comparison and cause-effect charts for comparison and cause-effect patterns, tables of attributes for descriptive patterns, tree and flow charts for temporal sequence and classification patterns, diagrams for descriptive patterns,

FIGURE 4-6   Poster of Causation Structure

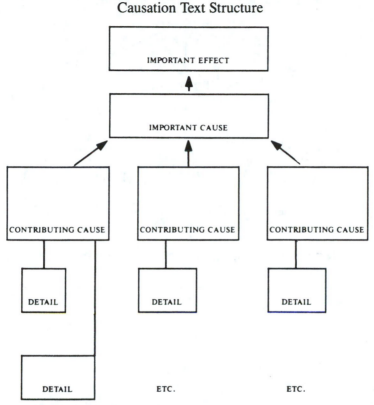

Causation Text Structure

Source: D. G. Richgels, L. M. McGee, and E. A. Slaton, "Teaching Expository Text Structure in Reading and Writing," in *Children's Comprehension of Text,* ed. K. D. Muth. (Newark, Del.: International Reading Association, 1989), p. 182. Reprinted with permission of Donald J. Richgels and the International Reading Association.

and outlines for main idea–detail structures (see Slater, Graves, & Piche, 1985). Figures 4-7 and 4-8 are examples of study guides that focus the students' attention on organizational patterns.

Pattern writing. You may also wish to use writing to increase awareness of expository structure. To construct a graphic organizer for a text read, begin with a blank organizer like the one used in Figure 4-6. Have the students brainstorm an appropriate topic that they are interested in writing about for some meaningful purpose, like submitting an article to the school newspaper or writing a letter to an editor of a local newspaper. Then ask them to fill in some possible content. After completing the organizer, they can write their articles or letters and evaluate whether using such patterns in their writing is useful for getting their point across.

FIGURE 4-7   Tree Chart Showing Major Concepts in Fifth-grade Science Chapter

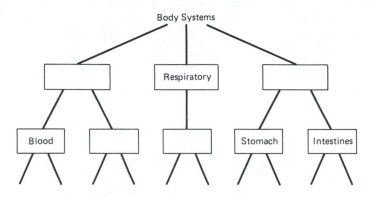

1. Fill in the four missing labels in the boxes in the chart.
2. Add two specific parts for each of the organs.

FIGURE 4-8   Comparison of Body Systems of Frog and Grasshopper (Ninth-grade Science)

BODY SYSTEMS	FROG	GRASSHOPPER
Digestive		
Respiratory		
Nervous		

1. Fill in this chart with brief descriptions.
2. In terms of which system are the frog and the grasshopper most nearly alike? Tell how they are the same.
3. In terms of which system are the frog and the grasshopper most greatly different? Tell how they are different.

Mapping. Another way to encourage students to use global connections is to encourage them to construct a diagram of these relationships (Hanf, 1971). Armbruster and Anderson (1980) found it to be a successful technique for improving middle school students' recall. They taught students specific techniques for diagramming six of the possible types of connections: examples, property, definition, comparison-contrast, temporal, and causal. Davidson (1982) has recommended a less highly structured approach. She suggests that each student be encouraged to diagram the passage structure in his or her own creative way. Then, students can compare their maps and discuss the differences. A map of a main idea–detail structure from a content-area text is given in Figure 4-9. Figure 4-10 shows how

FIGURE 4-9 Mapping of Main Idea–Detail Structure in Chapter on Puritan Values

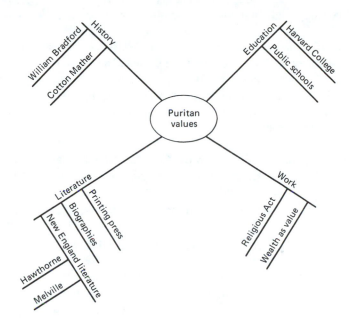

FIGURE 4-10 Alternative Map of Chapter on Puritan Values

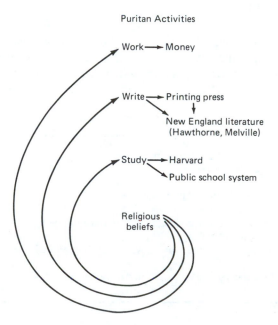

another student may have mapped the same chapter. This map stresses the causal relationship between the Puritan religious beliefs and their other activities. The tree chart used in the study guide in Figure 4-7 can also be regarded as a kind of map.

Hierarchical summary procedure.   Taylor (1982) has suggested the use of a hierarchical summary procedure to direct the students' attention to the organizational pattern. She recommends that this procedure be used with middle-grade students; when she did this, she found that it improved not only the amount recalled during reading but also the quality of the students' written compositions. The five steps of this procedure are as follows:

1. *Previewing.* Students preview a few pages of the assignment and generate the skeleton outline of numbers and letters for the sections indicated by sub-headings. The teacher may want to help them with this at first.
2. *Reading.* Children read in sections, filling in the outline for the section as they proceed.
3. *Outlining.* For each subsection, students write a main idea *in their own words.* Then, they fill in the supporting details *in their own words.* At the end of a major section, they write a main idea for the section *in their own words,* and they summarize the subsection into key phrases in the left margin.
4. *Studying.* After reading is completed, the students review their "hierarchical summaries."
5. *Retelling.* Finally, in partners, students orally retell what they learned from reading the assignment.

Teacher assistance and class discussion will be necessary as students are learning this procedure, but, gradually, they will be able to do it on their own. Figure 4-11 provides a fictional example of a short section of a student's hierarchical summary.

FIGURE 4-11   Section of Student Hierarchical Summary

I. Puritan cultural values that still influence our society
   A. Puritans respected education.

Puritan values affect us today

      Most towns built schools.
      Harvard College was supported by taxes.
      Today, we have public education for all.
   B. Puritans believed that work was for God and that leisure was bad.
      They disliked games and holidays.
      They associated wealth with work and poverty with illness. Thus, poor people were sinful.
      Today, we still respect people who work and have wealth.

Taylor (1986) has suggested that cooperative summarizing may be a useful variation of this procedure. She recommends that students be divided into heterogeneous groups of three. They can take turns reading subsections aloud, and, after each, they can complete the hierarchical summaries together. Because it is important for all students to participate, each student should suggest a topic, detail, or main idea at the appropriate point. Then the group can select from the suggestions or discuss how to combine them. Each member completes a hierarchical summary as the students work through the reading selection.

MACROSELECTION

Perhaps the most important step in effective macroprocessing is selecting the most important information to remember from the reading passage. Good readers tend to remember the more important information more often than they remember less important information (see Meyer, 1975), and evidence exists that younger students may have some trouble picking out what is important (Brown & Smiley, 1978). Students' ability to select what is important may also be related to the difficulty of the material; that is, they can do it well with easy material but have more trouble with more difficult material (see Brown, Smiley, & Lawton, 1977; Danner, 1976).

Good readers use various cues to decide what information is important. Van Dijk (1979) suggests that writers use what he calls "relevance signals," which can be graphic (for example, italics or boldface), syntactic (for example, word order), lexical (for example, "the important thing"), semantic (for example, a summary statement), or schematic (for example, text structure or organization). Afflerbach and Johnston (1986) found that good readers used contextual factors like prior knowledge, text structure factors, and their perception of the author and his or her intentions. Williams (1986) found that changing the basic form of organization changed the main ideas that were selected: Good readers select the information that is central to the form of organization being used.

Moreover, information can be "textually important" (that is, important to the author and highlighted with relevance signals in the text) or "contextually important" (that is, important to the reader depending on his or her purpose for reading) (Van Dijk, 1979). Winograd (1984) found that although the good readers in his study selected the most important information according to text factors, the poor readers seemed to select what was most interesting to them. Thus, poor readers may be more contextually based than good readers. Hare (1988) recommends that teachers tell students about the distinction between what she calls "author-based" (that is, text-based) and "reader-based" (that is, contextually based) decisions about important information. Students can be made aware of how they are making these decisions and how, why, and when different kinds of decisions are useful.

Macroselection Instruction

Macroselection instruction is a good example of reading process instruction that can easily be integrated into the curriculum in every content area at every grade level. Students can be told that part of good reading is picking out the important ideas to remember. After an assignment is read, students can be asked what was important and why. Talk with students about how the selected ideas are the ones most central to the overall organization. Did they use their prior knowledge about the topic to decide what was important? Are there any clues in the text that helped them with their decision? As students work on meaningful materials, comprehension activities can be designed to encourage them to make these choices. Actually, all the organizational activities suggested earlier in this chapter will help students to select what is important. Three other activities that probably encourage active selection follow. Each of these activities can be adapted for various ages and content areas.

Select the most important idea. Divide students into pairs or small groups. Have them read a section of the textbook or story in short segments. While reading each segment, have each student write down the *one* most important idea to remember. Students then compare their choices. As a team, they must choose only one. If appropriate, team answers can be compared for the whole class. Test items can later be selected from class choices. This activity has the advantage of being appropriate for students at various stages of independence on this strategy because it allows them to learn from each other.

Write a fair test. Involving students in writing tests can be a way of asking them to think about what is important. On the most dependent level, you can ask students to make up the test by selecting the most important questions from a list you provide. On a more independent level, they can make up the test from scratch. (This activity will encourage microselection as well as macroselection. Remember, all these processes interact!)

Rank the sentences. Stewart and Tei (1983) have suggested that students be given sentences in random order. They can then rank the sentences according to importance and reorder them so that the main idea is clear. The teacher should probably model this process first, discussing his or her decisions and the criteria for importance being used. Students should also be shown why selecting the important ideas can be useful to them. One possible variation might be to use student writing. Divide the students into pairs in which they rank and reorder sentences from their partner's essay. The author of the essay could have ranked them ahead of time. Then, the students could compare and discuss their rankings to see if the reader and the writer agree.

MACRORULES AND SUMMARIZATION

Often, selecting what to remember involves more than just lifting facts from the text. When students are trying to select what to remember, they will often decide to create a summary statement rather than select a statement from the assignment. Recently, it has become possible to be quite specific about the way students may arrive at summary statements. These statements seem to reflect several processes that can be used in conjunction with macroselection. The four *macrorules* that readers seem to use to create passage summaries can be described as follows (Brown & Day, 1983):

1. *Deletion.* Unimportant and redundant information is deleted.
2. *Superordination.* More general terms are substituted for groups of specifics.
3. *Selection.* General statements (topic sentences) are selected to retain [macroselection].
4. *Invention.* Explicit topic statements are invented when they are not stated.

Figure 4-12 gives an example of a typical summary and the rules used to derive it. Note how these rules work together to result in concise summary statements.

Research has substantiated the hypothesis that poor readers are less able to use summarization rules efficiently than are good readers (Winograd, 1984). In a study of children's use of these "macrorules," Brown and Day (1983) found that elementary school children (fifth-graders) seemed to know how to delete appropriately, but they did not use the other rules adequately. The invention rule seemed to be the most difficult and was seldom used before the high school level. Even tenth-graders used this rule in only one-third of the appropriate situations. Moreover, it seems that even college students sometimes have trouble summarizing (Taylor, 1983).

Finally, finding the main idea can be seen as the application of these macrorules at the paragraph level. Finding the main idea of a paragraph is simply paragraph summarization. If the main idea is stated explicitly, finding it involves *selection.* If it is not stated, finding it requires *invention,* a more difficult process. (Remember, finding the main idea is important for all the reasons that macroprocessing is important: helping readers to select what to remember and to organize the information for more efficient recall.)

Incidental Instruction: K–12

Students at all grade levels can be encouraged to do some kind of summarizing. This can be done in various regular classroom activities: book sharing, journal writing, paper researching, and so on. When students are summarizing for these meaningful tasks, they are deleting unimportant information, selecting important information, and creating general statements not directly given (superordination and invention). When you are leading discussions, you can model summarizing for them. Activities

FIGURE 4-12   Example of Summarizing

Europe and the United Stated neared a face-saving formula to rescue the World Trade Conference here but made little attempt to hide the fact that they were deeply divided about the future of the trading system.

A conference spokesman said the European Common Market appeared ready to sign a final communique but only after inserting paragraphs underlining their disagreement on fundamental matters.

For instance, one clause will pledge the 88 nations at the conference "to refrain from" new protectionist measures, but the Europeans, beset by recession and unemployment, rejected this pledge and insisted on inserting a milder paragraph stating that the Common Market would "resist" protectionism, the spokesman said. All other nations here, including the United States, planned to endorse the tougher clause.

Another paragraph, also endorsed by the rest of the conference, called for new rules on farm trade. The Common Market, whose subsidized farm exports have been under heavy U.S. attack, refused to go along with this.

The conference, scheduled to end Saturday, stretched over into Sunday in an attempt to avoid a total breakdown. [4]

Summary:

Europe and the United Stated neared agreement on the World Trade Conference, but they are divided about the future of the trading system. Members of the European Common Market were ready to sign an agreement, but only if they could make changes. For instance, they are less opposed to protectionism than are the other countries. They also refuse to go along with new rules on farm trade.

1. Delete information (crossed off with one line).
2. Use superordination (on circled information).
3. Select topic sentence (in gray).
4. Invent summary statements (for information in braces in article;   underlined sentences in summary)

[4]*Source:* R. C. Longworth, "Future of World Trade Dim After Rift at Geneva Parley," *Chicago Tribune,* Sunday, November 28, 1982.

in which students compare different students' summaries of the same material will result in an increased understanding of the material to be recalled as well as an increased understanding of summarizing.

Explicit Summarizing Instruction

Explicit rule instruction. The explicit instruction teaching model described in Chapter Two has been used effectively to teach summarization rules. Brown and Day (1981) found that selection seemed harder to learn than superordination, and that the poorer writers among the junior college students in their study needed explicit instruction in rule usage. They also found that with the most disabled students, instruction in invention was not effective. Evidently, a certain level of reading and writing ability is a prerequisite to learning to use this rule.

Hare and Borchardt (1984) effectively used explicit instruction to teach low-income, minority, high school students how to summarize using the rules provided in Figure 4-13. The first four rules help the students with managing their strategies. The next four are adaptations of the macrorules suggested by Brown and Day (1983). Finally, the students are directed to polish their summaries.

Rinehart, Stahl, and Erickson (1986) similarly used explicit instruction to teach sixth-grade students how to summarize. They taught the following four summarization strategies (p. 428):

1. Identify and select main information.
2. Delete trivial information.
3. Delete redundant information.
4. Relate main and important supporting information.

They also gave the students a checklist of self-monitoring questions containing the following (p. 438):

1. Have I found the overall idea that the paragraph or group of paragraphs is about?
2. Have I found the most important information that tells more about the overall idea?
3. Have I used any information that is not directly about the overall idea?
4. Have I used any information more than once?

This training improved the students' summaries of paragraphs with stated main ideas, but it did not improve their summaries of paragraphs that required invention. It also improved their recall of major information probably through its effect on the amount of that information in the students' notes.

Finally, Armbruster, Anderson, and Ostertag (1987) effectively combined instruction in text structure and summarization strategies to improve the students' summarization abilities. They also used an explicit instruction model to teach fifth-grade students about how to identify the problem-solution text structure and how to summarize such passages. First, they provided students with a schematic diagram of this structure (see Figure 4-14). They then provided them with the guidelines for writing a summary (see Figure 4-15). Note that these guidelines are related to the particular type of organizational pattern. Finally, the students practiced the strategy.

How short can you make it?   Writing and reading instruction overlap when you ask students to write summaries. One motivational approach might be to have

FIGURE 4-13   Rules for Summarizing

Four General Steps to Help with the Four+ Specific Rules for Writing a Summary

1. *Make sure you understand the text.* Ask yourself, "What was this text about?" "What did the writer say?" Try to say the general theme to yourself.
2. *Look back.* Reread the text to make sure you got the theme right. Also read to make sure that you really understand what the important parts of the text are. Star important parts.

Now Use the Four Rules for Writing a Summary

3. *Rethink.* Reread a paragraph of the text. Try to say the theme of that paragraph to yourself. Is the theme a topic sentence? Have you underlined it? Or is the topic sentence missing: If it is missing, have you written one in the margin?
4. *Check and double-check.* Did you leave in any lists? Make sure you don't list things out in your summary. Did you repeat yourself? Make sure you didn't. Did you skip anything? Is all the important information in the summary?

Four Rules for Writing a Summary

1. *Collapse lists.* If you see a list of things, try to think of a word or phrase name for the whole list. For example, if you saw a list like eyes, ears, neck, arms, and legs, you could say "body parts." Or, if you saw a list like ice skating, skiing, or sledding, you could say "winter sports."
2. *Use topic sentences.* Often authors write a sentence that summarizes a whole paragraph. It is called a topic sentence. If the author gives you one, you can use it in your summary. Unfortunately, not all paragraphs contain topic sentences. That means you may have to make up one for yourself. If you don't see a topic sentence, make up one of your own.
3. *Get rid of unnecessary detail.* Some text information can be repeated in a passage. In other words, the same thing can be said in a number of different ways, all in one passage. Other text information can be unimportant, or trivial. Since summaries are meant to be short, get rid of repetitive or trivial information.
4. *Collapse paragraphs.* Paragraphs are often related to one another. Some paragraphs explain one or more other paragraphs. Some paragraphs just expand on the information presented in other paragraphs. Some paragraphs are more necessary than other paragraphs. Decide which paragraphs should be kept or gotten rid of, and which might be joined together.

A Final Suggestion

+. *Polish the summary.* When a lot of information is reduced from an original passage, the resulting concentrated information often sounds very unnatural. Fix this problem and create a more natural-sounding summary. Adjustments may include but are not limited to: paraphrasing, the insertion of connecting words like "and" or "because," and the insertion of introductory or closing statements. Paraphrasing is especially useful here, for two reasons: one, because it improves your ability to remember the material, and two, it avoids using the author's words, otherwise known as plagiarism.

Source: V. C. Hare and K. M. Borchardt, "Direct Instruction of Summarization Skills," *Reading Research Quarterly,* 20 (1984), 66. Reprinted by permission of Victoria Chou Hare and the International Reading Association.

FIGURE 4-14 Problem-Solution Frame

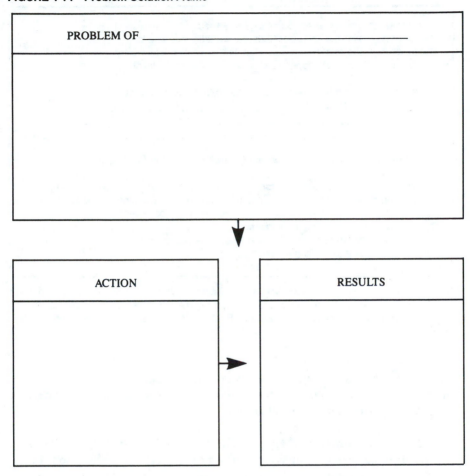

PROBLEM =   something bad; a situation that people would like to change

ACTION   =   what people *do* to try to solve the problem

RESULTS   =   what happens as a result of the action; the effect or outcome of trying to solve the problem

Source: B. B., Armbruster, T. H. Anderson, and J. Ostertag, "Does Text Structure/Summarization Instruction Facilitate Learning from Expository Text?" Reading Research Quarterly, 23 (1987), p. 335. Reprinted by permission of Bonnie B. Armbruster and the International Reading Association.

FIGURE 4-15   Guidelines for Summarizing Problem-Solution Passages

---

How to Summarize Problem-Solution Passages
Sentence 1—Tells who had a problem and what the problem is.
Sentence 2—Tells what action was taken to try to solve the problem.
Sentence 3—Tells what happened as a result of the action taken.

Pattern for Writing a Summary of a Problem-Solution Passage
_____ had a problem because _____ .
Therefore, _____ .
As a result, _____ .

Guidelines for Checking Summaries of Problem-Solution Passages
Check to see that:
1. Your summary has all of the information that should be in a summary of a problem-solution passage....Compare your summary with the original problem-solution passage to make sure that the summary is accurate and complete.
2. You have used complete sentences.
3. The sentences are tied together with good connecting words.
4. The grammar and spelling are correct.

Source: B. B. Armbruster, T. H. Anderson, and J. Ostertag, "Does Text Structure/Summarization Instruction Facilitate Learning from Expository Text?" *Reading Research Quarterly,* 23 (1987), p. 337. Reprinted by permission of Bonnie B. Armbruster and the International Reading Association.

students see how short they can make a summarizing statement. Students can work in pairs and compete or work as a team in competition with another team. They can work with published texts or with their own writing.

Summary blueprints.   Hare and Bingham (1986) suggest that teachers provide their students with summary blueprints, or graphic representations of the major structure of the passage that will guide them to select the main information. Figure 4-14, the diagram provided by Armbruster, Anderson, and Ostertag (1987) is one example of this. Figure 4-16 shows the blueprint for a narrative suggested by Hare and Bingham (1986). Students should be given the blueprint before reading. Then, classroom discussion can be used to encourage students to share their ideas about the categories and the important information. A class form could be completed on the board or overhead projector. Students can discuss why the information important to one person may not be so important to another person.

Select the best. Provide students with alternative summaries of the same passage. At an easy level, have one summary that includes unimportant information and one that includes all the important information. At a more difficult level, have one summary that uses only deletion and selection and one that uses invention. Ask students to select the better summary. Ask them to explain their choice. Garner,

FIGURE 4-16   Summary Blueprint

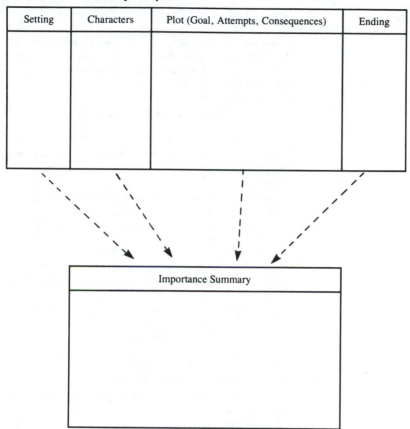

Source: V. C. Hare and A. Bingham, "Teaching Students Main Idea Comprehension," in *Teaching Main Idea Comprehension,* ed. J. Baumann. (Newark, Del.: International Reading Association, 1986), p. 182. Reprinted by permission of Victoria Chou Hare and the International Reading Association.

Belcher, Winfield, and Smith (1985) found that by the fourth grade, most students can recognize a good summary, but second-graders have some trouble with this (Hahn & Garner, 1985).

Finding the main idea. No shortage of activities exists for teaching students to find the main idea. Most traditional reading methods texts and classroom reading curricula include many of these. They range from straightforward drill to such activities as writing titles and drawing pictures. Unfortunately, there is much confusion about what is meant by the term "main idea." Cunningham and Moore (1986) have identified nine different types of main ideas that are supplied by good readers when asked to "decide what the main idea is" (see Table 4-5). Study this

TABLE 4-5   Definitions and Examples of Nine Main Idea Tasks

MAIN IDEA TASK	DEFINITION AND EXAMPLE
Gist	A summary of the explicit contents of a passage achieved by creating generalized statements that subsume specific information and then deleting that specific (and now redundant) information. "Locoweed is poison for horses."
Interpretation	A summary of the possible or probably implicit contents of a passage. "Horses don't always know what is good for them."
Key Word	A word or term labeling the most important single concept in the passage. "Horses."
Selective Summary– Selective Diagram	A summary or diagram of the explicit contents of a passage achieved by selecting and combining the most superordinate and important words and phrases (or synonyms for them) from a passage. "Horses go crazy, get sick, and die after eating locoweed."
Theme	A generalization about life, the world, or the universe that the passage as a whole develops, implies, or illustrates but which is not topic or key word specific. "Animal owners have a great responsibility for their charges."
Title	The given name of the passage. [Not applicable for "locoweed" passage.]
Topic	A phrase labeling the subject of a passage without revealing specific content from the passage. "What happens when horses eat locoweed."
Topic Issue	A single word, term, or phrase labeling a conceptual context for the passage. "Dangerous plants."
Topic Sentence Thesis Sentence	The single sentence in a paragraph or passage which tells most completely what the paragraph or passage as a whole states or is about. "Some horses are said to become 'loco' or insane from eating locoweed."
Other	Any response that cannot be classified as one of the other main idea types. These would include all literal and critical responses.

Source: J. W. Cunningham and D. W. Moore, "The Confused World of Main Idea," in *Teaching Main Idea Comprehension,* (Newark, Del.: International Reading Association, 1986), pp. 6–7. Reprinted with permission of James W. Cunningham and the International Reading Association.

table. What do you mean when you talk about finding the main idea? Cunningham and Moore (1986) take the position that "different types of main ideas are legitimate" (p. 7). The point is that teachers must be clear with students about what type of main idea is being discussed. Indeed, it might be useful to use a more specific term, like "topic sentence," "gist," or "theme," rather than the term "main idea" to make this clear.

Moreover, from a developmental standpoint, Williams (1984) found that the ability to find the main idea is probably based on classification skills. Baumann (1984) has suggested a kind of skill hierarchy for teaching main-idea skills that begins with classification, then microselection with individual sentences, then selection of topics and explicit main ideas of paragraphs, then invention of main ideas when they are implicit in paragraphs, and then, finally, selection of explicit and implicit main ideas of whole passages. He found that a direct teaching strategy using the taxonomy was effective for teaching sixth-grade students to perform these processes. It is important to remember that such instruction can occur within the context of natural reading tasks that students are completing for other purposes. Moreover, even if you do not wish to use focused, teacher-directed activities concerning specific subprocesses, it is useful to remember that students' abilities in this area develop throughout the school years, and performance is probably related to the complexity of the text, the length of the material, and the explicitness of the main idea.

One technique for helping students to invent a main idea when it is not stated explicitly in a topic sentence has been suggested by Irwin and Baker (1989), and is based on the suggestions of Baumann and Schmitt (1986). Students can be guided to fill in the main-idea wheel (see Figure 4-17) by first identifying the topic of the paragraph and placing it in the center of the wheel, then filling in the details in the spokes, and then looking at the details to determine what is being said about the topic. This is added below the topic in the center, or it could be listed below the wheel. Students can make main-idea wheels using each other's writing or other meaningful materials, but the most important step is helping them to use this strategy when they need to find main ideas to achieve some self-selected purpose (for example, taking notes in the library for a class presentation, studying for an important test, and so forth).

SUMMARY

Macroprocessing is the ongoing process of creating an organized set of summary ideas for the purpose of recall. Awareness of the organizational pattern is critical for effective macroprocessing. For stories, this entails having an awareness of the structure of a typical story; typical stories probably include one or more sets of the following categories: (1) setting, (2) initiating event, (3) internal response, (4) attempt, (5) consequence, and (6) reaction. Typical expository materials are organized according to one or more of the following patterns: (1) description, (2) temporal sequence, (3) explanation, (4) comparison-contrast, (5) definitions-examples, and (6) problem-solution. They can also be seen as having a main idea–detail organizational pattern.

FIGURE 4-17   Main-idea Wheel

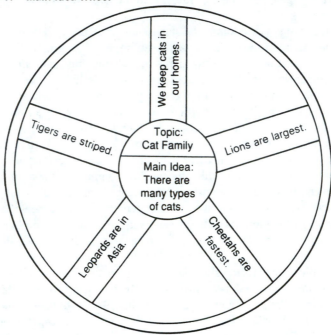

Source: J. W. Irwin, and I. Baker, *Promoting Active Reading Comprehension Strategies* (Englewood Cliffs, N.J.: Prentice Hall, 1989), p. 137.

Based on their awareness of the organization, students summarize by selecting the most important information (the information most related to the general topics in the organizational structure), deleting the unimportant information, substituting general terms for specifics, and inventing topic statements. Finding (or inventing) the main idea can be viewed as summarizing at the paragraph level.

The activities suggested in this chapter are designed to heighten students' awareness of organizational patterns and to increase their ability to select what is important and to summarize what they read. All can be used as part of the instruction in subjects in which students are reading for other purposes. Such integration is critical if students are to learn to use these strategies in natural reading tasks.

SELF-CHECK TEST

1. Define each of these summarization rules.
   deletion
   superordination

selection (macro-)

invention

2. What are the six important categories of information in a simple story?

3. List five types of organizational patterns in expository material. For each, tell what clue words might help a reader to identify that pattern. Write a sample paragraph for each.

4. List five specific types of main ideas.

5. Answer true or false.

_____ (a) Macroprocessing is important only when you just want to remember the gist of a passage.

_____ (b) The invention rule is the easiest to use.

_____ (c) Summarizing effectiveness depends on an awareness of the organizational pattern.

_____ (d) Awareness of the organizational pattern can result in more information recalled.

_____ (e) There is no relationship between microprocessing and macroprocessing.

_____ (f) There is no relationship between integrative processing and macroprocessing.

6. For each of these activities, tell which strategy it was designed to teach.

Select the best	Scrambled stories
Macrocloze	Retelling
Mapping	Pattern guide
How short can you make it?	Pattern writing
Story maker	Summary blueprints

SUGGESTED ACTIVITIES

1. If you are an primary grade teacher, select some of the books that your students like to read. What categories of information do you find (using the Stein and Glenn story grammar)? Are there any categories that need to be inferred? Try using the summary blueprint (p. 79) to summarize the story.

2. Use the story recipe (p. 61) to plan a simple story. Write the story. How many episodes does it have? Does it fit with a simple story grammar? Why or why not?

3. Study the content-area materials that your students normally read. What kinds of organizational patterns are used? What kinds of pattern guides could be used to focus your students' attention on these patterns? Would a main idea–detail guide be better? Make one of these guides.

4. Write a five-sentence summary of this chapter. What summarization rules have you used? Be specific for each sentence of your summary.

5. Collect a set of paragraphs designed to assess your students' abilities to find explicit (selection) and implicit (invention) main ideas.

FIGURE 4-1 (Answer) Simple Exercise in Analyzing Story Structure

Setting	Once there was a very tall girl named Alice. Alice
Initiating event	was the tallest girl in her class. All of her classmates
Internal response	made fun of her. This made her feel very bad. She
Attempt	even tried walking with her knees bent. that just
Consequence	made her look funny. Looking funny made her feel
Reaction	even worse.
	One day Alices' teacher said that they were going
	to have a guest speaker, and in walked the
	tallest woman Alice had ever seen. She was the star
Initiating event	of the local women's basketball team. She talked to
	the students about the new league, the games that
	had been played, and what it was like to be a
Internal response	professional athlete. Everyone admired her. Alice
Attempt	was very excited. She asked if she could, maybe,
	be a player someday. The woman replied that
Consequence	because she was so tall, she would have a better
	chance than many. For the first time, Alice was proud
Reaction	of being tall.

TABLE 4-3 (Answer) Simple Exercise in Identifying Organizational Patterns

SIMPLE PARAGRAPH	PATTERN USED?
The two groups used different approaches. One group tried to solve the problem alone, whereas the other group immediately began to look for someone to ask. One group divided the tasks among the individuals, and the other group did everything as a whole.	Comparison-contrast
Many reasons existed for the move from country to city. More jobs were in the city. More cultural events, shops, and educational opportunities were also in the city.	Explanation
A chemical change is a process by which new substances are created. Burning and rusting are examples of chemical changes.	Definition-examples
So many people were moving into the cities that many had trouble finding places to live. New homes were built at an amazing rate.	Problem-solution

REFERENCES

Afflerbach, P. P., & Johnston, P. H. (1986). What do expert readers do when the main idea is not explicit? In J. Baumann (Ed.), *Teaching main idea comprehension* (pp. 49–72). Newark, Del.: International Reading Association.

Armbruster, B. B., & Anderson, T. H. (1980). *The effect of mapping on the free recall of expository text* (Technical Report No. 160). Urbana-Champaign: Center for the Study of Reading, University of Illinois.

Armbruster, B., & Anderson, T. (1981). *Content area textbooks* (Reading Education Report No. 23). Urbana-Champaign: Center for the Study of Reading, University of Illinois.

Armbruster, B. B., Anderson, T. H., & Ostertag, J. (1987). Does text structure/summarization instruction facilitate learning from expository text? *Reading Research Quarterly, 23,* 331–346.

Baumann, J. (1982, December). Teaching children to comprehend main ideas. Paper presented at the annual meeting of the National Reading Conference, Clearwater, Florida.

Baumann, J. (1984). The effectiveness of a direct instruction paradigm for teaching main idea comprehension. *Reading Research Quarterly, 20,* 93–115.

Baumann, J. (1986). The direct instruction of main idea comprehension ability. In J. Baumann (Ed.), *Teaching main idea comprehension,* (pp. 133–178). Newark, Del.: International Reading Association.

Baumann, J., & Schmitt, M. C. (1986). The what, why, how, and when of comprehension instruction. *Reading Teacher, 39,* 640–646.

Bean, T. H., Singer, H., Sorter, J., & Frazee, C. (1982, December). Acquisition of summarization rules as a basis for question generation in learning from expository text. Paper presented at the annual meeting of the National Reading Conference, Clearwater, Florida.

Brown, A. L., & Day, J. D. (1981). Strategies and knowledge for summarizing texts: The development and facilitation of expertise. Unpublished manuscript, University of Illinois.

Brown, A. L., & Day, J. D. (1983). *Macrorules for summarizing texts: The development of expertise.* Urbana-Champaign: Center for the Study of Reading, University of Illinois.

Brown, A., & Smiley, S. (1978). *The development of strategies for studying prose passages* (Technical Report No. 66). Urbana-Champaign: Center for the Study of Reading, University of Illinois.

Brown, A., Smiley S., & Lawton, S. (1977). *The effects of experience on the selection of suitable retrieval cues for studying from prose passages* (Technical Report No. 53). Urbana-Champaign: Center for the Study of Reading, University of Illinois.

Calfee, R., & Curly, R. (1984). Structure of prose in the content areas. In J. Flood (Ed.), *Understanding reading comprehension* (pp. 161–180). Newark, Del.: International Reading Association.

Christie, D. J., & Schumacher, G. M. (1978). Memory for prose: Development of mnemonic strategies and use of higher order relations. *Journal of Reading Behavior, 10,* 337–344.

Cunningham, J. W., & Moore, D. W. (1986). The confused world of main idea. In J. Baumann (Ed.), *Teaching main idea comprehension* (pp. 1–17). Newark, Del.: International Reading Association.

Danner, F. W. (1976). Children's understanding of intersentence organization in the recall of short descriptive passages. *Journal of Educational Psychology, 68*, 174–183.

Davison, J. (1982). The group mapping activity for instruction in reading and thinking. *Journal of Reading, 26*, 52–56.

Elliot, S. N. (1980). Children's knowledge and use of organizational patterns of prose in recalling what they read. *Journal of Reading Behavior, 12*, 203–212.

Fishman, A. S. (1978). The effects of anaphoric reference and noun phrase organizers on paragraph comprehension. *Journal of Reading Behavior, 10*, 159–167.

Fitzgerald, J. (1989). Research on stories: Implications for teachers. In K. D. Muth (Ed.), *Children's comprehension of text* (pp. 2–36). Newark, Del.: International Reading Association.

Gabriel, H., Braun, C., & Neilsen, A. (1980, December). An investigation of the effects of textural organization on comprehension of good and poor readers. Paper presented at the annual meeting of the National Reading Conference, San Diego, California.

Garner, R., Belcher, V., Winfield, E., & Smith, T. (1985). Multiple measures of text summarization proficiency: What can fifth-grade students do? *Research in the Teaching of English, 9*, 140–153.

Gordon, D. J. (1989). Teaching narrative text structure: A process approach to reading and writing. In K. D. Muth (Ed.), *Children's comprehension of text* (pp. 79–102). Newark, Del.: International Reading Association.

Hahn, A. L., & Garner R. (1985). Synthesis of research on students' ability to summarize text. *Educational Leadership, 42*, 52–56.

Hanf, M. B. (1971). Mapping: A technique for translating reading into thinking. *Journal of Reading, 14*, 225–270.

Hare, V. C. (1988). New directions in thinking about main idea and main idea instruction. *The Reading Instruction Journal, 31*, 14–19.

Hare, V. C., & Bingham, A. (1986). Teaching students main idea comprehension: Alternatives to repeated exposures. In J. Baumann (Ed.), *Teaching main idea comprehension* (pp. 179–194). Newark, Del.: International Reading Association.

Hare, V. C., & Borchardt, K. M. (1984). Direct instruction of summarization skills. *Reading Research Quarterly, 20*, 62–78.

Irwin, J. W. and Baker, I. (1989) *Promoting Active Reading Comprehension Strategies.* Englewood Cliffs, NJ: Prentice-Hall.

Kintsch, W., & Greene, E. (1978). The role of culture-specific schemata in the comprehension and recall of stories. *Discourse Processes, 1*, 1–13.

Mandler, J. M., & DeForest, M. (1979). Is there more than one way to recall a story? *Child Development, 50*, 886–889.

McGee, L. M., & Richgels, D. J. (1985). Teaching expository text structure to elementary students. *The Reading Teacher, 38*, 739–748.

Meyer, B. J. F. (1975). *The organization of prose and its effects in memory.* Amsterdam: North-Holland.

Meyer, B., Brandt, D., & Bluth, G. (1980). Use of top-level structure in text: Key for reading comprehension of ninth-grade students. *Reading Research Quarterly, 16,* 72–103.

Morrow, L. M. (1986). Effects of structural guidance in story retelling on children's dictation of original stories. *Journal of Reading Behavior, 18,* 135–152.

Morrow, L. M. (1989). Using story retelling to develop comprehension. In K. D. Muth (Ed.), *Children's comprehension of text* (pp. 37–58). Newark, Del.: International Reading Association.

Richgels, D. J., McGee, L. M., & Slaton, E. A. (1989). Teaching expository text structure in reading and writing. In K. D. Muth (Ed.), *Children's comprehension of text (pp. 167–184). Newark, Del.: International Reading Association.*

Rinehart, S. D., Stahl, S. A., & Erickson, L. G. (1986). Some effects of summarization training on reading and studying. *Reading Research Quarterly, 21,* 422–438.

Rubin, A., & Gentner, D. (1979, December). An educational technique to encourage practice with high-level aspects of texts. Paper presented at the annual meeting of the National Reading Conference, San Antonio, Texas.

Slater, W. H., Graves, M. F., Piche, G. L. (1985). Effects of structural organizers on ninth grade students' comprehension and recall of four patterns of expository text. *Reading Research Quarterly, 62,* 189–202.

Smith, M., & Bean, T. W. (1983). Four strategies that develop children's story comprehension and writing. *Reading Teacher, 37,* 295–301.

Stein, N. (1979). How children understand stories: A developmental analysis. In L. Katz (Ed.), *Current topics in early childhood education* (Vol. 2). Hillsdale, N.J.: Ablex.

Stein, N. L., & Glenn, C. G. (1977). An analysis of story comprehension in elementary school children. In R. Freedle (Ed.), *Multidisciplinary approaches to discourse comprehension.* Hillsdale, N.J.: Ablex.

Stein, N. L., & Nezworski, T. (1978). The effects of organization and instructional set on story memory. *Discourse Processes, 1,* 177–193.

Stewart, O. & Tei, E. (1983). Some implications of metacognition for reading instruction. *Journal of Reading, 27,* 36–43.

Taylor, B. M. (1980). Children's memory for expository text after reading. *Reading Research Quarterly, 15,* 399–411.

Taylor, B. M. (1982). A summarizing strategy to improve middle grade students' reading and writing skills. *Reading Teacher, 36,* 202–205.

Taylor, B. M. (1986). Teaching middle grade students to summarize content textbook material. In J. Baumann (Ed.), *Teaching main idea comprehension* (pp. 195–209). Newark, Del.: International Reading Association.

Taylor, B. M., & Beach, R. W. (1984). The effects of text structure instruction on middle grade students' comprehension and production of expository text. *Reading Research Quarterly, 19,* 134–146.

Taylor, K. K. (1983). Can college students summarize? *Journal of Reading, 26,* 524–529.

Van Dijk, T. A. (1979). Relative assignment in discourse comprehension. *Discourse Processes, 2,* 113–126.

Vaughan, J. L. (1982). Use the conStruct procedure to foster active reading. *Journal of Reading, 25,* 412–422.

Vaughan, J. L., Stillman, P. L., & Sabers, D. L. (1978, December). Developing ideational scaffolds during reading. Paper presented at the annual meeting of the National Reading Conference, St. Petersburg, Florida.

Whaley, J. F. (1981). Story grammars and reading instruction. *Reading Teacher, 34,* 762–771.

Williams, J. R. (1986, August). Reading comprehension: Categorization, macrostructure and finding the main idea. Paper presented at the annual meeting of the American Psychological Association, Washington, D.C.

Williams, J. R. (1988). Identifying main ideas: A basic aspect of reading comprehension. *Topics in Language Disorders, 8,* 1–13.

Winograd, P. (1984). Strategic differences in summarizing texts. *Reading Research Quarterly, 19,* 404–425.

5

TEACHING ELABORATIVE PROCESSES

So far in our examination of the comprehension process, we have described a reader who chunks words into meaningful phrases and selects from those phrases the ideas to be remembered. That reader also ties the individual ideas into a coherent whole by noticing or inferring relationships among individual sentences and by summarizing the passage into general ideas and organizing the ideas around an organizational structure. The questions we must now ask are: Have we described everything a reader "comprehends" when he or she reads? Does this describe everything a reader does when trying to understand a passage? Do students ever report having comprehended anything other than micro, integrative, or macro information?

The answer is, of course, "Yes." Readers will often make inferences that are not necessary for microprocessing, integrative processing, or macroprocessing, but they are useful to that specific reader in that specific context. They are part of the meaning that he or she is constructing. (See the definition of comprehension in Chapter One.) These can be called "uninvited inferences" or *elaborations*. Readers often elaborate on the author's intended message.

ELABORATIVE PROCESSES

Elaborations can be defined as those inferences that are not necessary for microprocessing, integrative processing, or macroprocessing. Readers elaborate for many reasons. Elaborations improve recall (Reder, 1978) and increase enjoyment. The most typical types of elaborations are (1) making predictions, (2) integrating the information with prior knowledge, (3) forming mental images, (4) responding affectively, and (5) responding with higher-level thinking processes. The amount and type of elaboration used by a particular reader are related to that reader's purpose and prior knowledge.

This can be demonstrated by examining what different readers remember from reading the same passage. The underlined portions are the elaborations in what Susie and Sally have recalled.

> SUSIE: It was a story about a little girl who missed her father. She wondered if he loved her. Her mother told her to listen like she listened to other good sounds. I remember especially when she listened to the storm in the mountains. <u>It reminded me of when I was in Colorado last year.</u>
>
> SALLY: It was about a little girl who missed her father. <u>Fathers don't always come home. I had a friend once whose father didn't come home for three years. He was in a war. When he came home, everyone was happy.</u>

As can be seen from Sally's recall, not all elaborations are necessarily facilitative of recall of the passage being read. You may have had experience with children who infer so many extraneous details that their comprehension of the passage is actually reduced. Adams and Bruce (1980) have suggested that decisions about what to infer should be based on "the concept of good structure" (p. 4). Warren, Nicholas, and Trabasso (1979) suggest that good readers infer information that is "relevant to the progress of the narrative" (p. 44). All these authors are trying to suggest that an elaboration is appropriate to the extent to which it is related to the important ideas expressed in the text. Elaborations are also appropriate to the extent that they help the reader achieve his or her purpose. Although no exact rules can be developed to define this for all situations, most teachers are probably able to tell when students are elaborating appropriately and inappropriately.

PREDICTIONS

Many researchers in the field of reading comprehension stress the central role of prediction (see Collins & Smith, 1980, p. 4). Collins and Smith define predictions as "hypotheses about what will happen" (1980, p. 14). They suggest that good readers often read with various event and text structure expectations. These predictions probably help these readers to monitor their comprehension and direct their attention to important information.

Some possible types of predictions are given in Figure 5-1. When reading stories, students can make predictions about what will happen, based on such things as what they already know about the character, his or her motivation, or the situation itself. Titles and pictures also often contain hints of what is to come. The characteristics of the individual reader will also affect what predictions are made. The reader's prior knowledge, attitudes about the content, and purpose for reading can all

FIGURE 5-1   Possible Predictions Made by Readers of Stories

I.   Predictions of events based on...
  A. Character traits
  B. Character motivation
  C. Situational characteristics
  D. Signals in text
    1. Pictures
    2. Title
  E. Reader characteristics
    1. Prior knowledge
    2. Attitudes (affective responses)
    3. Purpose for reading
II. Structural predictions based on...
  A. Prior knowledge of genre
  B. Story grammar awareness

Source: Adapted from A. Collins and E. E. Smith, *Teaching the Process of Reading Comprehension,* Technical Report no. 182 (Urbana-Champaign: Center for the Study of Reading, University of Illinois, 1980) p. 16.

influence these predictions. Students can also infer what kinds of events are likely to come next based on the genre: in a mystery story, one set of events is likely; in a Greek tragedy, another set is more plausible. Moreover, predictions can also be based on the position of the information in the story structure. For instance, if the story has just presented an initiating event, the reader will probably expect an internal response. (See the discussion of story structure in Chapter Four.)

Note that the teacher can give students clues about what information might be used when asking prediction questions. For each category in Figure 5-1, a question could be formed. For instance, for I. A., Character traits, the teacher could ask, "What do you know about the character that would help you to predict what he or she might do next?" Other questions suggested by this table include: "What do you know about what the character wants that would help you to predict what he or she will do next?" "What do you know about the situation that would help you to predict what would happen next?" and so on.

Readers of expository texts also make predictions (see Figure 5-2). These predictions are often based on prior knowledge about the topic. For instance, if one is reading about slavery immediately prior to the Civil War, one might expect that the Underground Railroad will be mentioned. Predictions can also be based on what one knows about certain causal relationships; if one is reading about a series of conflicts between two powerful Western countries in the nineteenth century, one might predict that these conflicts are leading up to a war. (See Chapter Seven for a discussion of the importance of prior knowledge.)

Moreover, content expectations in expository materials are also largely based on structural considerations. If one is reading a long list of details, one might be

FIGURE 5-2   Possible Predictions Made by Readers of Expository Texts

I. Content predictions based on...
   A. Prior knowledge of the topic
   B. Prior knowledge of causality
      1. Physical
      2. Political
      3. Psychological
      4. Other
II. Structural predictions based on ...
   A. Prior knowledge of content-area–related organizational patterns
   B. Organizational patterns in prior text
   C. Signals in text
      1. Headings
      2. Titles
      3. Introductions
      4. Transitional statements
      5. Tables, charts, etc.

predicting what the main idea will be, or vice versa. If one has been reading about a problem, one might expect the solution to follow; examples might be expected after a definition; and so on. Thus, an understanding of organizational patterns is probably useful for prediction.

Organizational patterns can be predicted on the basis of at least three aspects of the text: (1) the content area, (2) the prior text, and (3) direct signals. For instance, if one were reading social studies, one would predict that chronology and cause-effect are more likely to be used than definition-example, whereas the opposite might be true for science. If the previous section were entirely chronological, this would strengthen this position. Finally, if the subheading were, "Major Conflicts from 1920 to 1935," the prediction would be further substantiated.

General Instruction in Making Predictions

Students can be encouraged to make predictions at all grade levels and in all subjects. Because predictions are often based on prior knowledge, discussion of predictions should probably be preceded by some discussion of what students already know. Asking students to make predictions when looking over an assignment you are giving can often motivate them at the same time that it increases their comprehension. Group discussion of various student predictions can allow students to be exposed to each other's reasoning processes. Stress that it is not important to be right all the time. Many good predictions do not match the decisions made by the author. Sometimes, the author wants to surprise the reader by including an outcome that no one would predict. Share your own predictions, whether right or wrong. What information did you use? Try to demonstrate how one might use all the information in Figure 5-1 or 5-2 as appropriate. Use explicit instruction in predicting for students who do not seem to use this strategy effectively.

Activities that Encourage Prediction

Gist strategy. Schuder, Clewell, and Jackson (1989) have suggested that students be taught to use prediction as a comprehension strategy for expository materials using the "gist" procedure provided in Figure 5-3. The teacher leads the students through the directions listed in the left-hand column while using the prompts on the right to direct the discussion. After a few lessons, the students will begin to

FIGURE 5-3   Directions and Prompts for Helping Students Get the Gist of Exposition

DIRECTION	PROMPT
Prereading In the next (two) minutes, scan the…(page, chapter, unit) to see what it is going to be about. Record predictions about topic and gist on board, chart paper, or overhead.	1. What do you think this…(chapter, unit, page) is going to be about? What makes you think so? 2. What do you think…(the text) is going to tell you about…(predicted topic)? What makes you think so?
During reading Read the first/next…(paragraph or larger chunk) to find out if it supports your prediction. List and/or diagram relationships between evidence and statements of gist on the board, chart paper, or overhead. Record changes, if any, in statements of predicted gist.	3. Did you find evidence that supports your prediction? What was it? 4. Did you find evidence that does not support your prediction? What was it? 5. Do you want to change your prediction at this point? If not, why not? If you do, how do you want to change it?
Postreading Think about what you have just read. Make a final revision of the statement about the gist. Record final changes, if any.	6. Do you want to make any changes in your statement of what this is about? If yes, what changes do you want to make? Why do you want to make those changes? 7. What did you learn that you did not know before reading?
Discuss.	

Questions may be omitted if the students supply the information prior to prompting.
Note: Prompts are recursive as the students entertain multiple hypotheses and/or move to new chunks of text or read other texts on the same topic.

Source: T. Schuder, S. F. Clewell, and N. Jackson, "Getting the Gist of Expository Text, in *Children's Comprehension of Text,* ed. K. D. Muth. (Newark, Del.: International Reading Association 1989), p. 230. Reprinted with permission of Ted Schuder and the International Reading Association.

respond to the prompts without being asked. Then, they are ready to take on the roles of prompter and recorder. The goal would be internalization of the entire process as a self-monitoring activity.

Directed reading-thinking activity.   Stauffer (1969) has suggested that some students could be led through a text in segments. For each, the students examine text cues and other information, make a prediction, and read to verify that prediction. Predictions can be written on the board before reading. After reading the segment, students can discuss whether their predictions were accurate. Be sure to encourage students to discuss the reasons for their predictions.

Writing activities.   Students can be actively involved in writing predictions for their independent reading materials or for each others' stories. For instance, when students are reading a book with several chapters, they can keep a list of predictions made at the end of each chapter in a reading response journal (see p. 104). Students can also share their stories with each other omitting the final section and asking their peers to predict the ending. These can be exchanged, read orally, or circulated around the class with different students suggesting different endings.

OTHER PRIOR-KNOWLEDGE ELABORATIONS

All elaborations, including predictions, require prior knowledge. Reder (1978) has presented a model of elaboration that stresses the role of the reader's prior knowledge. She points out that each word or idea in the passage being read evokes a unique set of associations for each reader. The particular elaboration chosen from this set of associations would be the one most consistent with the passage being read. Moreover, as Reder (1978) points out, "How much one elaborates depends upon previous experience with the material, inherent interest in the subject matter, understanding of the text, time allotted to read it, concentration and general tendency to elaborate" (p. 72). Elaboration that integrates new ideas with past experiences clearly improves recall (Reder, 1980).

Let us look at some examples of possible prior-knowledge elaborations other than predictions. Jill, Jack, and John are each commenting on the first four paragraphs of *The Heart of Darkness* by Joseph Conrad. Note how each comment is valid, yet how they differ according to the students' prior experience. Each of these students is actively interacting with the material and will probably remember more than those students who do not use prior-knowledge elaborations. Yet each of these students will probably remember very different things.

> JILL: I think the fact that Marlow looks like an idol is an important symbol. It's like when *The Idiot* had so many aspects of a Christ figure. Religious symbolism usually carries deeper meeting.

JACK: This whole scene reminds me of the night I spent on a steamer on the Mississippi. As in this scene, the river seemed to stretch out forever; there was no separation between water and sky. Everything was hazy, and there was a sense of approaching gloom as the sun set. It really gave me the creeps.

JOHN: I like the description of the Director of Companies as looking "nautical." It made me think of an old sea captain I knew as a kid. Like this character, he liked to look out to sea. I picture him with a seaman's cap, a beard, and a pipe. I think it also indicates that he is hardened and is quiet and used to being alone, always dreaming about the old days.

Of course, prior-knowledge elaborations can be inappropriate if they stray too far from the text. (For an example, see Sally's recall at the beginning of this chapter.) In the examples, the students are connecting images in the text with things they have experienced, so we would probably characterize these elaborations as appropriate. Without knowing the students' purposes for reading, we cannot say that one is better than another.

Incidental Instruction in Prior-Knowledge Elaboration

If students are actively interacting with the content they are reading, they will make prior-knowledge elaborations. Good readers will gear these elaborations toward specific purposes. Thus, encouraging students to think about what they already know before reading, giving them a purpose for reading, and getting them actively involved in the material will all be useful for encouraging prior-knowledge elaborations. Prereading purposes such as "Think about how this relates to what we studied in Chapter Three" or "While you are reading, think about other people you know who are like this" will lead to prior-knowledge elaborations. The teacher's attitude toward elaborations that are shared during class discussions will also make a difference.

Explicit Instruction in Prior-Knowledge Elaborations

In a remedial situation, you may wish to use explicit instruction including explaining, modeling, questioning, and practicing independently. While you are reading aloud to the students, pause and share appropriate prior-knowledge elaborations. Tell the students that good readers actively think about what they are reading and actively relate it to what they already know or have experienced. Tell them that this helps them to understand, remember and enjoy what they are reading. Then have the students model the procedure for you. Have them read orally, pausing to talk about what they already know about what is being said. Figure 5-4 shows how a teacher can follow this procedure with a small group in the fourth grade. Several other specific activities for guiding students to use their prior knowledge appropriately are provided in Chapter Seven of this text.

FIGURE 5-4   Teaching of Prior-Knowledge Elaboration

FOURTH-GRADE TEACHER MONOLOGUE
"Now, while you're reading this section, I want you to think constantly about what you already know about what's being said. That will help you understand and remember it better. It's especiallly helpful to do this while reading in your social studies book, so you can better understand the people you are reading about. Let me show you what I mean. Let's look at page 130."
(Teacher reads a few sentences.)
"Well, it says mining helped them have jobs, so it was very important. Why is that important? I have a friend who didn't have a job for a long time. He didn't have any money because of it. He couldn't pay his bills and had to move to a tiny apartment with no windows. He couldn't afford to buy new clothes or good food. The people I know who have jobs have bigger homes, new clothes, and good food. So, if mining helped the people have jobs so they could have these things, I can see why it was so important!
"Let's read on." (Student reads until teacher asks him to stop.)
"So, here it says that life in the city was very different from life in the villages. What do you already know about cities and villages that will help you understand this?"
(Students reply with their prior experiences. Teacher leads them to draw conclusions and summarize differences.)

MENTAL IMAGERY

Paivio (1986) has hypothesized that cognition really involves two processing systems—a verbal linguistic system and a nonverbal imaging system: "both verbal and imaginal contexts and associations contribute to the reader's psychological organization of text" (p. 227). Forming mental images as we read does seem to increase the amount we understand and recall. Gambrell and Boles (1986) found that poor readers receiving instructions before reading to form mental images were more likely to detect text inconsistencies than were poor readers who received general reading instructions. Steingart and Glock (1979) found that college students instructed to image while they read concrete materials recalled more and made more inferences than did students instructed to repeat the passage to themselves. Research seems to indicate that poor comprehenders are more likely to be helped by imagery instructions than are good comprehenders. (see Golinkoff, 1975–76). Also, evidence exists that students who can be characterized as "picture learners" are more likely to be helped by imagery instruction than those who are not (Levin, Divine-Hawkins, Kurt, & Gutemann, 1974). Finally, Sadowski, Goetz and Kangiser (1988) have reported that the imagery reports of the college students in their study varied: "Although these reports were quite similar in many ways, there was a element of richness and variety to them that indicated a somewhat unique imaginative experience for each reader" (p. 333).

Incidental Instruction in Mental Imagery

On a practical level, because it will help some of your students, forming vivid mental images can be encouraged when it is applicable for the material at hand. Various activities can be used: writing elaborative descriptions, describing sounds and smells that are brought to mind during reading, drawing pictures to illustrate the material, and so on. In the content areas, concrete demonstrations of scientific principles, pictures, movies, and cultural artifacts, for example, will also probably facilitate comprehension by making it possible for students to visualize while they are reading. Guided imagery writing before reading can facilitate involvement. For instance, lead students to visualize the world as it would be after a nuclear war. Have them close their eyes and visualize as you describe some of the effects. Then have them write descriptions. Then have them read about arms reduction negotiations. Remember that students will vary in the extent to which mental images are interesting and useful, so you may wish to provide alternative activities for some children in some situations.

Specific Activities for Encouraging Imaging Strategies

If you think that a specific student or group of students might benefit from training in forming mental images, then you can construct specific activities that seem to be useful for this. The first step is making sure that students are prepared. Students can appropriately image only when they have adequate prior experience with the images involved. If you think this might be a problem, bring in some pictures or films with settings or images similar to those involved in the reading selection. If necessary, describe some of the important mental pictures before students actually read the text. Then, writing and drawing activities can be used to encourage imaging.

Writing activities. Have students select an event in their lives that they would like to describe. Encourage them to fill in a chart including a column for each of the following sensory experiences that they remember: sights, sounds, smells, tastes, and feelings. They could then write the description using as many vivid images as possible. To connect this to reading, have them exchange papers and read each others' descriptions. Then, they could tell what they liked and remembered about the images in each other's papers, or they could draw illustrations for each other. You could also do a similar writing activity by reading to the students first. Then ask them to fill in a senses chart and write about the images that came to mind as you read.

Drawing activities. Drawing activities can also be used to encourage mental images and to help students compare their images with each other. (Remember to stress that good readers will often differ in the details that they imagine.) For young children, read the children a picture book without showing them the pictures. Then ask them to draw the illustrations. Make a new book using the pictures from the class. For all grades, you may wish to involve them in illustrating their own and others' writing. Stories they have written work especially well for this activity.

AFFECTIVE RESPONSES

An emotional response, especially one intended by the author, is part of the comprehension process. Spiro (1984) has suggested that subjective reactions may actually facilitate or interfere with recall. Moreover, the importance of affective responses has been demonstrated in the research of Golden and Guthrie (1986) in which students who identified with a particular character identified the central conflict of the story as pertaining to that character. Similarly, the comprehension taxonomy presented by Smith and Barrett (1979) also includes affective responses are part of comprehension. In this taxonomy, the category of "appreciation" includes affective responses related to such factors as (1) emotional responses to plot or theme, (2) identification with characters and incidents, and (3) reactions to the author's use of language. In the activities that follow, "reactions to the author's use of language" is interpreted as reactions to connotations and figurative language. Moreover, I have also added "bibliotherapy" or reading for personal growth to this list of possible affective responses.

Again, as with other elaborations, readers who are interacting with the text affectively are being more active than those who are not, and these active, involved readers will probably remember more or different things than will those who are not reacting affectively. One point to remember, however, is that affective reactions are not always appropriate for every purpose. For instance, a literature teacher teaching "The Tell-Tale Heart" by Edgar Allen Poe can encourage an affective response with a dramatic reading with lights off and candles lit. In contrast, a social studies teacher may wish to warn students that an editorial is loaded with emotional language designed to persuade them, thus helping them to resist their affective responses. (The latter instruction would involve higher-level thinking responses, especially analysis; see the description of analysis later in this chapter.)

Incidental Teaching of Affective Responses

All teacher should realize that affective responses are a sign of an active approach to reading, though the extent to which they are discussed in normal classroom situations depends on the objectives of the lesson. Perhaps the most common situation in which such discussions occur is when students are reading literature. For stories, novels, poems and plays, affective response is an essential part of understanding (see Sadowski, Goetz, & Kangiser, 1988). Indeed, Rosenblatt (1978, 1989) has reminded us that readers assume at least two stances in their approach to any act of reading. If engaged in "efferent reading," the reader's attention is focused on acquiring something to remain after reading is over such as information, a solution to a problem, a procedure to be carried out, and so forth. If engaged in "aesthetic reading," on the other hand, "the reader's attention is centered directly on what he is living through during his relationship with that particular text" (1978, p. 25). In aesthetic reading, the emphasis is placed on the experience itself. Thus, "the aesthetic reader experiences and savors the qualities of the structured ideas, situations, scenes, personalities and emotions that are called forth and participates in the tensions, conflicts, and resolutions as they unfold" (1989, p. 159). Clearly, such aesthetic reading involves affective response, and, as Winograd and Smith (1987) point out, "aesthetic reading is what turns people into motivated lifelong readers" (p. 306).

Activities for Encouraging Affective Responses

Many activities for facilitating emotional responses can be created for specific situations. A few suggestions for each type of affective response are given in the paragraphs that follow.

Emotional response to plot or theme.   Emotional responses to plot or theme can be facilitated in prereading discussion by asking students to think about similar events that they have experienced before reading the selection. Similarly, postreading discussions of how similar events or themes apply to their own lives will help them to respond affectively. Finally, role playing critical scenes from the plot may help students to sense the emotional impact of the events. Students should be encouraged to understand why they have responded in the way that they have. In this way, reading can be used to learn about the self as well as others (Probst, 1989).

Identification with characters.   Again, discussions in which students think about how they would feel if they were one of the characters will facilitate identification with that character. Also, students can be told that they will be asked to do a postreading writing or speaking activity in which they take on the persona of one of the characters. These may involve writing the character's diary, writing a letter from one character to another, writing the same story from a different character's point of view, or dramatizing part of the story. Finally, students can be asked such questions as "How would you feel if this happened to you?" and "How did X feel?" Then, they can compare their own anticipated reactions with those of the characters.

Connotations and figurative language.   Students should be taught that words have both *denotations,* literal meanings, and *connotations,* implications beyond the literal meanings that are often emotional in character. Students can compare pairs of words or phrases, such as "female parent" and "mother," that have the same denotations but different connotations. They can discuss authors' word choices and suggest other words that would change the story because of their

TABLE 5-1   Examples of Types of Figurative Language

DEFINITION	EXAMPLE
Simile: two dissimilar things said to be alike; uses word "like" or "as"	My heart sank like a stone.
Metaphor: same as simile but words "like" and "as" are not used	All the world's a stage.
Personification: representing a thing or animal as a person	His money said it all.

connotations. They can be asked to point out how their reaction to a story or essay was affected by the connotations of specific words. This will lead directly to the higher-level thinking process of analysis.

Figurative language, like connotation, involves meaning that goes beyond the most literal interpretation. The commonest types of figurative language are simile, metaphor, and personification (see Table 5-1). Students should be encouraged to discuss the connotations of such expressions when these expressions occur in their reading assignments.

Bibliotherapy.   Many have suggested that responsive reading can be useful for solving personal problems. That is sometimes called "bibliotherapy." Hafner (1977) suggests that this process occurs through identification with a character, catharsis, and insight (p. 329). (He has also provided an annotated bibliography of books that can be used for such a purpose.) Certainly, teachers should not regard themselves as psychotherapists, but by helping students find books for this purpose, they can help students learn that responsive reading is a useful resource for personal growth.

HIGHER-LEVEL THINKING RESPONSES

When we are speaking of elaborative processes, it is impossible to separate "reading" from "reasoning." When we are reading, we often engage in many types of "higher-level" thinking processes. For instance, transferring information to apply in new situations, analyzing the reasoning used by the author, integrating ideas into a creative idea or product, and making judgments about what is being read are all higher-level thinking responses that can be a part of a reading act. Bloom (1956) originally called these processes "application," "analysis," "synthesis," and "evaluation," respectively.

Extensive teaching suggestions concerning these processes can be found in Sanders (1966), Burmeister (1978), and others. Although teachers tend to reserve this instruction for older and better readers, students of *all* ages and ability levels should be asked to use these thinking processes during and after reading. Moreover, no one type of thinking should be viewed as inherently more difficult than any other; for instance, some evaluation questions can be easier than some applications questions, and so on. Finally, all these processes can be encouraged in all content areas as well as in reading classes.

Application

Basically, application is the process of deciding what information to apply in a new situation and applying it appropriately. In a true application task, the teacher does not tell the students what they are to apply. Rather, the students realize that a given piece of information is applicable. Many teachers think that the content they are teaching has not been fully comprehended unless the students can apply it independently.

Examples of application activities can be found in all the content areas. In math and science, word problems often require students to decide which reasoning or mathematical process to use and then to apply it. In social studies, students are applying information if they read a chapter on a given culture and then later accurately predict how someone in that culture will react. You can probably think of numerous other examples. The important point to remember is that if you must tell the students what information to apply, they have not yet reached the application level of thinking for that piece of content.

Analysis

Analysis can be seen as the process of breaking the information into its component parts and assessing one's own thought processes in relation to those parts. For instance, students are engaged in a analysis when they point out that an author's premises do not lead to the stated conclusion(s) or when they note that the author has used biased language. This is sometimes called "critical reading." Burmeister (1978) lists the following activities as examples:

1. Making judgments related to the authenticity of a source of information.
2. Distinguishing between fact and opinion.
3. Analyzing propaganda.
4. Detecting fallacies of reasoning.

Pearson and Johnson (1978) recommend that students be taught to detect bias in writing by recognizing emotionally laden words as well as the use of propaganda techniques, such as implication by association, half-truths, and overgeneralization. The paragraphs that follow contain brief descriptions of these processes and a few possible activities for teaching each of them. Similar activities are often found in basal reader series.

Source credibility.   Students should develop the habit of assessing the possible credibility of each author. For instance, a gardener may be a less credible source than a physician if the article is about treating human bacterial diseases. This is not to say that both viewpoints should not be considered but, rather, to point out that the reliability of the source must be considered an important piece of information. Activities in which the students read different types of authors discussing the same topic and worksheets in which possibly credible authors are to be matched with appropriate statements are examples of activities that teach students to analyze the credibility of authors.

Fact versus opinion.   Students must be able to distinguish facts, such as "It is 40 degrees today," from opinions, such as "It is cold today." The first of these statements is objectively verifiable; the second is a matter of opinion. Have students rewrite factual statements as opinions, and vice versa. Have students underline facts and circle opinions in newspaper articles or even in each other's papers. Frager and Thompson (1985) have suggested that students could benefit by reading conflicting reports on the same event. Then, they could list the facts and opinions in each to see if this helped them to understand the differences in the authors' views.

Propaganda.   Typical propaganda techniques are illustrated in Table 5-2. Students can be asked to find examples of these in advertisements, editorials, and political speeches. In school campaigns, they can watch for when they use them themselves!

Fallacies of reasoning.   A thorough explanation of possible reasoning fallacies is beyond the scope of this book. For an excellent discussion of eight common fallacies, see Burmeister (1978). Other discussions can be found in books on critical reasoning.

Emotionally laden words.   Perhaps the easiest type of biased writing for students to detect is the use of emotionally laden words. Students can be taught to circle emotionally laden words in newspaper articles and persuasive essays. They can rewrite such passages with the language changed so as to eliminate the bias, or they can compare the words used in articles with opposing points of view. They can also look at each other's essays in this way.

Synthesis

Synthesis is the process of combining separate pieces of knowledge to come up with knowledge that is new, at least new to the person doing the thinking. It is the process of thinking creatively. In a sense, all elaborations fall into this category, and, as with elaborations, this type of thinking is encouraged only when the teacher abandons the "one right answer" approach and encourages divergent responses. Activities that

TABLE 5-2   Typical Propaganda Techniques

NAME	DEFINITION	EXAMPLE
Name calling	Calling people or things by names with pleasant or unpleasant connotations designed to evoke emotional response	1. Calling local politician a "communist" 2. Calling one politician "skinny" and another "slim"
Implication by association	Using testimonies of trusted people or associating a person or thing with pleasant or unpleasant concepts	1. A distinguished actor tells about how he uses a given product every day. 2. Calling a product something like "The All-American Pen"
Half-truths	Omitting qualifying details or using one truth to imply an opinion	Quoting a noted authority but leaving off the qualification: "If the world were different, this would be great" becomes "This would be great."
Overgeneralizations	Stating sweeping generalizations as if they were facts; failing to give critical details	1. "This vacuum cleaner is the best that has ever been made." 2. "If I am elected, I will work toward ending war and poverty."
Bandwagon	Appealing to the reader's desire to belong: the "everyone does it" approach	"Over two million people have already bought our product."

encourage synthesis often require some sort of creative product, such as a play, a story, or a plan of operation. Examples of activities are rewriting a story as it would occur in a different culture, writing a fictional description of a day in the life of an historical figure, predicting what the world would be like if one natural law were changed, and planning political action after reading about a political issue.

Evaluation

Finally, evaluation involves first deciding on the evaluation criteria and then evaluating the ideas as good or bad, right or wrong, just or unjust, and so on, on the basis of those criteria. For instance, a student who recalls what a critic has said about a play is not evaluating it himself or herself. If, conversely, the student decides independently what makes a play good, and then judges the play according to those criteria, that student is evaluating the quality of that play.

Activities in which students assume the role of decision maker can help them to appreciate the importance of this type of thinking. For instance, students can pretend to be members of the Food and Drug Administration setting up criteria to be used for the approval of a new drug; they can be asked to pretend that they are politicians who must vote on pending legislation. Such tasks involve reading for information, setting up criteria, and making difficult evaluative decisions.

FINAL CONSIDERATIONS FOR TEACHING ELABORATION

At least three considerations are relevant to the teaching of all five elaborative processes discussed in this chapter. First, teachers must abandon the "one right answer" approach if they are to encourage elaborations. Elaborations are usually personal responses, which will differ from reader to reader. Students need to feel that their reasoning process will be valued. Because elaborations are divergent responses, they are difficult to grade, but this does not mean that they are not an important part of the comprehension process.

Second, elaborative processes are not for only those students who have fully mastered microprocesses, integrative processes, and macroprocesses. Students in all grades and all ability levels can elaborate on the meanings they encounter during readings tasks. In fact, the ability to elaborate can facilitate microprocesses, integrative processes, and macroprocesses as much as the reverse.

A good general strategy for teaching all elaborative processes is first to explain and model the procedure yourself, then to encourage students to model it for you and for each other, and then to provide tasks that encourage the particular type of elaboration (explicit instruction). For instance, if you would like to encourage the formation of vivid mental images, begin by describing your own images to the students after you have all read an image-evoking passage. Then have them read another one, pausing to tell you about their images. Then ask them to read silently while focusing on the formation of vivid mental images. A similar procedure can be used to encourage all elaborative processes, including the higher-level thinking responses of application, analysis, synthesis, and evaluation.

Finally, writing activities of all kinds are especially useful for helping students to elaborate when reading. For instance, students can keep *reading-response journals* in which they record their responses at the end of each day of reading or at the end of each book they read, for instance. You can provide them with a set of possible opening statements to help them get started. These might include such lead-ins as: "When I was reading this I felt..." (affective response). "When I read this, I pictured..." (mental imagery). "This reminded me of..." (prior-knowledge elaboration). "I had expected that..." (prediction). "I liked it (did not like it) because..." (evaluation). A list like this one can be kept on a bulletin board to help students when they are having trouble responding. You can also have students write such free-form responses after you read to them or after they have listened to another student read his or her piece of writing. Other suggestions for using writing have been provided throughout this chapter.

SUMMARY

Good readers often go beyond microprocesses, integrative processes, and macroprocesses. They elaborate on the text in ways that facilitate recall and make the information more useful or enjoyable to them. Elaborations can be appropriate or inappropriate depending on their effectiveness in facilitating the reader's purpose.

There are many types of elaborations, including (1) making predictions, (2) integrating the information with prior knowledge, (3) forming mental images, (4) responding affectively, and (5) responding with higher-level thinking processes. Predictions are based on the content and the structure of what is being read as well as on the reader's prior knowledge, attitude, and purpose. Affective responses include emotional responses to the plot or theme, identification with characters, and affective reactions to word connotations and figurative language. Finally, higher-level thinking processes include application, analysis, synthesis, and evaluation and can be taught in all content areas as well as in reading classes.

Teachers encourage elaborations when they reject the "one right answer" approach and encourage personal interaction with the material. Elaborations should not be judged on the basis of their "rightness"; rather, they should be judged on the basis of the quality and relevance of the processes involved. Students at all grade and ability levels and in all content areas should be encouraged to elaborate in all of the ways suggested in this chapter.

SELF-CHECK TEST

1. Choose either expository or narrative material, and list the factors on which readers base their predictions.
2. List five types of elaborative processes.
3. Define the following.

   structurally based prediction

   connotation

   application

   analysis

   synthesis

   evaluation

   aesthetic reading

efferent reading

gist strategy

reading-response journal

4. Fill in the blanks.

    (a) High-picture learners should be encouraged to _____

    (b) The first step in teaching prediction is _____

    (c) Appropriate elaborations are _____

    (d) A student may be unwilling to make a prediction because _____

5. Answer true or false.

    ____ (a) First-grade students should not be expected to elaborate.

    ____ (b) Elaboration processes interact with microprocesses, integrative processes, and macroprocesses.

    ____ (c) All elaborations facilitate recall.

    ____ (d) Affective responses should always be encouraged.

    ____ (e) All students will make the same prior-knowledge elaborations.

    ____ (f) Thinking and reading are two separate things.

    ____ (g) The "one right answer" approach encourages elaborations.

    ____ (h) Detecting propaganda is an example of synthesis.

    ____ (i) Judging quality is an example of analysis.

SUGGESTED ACTIVITIES

1. Ask some students to make predictions after reading the introduction to a reading assignment. Write down each prediction. For each response, tell what information the student is using as a basis for the prediction.

2. Practice making predictions yourself. For one day, write down a prediction each time you begin to read something. On what basis are you making these predictions?

3. Begin a reader-response journal of your own. Try to write a response whenever you read something interesting. What kinds of responses do you tend to make? Why?

4. Keep track of how much efferent and aesthetic reading takes place in your own life and in your classroom. Is this the balance that you prefer? Why or why not? Is this the balance that is best for your students? Why or why not?

5. During a reasonably long reading task, monitor your own elaborative processes. To what extent do you use each type? To what extent is this a result of your purpose for reading? How much is your prior knowledge affecting these

elaborations? In what specific ways are your purpose, your prior knowledge, and your preferred method of reading interacting?

REFERENCES

Adams, M., & Bruce, B. (1980). *Background knowledge and reading comprehension* (Reading Education Report No. 13). Urbana-Champaign: Center for the Study of Reading, University of Illinois.

Bloom, B. (1956). *Taxonomy of educational objectives. Handbook I: Cognitive domain.* New York: David McKay.

Burmeister, L. E. (1978). *Reading strategies for middle and secondary school teachers.* Reading, Mass.: Addison-Wesley.

Collins, A., & Smith, E. E. (1980). *Teaching the process of reading comprehension* (Technical Report No. 182). Urbana-Champaign: Center for the Study of Reading, University of Illinois.

Frager, A. M., & Thompson, L. C. (1985) Conflict: The key to critical reading instruction. *Journal of Reading, 28,* 676–683.

Gambrell, L., & Boles, R. J. (1986). Mental imagery and the comprehension-monitoring performance of fourth- and fifth-grade poor readers. *Reading Research Quarterly, 21,* 454–464.

Golden, J. M., & Guthrie, J. T. (1986). Convergence and divergence in reader response to literature. *Reading Research Quarterly, 21,* 408–421.

Golinkoff, R. M. (1975–1976). A comparison of reading comprehension processes in good and poor comprehenders. *Reading Research Quarterly, 4,* 623–659.

Hafner, L. E. (1977). *Developmental reading in middle and secondary schools.* New York: Macmillan.

Levin, J. R., Divine-Hawkins, P., Kerst, S. M., & Gutemann, J. (1974). Individual differences in learning from pictures and words: The development and application of an instrument. *Journal of Educational Psychology, 68,* 296–303.

Paivio, A., (1986). *Mental representations: A Dual Coding Approach.* New York: Oxford University Press.

Pearson, P. D., & Johnson, D. D. (1978). *Teaching reading comprehension.* New York: Holt, Rinehart and Winston.

Probst, R. E. (1989). Teaching the reading of literature. In D. Lapp, J. Flood, & N. Farnan, (Eds.), *Content area reading and learning: Instructional strategies,* (pp. 179–186). Englewood Cliffs, Prentice Hall.

Reder, L. M. (1978). *Comprehension and retention of prose: A literature review* (Technical Report No. 108). Urbana-Champaign: Center for the Study of Reading, University of Illinois.

Reder, L. M. (1980). The role of elaboration in the comprehension and retention of prose: A critical review. *Review of Educational Research, 15,* 5–53.

Rosenblatt, L. M. (1978). *The reader, the text, the poem: The transactional theory of the literary work*. Carbondale: Southern Illinois University Press.

Rosenblatt, L. M. (1989). Writing and reading: The transactional theory. In J. Mason, (Ed.), *Reading and writing and connections*, Boston: Allyn and Bacon, 153–176.

Sadowski, M., Goetz, E., & Kangiser, S. (1988). Imagination in story response: Relationships between imagery, affect, and structural importance. *Reading Research Quarterly, 23*, 320–336.

Sanders, N. (1966). *Classroom questions: What kinds?* New York: Harper & Row.

Schuder, T., Clewell, S. F., & Jackson, N. (1989). Getting the gist of expository text. In K. D. Muth, (Ed.), *Children's comprehension of text* (pp. 224–243). Newark, Del.: International Reading Association.

Smith R. J., & Barrett, T. C. (1979) *Teaching reading in the middle grades*. Reading, Mass.: Addison-Wesley.

Spiro, R. J. (1984). Consciousness and reading comprehension. In J. Flood (Ed.), *Understanding reading comprehension*. (pp. 75–81) Newark, Del.: International Reading Association.

Stauffer, R. G. (1969). *Directing reading maturity as a cognitive process*. New York: Harper & Row.

Steingart, S. K., & Glock, M. A. (1979). Imagery and the recall of connected discourse. *Reading Research Quarterly, 15*, 66–83.

Warren, W. H., Nicholas, D. W., & Trabasso, T., (1979). Event chains and inference in understanding narratives. In R. O. Freedle (Ed.) *New directions in discourse processing* (Vol. 2,). Hillsdale, N.J.: Lawrence Erlbaum.

Winograd, P., & Smith, L. (1987). Improving the climate for reading comprehension instruction. *Reading Teacher, 41*, 304–310.

6

TEACHING METACOGNITIVE PROCESSES

Baker and Brown (1980) define a student's metacognitive skills as "the knowledge and control he has over his own thinking and learning activities" (p. 2). In a summary of research on metacognition, Garner (1987) has stated that "younger children (particularly those in kindergarten or in grades 1 or 2) know substantially less than older children (particularly those in grades 5 and 6) about themselves, the tasks they face, and the strategies that they employ in the area of memory, reading, and attention" (pp. 35–36). Similar findings are available for comparing good and poor readers (see Garner, 1987). In a way, this entire book is about improving students' metacognition, because it is about increasing their knowledge about reading strategies as well as facilitating their control over such strategies. Teaching methods like those described in Chapter Two, which involve direct explanation of strategies, questions about strategies, and substantive feedback about strategies, all promote conscious awareness and control of cognitive processes, or *metacognition*.

Jacobs and Paris (1987) divide metacognition into two categories: (1) self-appraisal and (2) self-management. These are similar to Baker and Brown's categories of knowledge and control. Self-appraisal involves declarative knowledge about cognition; this would include statements typically beginning with "that"—for instance, that prior knowledge is important for reading comprehension. It also includes procedural knowledge or knowledge about how to do things, and conditional knowledge or knowledge about why and when certain strategies are important. Self-management includes planning, evaluating, and regulating strategies.

For the purpose of this book, *metacognitive processing* can be defined as selecting, evaluating, and regulating reading comprehension strategies. The selection of a specific strategy in a specific situation can be called a *metacognitive decision*. Moreover, the Baker and Brown (1980) division of metacognitive processes into those that are necessary for "reading for meaning" and those that are necessary for "reading for remembering" (p. 5) will also be used in this chapter.

The most important metacognitive process used by readers to get *meaning* is monitoring their own comprehension for success or failure. Good readers know when they have or have not understood something, and they know what to do when their comprehension breaks down. Reading for *remembering* involves the conscious selection of the recall-facilitating basic processes discussed earlier in this text such as summarizing, organizing, and elaborating as well as the application of many processes that have traditionally been called "study skills": underlining, note taking, previewing, rehearsing, and reviewing. These are consciously selected to enhance basic processes.

Finally, Paris and Winograd (1989) have suggested that definitions of metacognition should be expanded to include the affective and motivational aspect of thinking as well. Students' willingness to monitor and regulate their reading processes actively will be affected by influenced factors like self-concept, expectation for success, value attached to the activity, and so forth. These motivational factors will be discussed in Chapter Seven.

BASIC PROCESSES, COMPREHENSION CONTEXTS, AND METACOGNITIVE DECISIONS

Good readers often adjust their use of comprehension processes according to the three comprehension contexts. (You will remember from Chapter One that these included the reader, textual, and situational characteristics.) Each time a reader decides to use a specific process in a specific way because of a specific context, he or she is making a metacognitive decision. (Note that using elaboration to facilitate recall is still elaborative processing, but *making the conscious choice* to emphasize it is a metacognitive process.)

For instance, the reader must consider his or her own prior knowledge: If he or she lacks the necessary background information he or she may choose to read slowly, resolving problems by referring to another source. Easy material with which he or she is familiar can be read more quickly with an emphasis on summarizing the important points.

Similarly, different types of texts will require different processes. A poem may require affective response, whereas an essay may require analysis to be understood fully. A clearly organized text will require less macroprocessing effort than will one whose main points are obscure and unrelated.

Finally, the total situation, including the purpose for reading, will also affect metacognitive choices about basic processes. If the purpose for reading the poem mentioned above were to understand imagery, then imaging while reading might be more important than affective response. If the purpose were to understand rhythm and meter, then slow oral reading, with an emphasis on chunking, would be essential, and the decision to read in this way is a metacognitive one. (See Chapter Nine for a complete discussion of reading purposes and methods.)

Instruction in Metacognitive Decision Making

You can involve your students in metacognitive decision making when they are planning their approach to specific tasks. Guide them in evaluating how their own prior knowledge, the difficulty of the text, and their purpose for reading can help them to determine their reading strategies. (Remember from Chapter One that a reading strategy is a reading process that is consciously selected to achieve a specific goal. Some examples of specific strategies are provided in Chapter Nine, Table 9-1.) Encourage them to discuss their planned strategies with each other. Then, after reading, encourage them to evaluate the efficacy of the strategy they chose. Did they change strategies along the way? Why or why not? Would they use this strategy again? Such strategy discussions can occur in individual conferences, small-group meetings, or large-group discussions.

You can also help your students to make their metacognitive decisions conscious by asking them to write about their strategies. For instance, when they take a test in a content area, ask them to first write a short paragraph about what strategies they used to study for the test. Then, after the test, return these papers and ask them to write briefly about how well their strategy worked and how they might want to study differently in the future. When students are about to engage in a new kind of reading, like reference reading in the library for a classroom report, ask them to take a minute and write down exactly what procedure they plan to use.

Reading Comprehension Interview

Wixson, Bosky, Yochum, and Alvermann (1984) have developed an interview procedure for assessing intermediate- and middle- school-level children's awareness of the demands of different reading tasks (see Figure 6-1). This interview includes questions about student strategies for actual classroom materials including a basal reader, a content-area textbook, and comprehension worksheets (see directions on interview). The whole procedure takes about thirty minutes, and the teacher is free to ask other questions. A summary sheet can be completed to analyze student responses (see Figure 6-2). Through the use of an interview such as this, the teacher can gain valuable information about a student's awareness of appropriate reading methods and purposes. You may wish to make up a similar interview of your own.

FIGURE 6-1   Reading Comprehension Interview

Name: Date:
Classroom teacher: Reading level:
                                                   Grade:

Directions: Introduce the procedure by explaining that you are interested in finding out what children think about various reading activities. Tell the student that he or she will be asked questions about his/her reading, that there are no right or wrong answers, and that you are only interested in knowing what s/he thinks. Tell the student that if s/he does not know how to answer a question s/he should say so and you will go on to the next one.

General probes such as "Can you tell me more about that?" or "Anything else?" may be used. Keep in mind that the interview is an informal diagnostic measure and you should feel free to probe to elicit useful information.

1. What hobbies or interests do you have that your like to read about?
2. a. How often do you read in school?
   b. How often do you read at home?
3. What school subjects do you like to read about?

Introduce reading and social studies books.

Directions: For this section use the child's classroom basal reader and a content area textbook (social studies, science, etc.). Place these texts in front of the student. Ask each question twice, once with reference to the basal reader and once with reference to the content area textbook. Randomly vary the order of presentation (basal, content). As each question is asked, open the appropriate text in front of the student to help provide a point of reference for the question.

4. What is the most important reason for reading this kind of material? Why does your teacher want you to read this book?
5. a. Who's the best reader you know in _____?
   b. What does he/she do that makes him/her such a good reader?
6. a. How good are *you* at reading this kind of material?
   b. How do you know?
7. What do you have to do to get a good grade in _____ in your class?
8. a. If the teacher told you to remember the information in this story/chapter, what would be the best way to do this?
   b. Have you ever tried _____?
9. a. If your teacher told you to find the answers to the questions in this book what would be the best way to do this? Why?
   b. Have you ever tried _____?
10. a. What is the hardest part about answering questions like the ones in this book?
    b. Does that make you do anything differently?

Introduce at least two comprehension worksheets.

Directions: Present the worksheets to the child and ask questions 11 and 12. Ask the child to complete portions of each worksheet. Then ask questions 13 and 14. Next, show the child a worksheet designed to simulate the work of another child. Then ask question 15.

11. Why would your teacher want you to do worksheets like these (for what purpose)?
12. What would your teacher say you must do to get a good mark on worksheets like these? (What does your teacher look for?)

Ask the child to complete portions of at least two worksheets.

13. Did you do this one differently from the way you did that one? How or in what way?
14. Did you have to work harder on one of these worksheets than the other? (Does one make you think more?)

Present the simulated worksheet.

15. a. Look over this worksheet. If you were the teacher, what kind of mark would you give the worksheet? Why?
    b. If you were the teacher, what would you ask this person to do differently next time?

Source: K. Wixson, A. Bosky, M. Yochum, and D. Alvermann, "An Interview for Assessing Students' Perceptions of Classroom Reading Tasks," *Reading Teacher* 37 (1984), 348. Reprinted with permission of the authors and the International Reading Association.

FIGURE 6-2   Summary Sheet: Reading Comprehension Interview

Name: Date:
Classroom teacher: Reading level:
                                     Grade:

1. What does the child perceive as the goal or purpose of classroom reading activities? (see questions 4 and 11)

   Basal reader:
   Content textbook:
   Reading worksheets:

2. What criteria does the child use to evaluate his/her reading performance? (questions: 5, 6, 7, 12, and 15)

   Basal reader:
   Content textbook:
   Reading worksheets:

3. What strategies does the child indicate s/he uses when engaging in different comprehension activities? (questions: 8, 9, 10, 13, and 14)

   Remembering information
     Basal reader:
     Content textbook:
   Answering questions
     Basal reader:
     Content textbook:
     Reading worksheets:

Source: K. Wixson, A. Bosky, M. Yochum, and D. Alvermann, "An Interview for Assessing Students' Perceptions of Classroom Reading Tasks," *Reading Teacher* 37 (1984), 350. Reprinted with permission of the authors and the International Reading Association.

READING FOR MEANING: COMPREHENSION MONITORING

The evaluating of the success or failure of the meaning-making process (comprehension) and the regulating of strategies to remedy comprehension problems is often called *comprehension monitoring*. Good readers are more effective comprehension monitors than are poor readers. For instance, good readers are more able to detect passage inconsistencies and to search previous and subsequent text to check for information than are poor readers (DiVesta, Hayward, & Orlando, 1979; Garner, 1980; Garner & Reis, 1981).

Collins and Smith (1980) define *comprehension monitoring* as "the student's ability both to evaluate his or her ongoing comprehension processes while reading through a text, and to take some sort of remedial action when these processes bog down" (p. 3). They recommend teaching students what difficulties might occur and what good readers do when these difficulties do occur. Their taxonomy of comprehension failures is given in Figure 6-3. Note that the first two main categories—failure to understand a word and failure to understand a sentence—describe microprocessing failures; the third category—failure to understand how one sentence relates to another—describes integrative processing failures; and the last

FIGURE 6-3   Taxonomy of Comprehension Failures

1. Failure to understand a word
   a. Novel word
   b. Known word that doesn't make sense in the context
2. Failure to understand a sentence
   a. Can find no interpretation
   b. Can find only vague, abstract interpretation
   c. Can find several possible interpretations (ambiguous sentence)
   d. Interpretation conflicts with prior knowledge
3. Failure to understand how one sentence relates to another
   a. Interpretation of one sentence conflicts with another
   b. Can find no connection between the sentences
   c. Can find several possible connections between the sentences
4. Failure to understand how the whole text fits together
   a. Can find no point to whole or part of the text
   b. Cannot understand why certain episodes or sections occurred
   c. Cannot understand the motivations of certain characters

Source: A. Collins and E. Smith *Teaching the Process of Reading Comprehension,* Technical Report No. 182 (Urbana-Champaign: Center for the Study of Reading, University of Illinois, 1980), p. 8. Reprinted by permission.

category—failure to understand how the whole text fits together—roughly corresponds to macroprocessing failures.

One of the reasons that good and poor readers differ in their ability to monitor their comprehension may be that they use different standards for evaluation. Baker (1985) has identified seven possible standards used by good readers. These are listed below. The situations given in parentheses describe the violation of the standard.

1. Lexical (An individual word is not known or does not make sense.)
2. External consistency (The information is not consistent with one's prior knowledge.)
3. Internal consistency (Ideas within the passage conflict with one another.)
4. Syntax (The syntax does not make sense.)
5. Integrative cohesiveness (The relationship between sentences does not make sense—that is, a connective, anaphoric reference or other implied integrative information is nonsensical; Baker calls his "propositional cohesiveness".)
6. Organizational cohesiveness (The relationship between this idea and the overall structure is unclear; Baker calls this "structural cohesiveness".)
7. Informational completeness (The information necessary to achieve the author's stated goal is not all included.)

In a study of fourth- and sixth-grade students' identification of passage inconsistencies, Baker (1984) found that older and better readers used different standards, especially when told to do so. In contrast, younger and poorer readers relied exclusively on the lexical standard.

This overreliance on lexical evaluation may be related to other processing deficits: Casazza (1989) found that poor college readers given explicit macroprocessing instruction were more likely to detect passage inconsistencies than students receiving traditional comprehension practice activities. In a study involving fourth- and fifth-grade poor readers, Gambrell and Boles (1986) found that students given instructions to use mental imagery were more likely to detect passage inconsistencies than students given general reading instructions. Given the interactive nature of comprehension processes, it is reasonable to assume that using various effective comprehension strategies will aid in the monitoring of comprehension and the detection of problems as well as the remedying of those problems.

Figure 6-4 gives the remedies that Collins and Smith (1980) suggest be taught to students. Note that these remedies are presented in order from the least disruptive to the most disruptive, and they should probably be tried in this order. For instance, ignoring and reading on and suspending judgment are less disruptive than stopping to form a tentative hypothesis, so such strategies should be tried first. Formation of a hypothesis would be used when ignoring and suspending judgment were inadequate. Thus, it is also important to teach students how to decide when to give up on one strategy and move on to another. You may also wish to have your students make up their own list of remedies.

The fifth strategy of Collins and Smith's (1980) list, *text reinspection*, is not often used but appears to be teachable (see Garner, 1987, pp. 113–114). Moreover, when poor readers do use this strategy, they tend to use "undifferentiated reading" of the entire text rather than thoughtful text sampling (Garner, Macready, & Wagoner, 1984). Garner, Hare, Alexander, Haynes, and Winograd (1984) successfully taught text reinspection to upper elementary and middle school students enrolled in a remedial reading clinic using direct explanation of the strategy in repeated practice situations. They suggest that, because many students seem to believe that text reinspection is "illegal," classroom discussion of its utility in ordinary situations is usually needed.

FIGURE 6-4   Possible Remedies for Comprehension Failures

1. *Ignore and read on,* because this information is relatively unimportant.
2. *Suspend judgment,* because it is likely to be cleared up later.
3. *Form a tentative hypothesis* to be tested as reading continues.
4. *Reread the current sentence(s)* or look for a tentative hypothesis.
5. *Reread the previous context* to resolve the contradiction.
6. *Go to an expert source,* because it simply does not make sense.

Source: A. Collins and E. Smith, *Teaching the Process of Reading Comprehension, Technical Report No. 182 (Urbana-Champaign: Center for the Study of Reading, University of Illinois, 1980). Reprinted by permission.*

Teaching students how their comprehension can break down, developing their awareness of when these breakdowns occur, and giving them some strategies to use for remedying the situation will help them to become more active, confident readers. Good readers are not consciously aware of comprehension monitoring until a "triggering event" signals a failure (Baker & Brown, 1980, p. 9). Students simply need to learn what to do when that triggering event (see Figure 6-3) occurs.

Incidental Monitoring Instruction

Comprehension monitoring can be encouraged in various situations, including content-area classes. Whenever students do not understand what they are reading, they should be encouraged to clarify the source of the breakdown. For instance, if students say that they did not understand a newspaper article on a current event, ask them why. They may discover that specific vocabulary words were causing them problems or that they did not have adequate prior knowledge, or that the main point was unclear. Then, they can be shown how to take the appropriate remedial steps to facilitate their own comprehension. Thus, they can learn to be active, independent readers who are not dependent on having teachers and experts available to help them.

Explicit Monitoring Instruction

Assessment.   One way to assess your students' abilities in the area of comprehension monitoring is to provide them with paragraphs in which the information is inconsistent. Which students notice? What do they do about it? Another procedure is to ask students if they have comprehended something they have read. Then, give a test of their comprehension. Have they predicted accurately? Finally, ask poor comprehenders what they do when they come to something they do not understand. If they say, "I don't know," or "I ask someone," then they may lack effective strategies for comprehension monitoring.

Comprehension-rating procedure.   The following instructional procedure has been developed by Davey and Porter (1982) and has been used successfully with middle school poor comprehenders. This "comprehension-rating procedure" involves four steps. (Note that the use of nonsense words has been criticized by some as discouraging reading for meaning and as an artificial reading activity. It is not necessary for using this procedure.)

Step 1 was designed to encourage the students to have a "meaning orientation to print" (Davey & Porter, 1982, p. 199). The teacher modeled this orientation by talking about the centrality of comprehension and her own comprehension breakdowns and remedial strategies. Then, she modeled these strategies while reading aloud, using materials with words omitted or with nonsense words substituted for some of the real ones.

Step 2 was designed to help the students focus on meaning. Students read materials using real or nonsense words and indicated whether or not they understood.

This activity moved from sentences to paragraphs and from oral to silent work, as the students progressed.

In Step 3, a third possible response was included. Students indicated whether they understood well, whether they sort of understood, or whether they did not understand at all. They also indicated the source of their comprehension failures.

Finally, in Step 4, students were directly taught various fix-up strategies. These were divided into word-level and idea-level strategies. Each was demonstrated and practiced. The obvious follow-up procedure is to encourage students to use these monitoring strategies throughout the year on various types of materials.

What-I-Know (W-I-K) Textbook Comprehension Monitoring   (see Heller, 1986). Before a content area reading assignment, distribute W-I-K worksheets to students (see Figure 6-5). Before reading, encourage them to assess what they already know by listing general concepts in the first column. Also ask them to determine their purpose for reading and to write this on the sheet at the bottom. Then, while they are reading, they should fill in new information related to their purpose in column B while writing confusing concepts and questions they have while reading in column C. Have them focus on knowing what they do and do not understand and why. When they are finished, they can synthesize the information that is related to their initial purpose at the bottom. You may wish to model this approach first for one reading section using the overhead or chalkboard or to have a complete sheet of your own to put up when they are finished. Always follow this activity with a

FIGURE 6-5   What-I-Know Sheet

COLUMN A WHAT I ALREADY KNEW	COLUMN B WHAT I KNOW NOW	COLUMN C WHAT I DON'T KNOW
kangaroos	animals with a pouch	carnivores
Australia a continent	dry climate	why few predators
koala bears	spiny anteater and	in Australia
	duck-billed platypus	Is a predator
southern hemisphere	special class of animals:	a carnivore
	monotremes	
possums	egg-laying mammals	
	kangaroo babies = joeys	
	kangaroo herd = mob	

ANSWER TO THE PURPOSE QUESTION: Marsupials are different from other animals in the following ways: They raise their young in a pouch. Most live in Australia or New Guinea. They are very small at birth, crawl from the birth canal to the mother's pouch, attach to the mother's milk gland, and develop into maturity in the pouch.

Source: J. W. Irwin and I. Baker *Promoting Active Reading Comprehension Strategies* (Englewood Cliffs, N.J.: Prentice Hall, 1989), p. 224.

discussion (either large or small group) of their reading strategies, confusions, remedies for confusions, and so forth.

Text Lookbacks.   Reis and Leone (1985) have suggested a three-day procedure for teaching remedial students to use text reinspection. On the first day, explicit instruction focuses on the question: "Why should I look back?" (Answer: To find information I cannot remember.) On the second day, the instruction can focus on: "When should I look back?" (Answer: When the question asks about something the author said that I cannot remember. I need not look back when the question asks what I think.) On the third day, the instruction can focus on: "Where should I look?" Students can practice skimming for information and other strategies for getting the answers to specific questions.

Comprehension code.   Tell the students that they will be using a code to evaluate their texts (see Smith & Dauer, 1984). If students cannot write in their books, give students strips of paper to affix to the margin. With the students, develop a code. For example, for a social studies text the code might be: A = agree, B = bored, C = confused, D = disagree, and M = main idea. Another code might be: C = clear, D = difficult, I = important, S = surprising. Encourage students to have ownership of the activity by making up their own code. Have the students record their responses as they read and then use their responses to direct class discussion. You may wish to focus specifically on monitoring ratings like C = confused or D = difficult to talk about remedies for comprehension difficulties.

READING FOR REMEMBERING: STUDYING

As has been discussed, good readers stop and adopt a remedial strategy when they realize that microprocesses, integrative processes, or macroprocesses have broken down. Good readers also select, evaluate, and adjust their strategies to remember certain parts of what they are reading. This has traditionally been called studying.

Comprehension Processes as Directed Study Strategies

Many of the processes discussed earlier in this book affect how much and what is remembered after reading. Macroprocesses and elaborative processes provide the most obvious examples of processes that might be chosen to increase recall. For instance, summarizing and noting the author's organization should be recommended as study strategies. Indeed, many of the activities suggested in Chapter Four, such as the hierarchical summary procedure and mapping can be used as study strategies (see pp. 68–71). Finally, elaborations such as imaging and integrating with prior knowledge have clear effects on recall and can also be taught as self-selected study strategies (see Chapter Five).

Self-questioning for Remembering

Another study strategy that has not been previously mentioned is self-questioning. Initial experimentation with this technique has indicated that it may be even more effective for low-ability students than for high-ability students (André & Anderson, 1978–79). Moreover, the technique is probably more effective if students are trained to do it correctly. André and Anderson point out that students should probably be trained first to identify the main idea (on which they will base their question) and then to form a question that either asks for new examples of the ideas presented (preferable) or asks directly about the concept presented, using a paraphrased format.

Figure 6-6 shows a fifth-grade student effectively using a self-questioning technique to guide her own studying. Note the amount of "metacognitive" thinking that is going on.

Before students will be willing to do self-questioning, you will have to convince them that the technique works. One way to do this is by having a classroom demonstration. When they have all read a passage, give a difficult "pop quiz." Then, they can see how much they don't remember. For the next section of the text, give them sample self-questions to answer while they read. Then, give another quiz. They will probably all do much better. This may motivate them to want to learn the technique.

Self-questioning can also be taught by moving students slowly from dependence on the teacher to independent application. On the most dependent level, you will need to supply the questions for the students to answer. Student answers can be compared and discussed, so that they can learn to recognize an answer that is clear, complete, and in their own words. Then, students can practice writing their own "self-questions." Again, students can compare questions, so that they learn to recognize and write questions that focus on the most important points and ask for examples whenever possible. Finally, students will be able to use this study technique independently, although you might wish to collect some written evidence for a while.

Traditional Study Strategies

If you have ever been exposed to study strategies, then self-questioning probably reminded you of the second step of a traditional study system.[1] All these systems recommend that students (1) preview the material; (2) focus their attention on key concepts; (3) rehearse the material at intervals, preferably in their own words; and (4) review the material as a whole after reading. Some also recommend taking notes and reflecting (or elaborating) on the material during or after reading. Self-question-

[1]Examples include SQ3R (Survey, Question, Read, Recite, Review), PQ4R (Preview, Question, Read, Recite, Review, Reflect), and OK5R (Overview, Key idea, Read, Record, Recite, Review, Reflect) (Robinson, 1961; Thomas & Robinson, 1977; Pauk, 1974, respectively). For a description of at least one system, see almost any text on study skills or secondary reading methods.

FIGURE 6-6   Use of Self-Questioning

TEXT READ	STUDENT THOUGHTS
LESSON 3. MINERS AND RANCHERS The hope of finding gold or silver brought many settlers to the last West. Large numbers of people had moved to California during the gold rush of 1849. More followed in gold, silver, and copper rushes in the 1860s and 1870s.	OK; now, why did people move to the West in the late 1800s? To find gold, silver, and copper, of course. That was easy.
"Boom towns" grew up almost overnight where metals were found. When one person made a strike, more rushed in to search for ore. A few struck it rich. Most did not. Many of them stopped searching and went to work for companies that made a business of mining. Some opened stores or businesses to serve the miners. But most of them became ranchers or farmers.	What was a "boom town"? Well, I guess it was a town that grew up around where people found gold. When people didn't find any, they became the other things for the town, like store owners. I wonder where they got the word "boom." I'll ask the teacher tomorrow.
Many western people, especially on Mexican land, had ranched for years before the Civil War. After the war, the ranching business got a big boost. This happened for two reasons. One, railroads were built across the country to the West Coast. Two, the killing of the buffalo opened new lands for cattle.	Why did all these new Westerners go into ranching? I guess because there was plenty of land and because they could ship the meat by train. They must have run out of gold. I don't know what it had to do with the Civil War. I'll read on to see if it comes up again.
The cattle were raised on the grassy plains. When they were big enough, they were shipped east by train. However, first they had to get to the railroads. This was done by means of a cattle drive. A cattle drive was not a drive at all. It was a very long walk. Cowboys on horses forced the cattle to walk hundreds of miles over dusty trails. Their goal was to reach the cattle pens next to the railroad tracks in Sedalia, Missouri, or Abilene, Kansas, or some other cow town.	What was a "cattle drive"? Well, it was when they had to walk the cattle to the railroad stations. I guess they sent the cattle on the trains while they were still alive. Then, they killed them in the East . . .

Source: Joan Schreiber and others, *America Past and Present* Copyright © 1983 by Scott, Foresman and Company Chicago, IL. Reprinted by permission.

ing probably helps the student with the second and third strategies—that is, it helps them to focus their attention and rehearse the material at intervals. Let us examine each of these strategies in terms of alternative ways of doing them and ways that you can teach them to your students.

Previewing. Previewing a reading passage usually involves reading the introduction and summary and looking at the titles, subheadings, and pictures.

During this process, the reader should be thinking about what he or she already knows about the topic and about what the organizational structure is going to be. He or she may also want to make predictions. If using something like the hierarchical summarization strategy suggested by Taylor (1982) (see Chapter Four), he or she will also write down a skeletal outline during previewing. Thus, previewing allows the reader to begin to mobilize prior knowledge, macroprocessing, and prediction abilities to facilitate comprehension and recall.

Previewing can be taught by guiding students through the process whenever you want them to study/read. Simply allow enough time to do this when you give the assignment. At first, you may need to model the thinking process. Then, they can model it back to you. Eventually, they will be able to do it silently, and, finally, they can be asked to do it as part of the reading assignment. For these last two stages, you may wish to require some sort of written product, such as a skeletal outline or a set of predictions.

Focusing attention.   Many study systems recommend turning each sub-heading into a question to be answered while reading. Others recommend simply looking for the key idea of each paragraph. Self-questioning is a version of this. The point is that the reader should be aware of what information is important for his or her purpose and then focus attention on that information.

You can help to focus the students' attention by giving them a purpose for reading or a study guide (see Chapter Nine). Eventually, however, students need to learn a focusing strategy they can use on their own. Thus, it would probably be useful for you to guide students through initial content-area chapters, asking them to decide how they will focus their attention for each section.

Rehearsing during reading.   Every educational psychology text tells you about the importance of rehearsal for recall. It is important to note, however, the difference between superficial and meaningful rehearsal (see Bransford, 1979). Although simply repeating something to be remembered may help retain it for short-term recall, long-term recall requires a more meaningful rehearsal. Thus, it is important to teach students to rehearse information by using their own words, thinking about how it conceptually relates to other information, and so on.

Rehearsal occurs when students mentally or orally answer the questions they have formed to focus their attention, when they write those answers into their hierarchical summaries, when they summarize paragraphs in the margin, when they underline or take notes, and when they answer the questions on a study guide. Rehearsing should be done at the end of *each section* of the chapter. Some students find that making a tape recording of their summaries of each section is useful. (Though the tape can be used for review, it is probably useful because it required them, while they were reading, to rehearse important information periodically in their own words.)

Rehearsal can be taught as part of the self-questioning study technique. If you would like to teach it as single technique, you may wish to do a demonstration similar to that suggested for self-questioning in which students are dramatically shown its effectiveness. You may also wish to require that rehearsal be done in writing, so that you can monitor progress.

   Underlining and note taking.   The research that has been done on the effectiveness of underlining and note taking as compared with just rereading the material has not been very positive (see Anderson, 1980). The real benefit of these strategies may simply be that they reduce the material to a manageable size for future study. In some classes, this can be important, especially at the college level. Several of the macroprocessing procedures recommended in Chapter Four of this text also require note taking and would probably help guide the more dependent students to take more meaningful notes.

   The points to remember if you decide to teach underlining or note taking are that the reader should (1) actively mark or transform the material into his or her own words, (2) be selective, and (3) look for the organizational pattern. Also, as you know, simply telling the students to do these things will not be sufficient for most students. You need to provide them with good models and then collect their work and give them feedback as they progress.

   An excellent description of ways to underline and take notes is available in Pauk (1974). Briefly, for underlining and text marking, Pauk urges students to consider the following (pp. 153–154):

1. Finish reading before marking.
2. Be extremely selective.
3. Use your own words.
4. Be swift.
5. Be neat.

He also suggests that students use a systematic symbol system. Suggestions for this are given in Table 6-2.

   For note taking, Pauk similarly urges students to finish reading each section before writing, to be selective, to use their own words, and to work quickly. He also recommends that they write in full sentences and that they summarize the notes with key words written in the left-hand margin. The key words in margins could be used for review and recitation while the right-hand side is covered.

   Reviewing.   Rehearsing after the entire reading assignment has been completed will also promote recall. Students can be encouraged to go back over the same items examined during previewing; the introduction, summary, graphic aids, and subheadings. For each subheading, they should summarize the related section in their own words. If they marked the text or took notes, then putting summary terms in the margins and reciting from those might provide a useful review. The important point

TABLE 6-2   Suggestions for Marking Textbooks

EXPLANATION AND DESCRIPTION	SYMBOLS, MARKINGS, AND NOTATIONS
1. Double lines under words or phrases signify the main ideas.	Radiation can produce mutations . . .
2. Single lines under words or phrases signify supporting material.	comes from cosmic rays . . .
3. Small circled numbers above the initial word of an underlined group of words indicate a series of arguments, facts, ideas, either main or supporting.	Conditions change . . . ① rocks rise . . . ② some sink . . . ③ the sea dashes . . . ④ strong winds . . .
4. Rather than underlining a group of three or more important lines, you may use a vertical bracket in the outer margin.	[had known . . . who gave . . . the time . . . of time . . .
5. One asterisk in the margin indicates ideas of special importance; two, ideas of unusual importance; and three, ideas of outstanding importance: reserved for principles and high level generalizations.	*When a nuclear blast is . . . **people quite close to the . . . ***The main cause of mutations . . .
6. Circle key words and terms.	The (genes) are the . . .
7. Box in the words of enumeration and transitions.	[fourth,] the lack of supplies . . . [furthermore,] the shortage . . .
8. A question mark in the margin, opposite lines you do not understand, is an excellent reminder to ask the instructor for clarification.	? | The latest . . . | cold period . . . | about 1,000,000 . . . | Even today . . .
9. If you disagree with a statement, indicate that in the margin.	*Disagree* | Life became . . . | on land only . . . | 340 million years . . .
10. Use the top and bottom margins of a page to record any ideas of your own that are prompted by what you have read.	*Why not use carbon dating?* *Check on reference of fossils found in Tennessee stone quarry.*
11. On sheets of paper that are smaller than the pages of the book, write longer thoughts or summaries, then insert them between the pages.	*Fossils* *Plants = 500,000,000 years old* *Insects = 250,000,000 " "* *Bees = 100,000,000 " "* *True fish = 350,000,000 " "* *Amphibians = 300,000,000 " "* *Reptiles = 300,000,000 " "* *Birds = 150,000,000 " "*
12. Even though you have underlined the important ideas and supporting materials, still jot brief summaries in the side margins.	*adapt ------- fossil ------- layer -------*

Source: Walter Pauk, *How to Study in College* Third Edition, p. 155. Copyright © 1974 by Houghton Mifflin Company. Used by permission.

is that they look away from the page to recite the information rather than simply reading sentences over without meaningfully rehearsing them.

You will probably want to model this procedure first. You may want to walk them through a review on the day each assignment is due. Reviewing the next day, however, is not the same as reviewing at the end of reading when the information is still fresh. Try a classroom experiment. For two weeks, have half the students review at home while the other half does not. (Make sure that ability levels are the same in each half.) As often as possible, show how the review group has superior recall.

A total study approach. Even after students understand all of the aforementioned strategies, they may need a way to put them all together into a systematic approach. One way is to have students think in terms of what they want to do (1) before (previewing), (2) during (focusing and rehearsing), and (3) after reading (reviewing) (see Anderson, 1980). Indeed, students should be taught that the difference between study reading and leisure reading is that, for the former, additional activities at all three of these stages are needed.

Finally, for most students, trying to learn all of these stages at once is discouraging. It just looks like too much work. Thus, you will probably want to introduce these stages one at a time, making sure that each has become habitual and "easy" before moving on to the next.

Teaching Study Skills: K–12

Although the procedures described in the foregoing paragraphs are primarily geared for older students, it would probably be useful to begin to encourage these habits as soon as students are engaged in trying to remember material. Elementary students can be asked to write summaries of reading assignments, which can be kept in a loose-leaf notebook and studied before the test. Before reading, students can be directed to preview the material and to decide what should be remembered. After reading, students can divide into pairs to "test" each other. This would require them to rehearse aloud. Finally, just teaching younger students to preview, read, and then review will probably lay a foundation for more sophisticated strategies to be used later.

SUMMARY

Metacognitive processing (in the area of reading comprehension) is selecting, evaluating, and regulating ones's comprehension strategies to achieve a specific goal. This includes selecting comprehension strategies (making metacognitive decisions), monitoring one's own comprehension for success or failure, taking remedial action when necessary, and selecting study strategies when recall is important. Study strategies include self-questioning, previewing, focusing attention, rehearsing, underlining, note taking, and reviewing. Students adjust their approaches according to their own abilities, the characteristics of the material, and the specific task involved. For a more thorough discussion of these factors, see Part Two of this text (Chapters Seven through Nine).

SELF-CHECK TEST

1. Define the following terms.

   metacognitive processes
   conditional knowledge
   lexical standard
   external consistency standard
   metacognitive decision
   comprehension monitoring
   text reinspection
   comprehension-rating procedure
   W-I-K
   comprehension code
   self-questioning
   previewing
   focusing
   rehearsal

2. Fill in the missing comprehension failures.

   (a) Failure to understand a word
       i. Novel word.
       ii.
   (b) Failure to understand a sentence
       i. Can find no interpretation.
       ii.
       iii. Can find several possible interpretations (ambiguous sentence).
       iv.
   (c) Failure to understand how one sentence relates to another
       i. Interpretation of one sentence conflicts with another.
       ii.
       iii. Can find several possible connections between the sentences.
   (d) Failure to understand how the whole text fits together
       i.
       ii. Cannot understand why certain episodes or sentences occurred.
       iii.

3. List five important study strategies.

4. List six possible comprehension remedies.

5. Answer true or false:
   _____ (a) The comprehension rating procedure is a way the teacher can assess the students' comprehension.
   _____ (b) Ignoring a comprehension breakdown is always ineffective.
   _____ (c) Self-questioning is only for college students.
   _____ (d) Students must be taught to rehearse verbatim from the book.
   _____ (e) Many students need to be convinced that study strategies are worth the time.
   _____ (f) All students know when they have failed to understand.
   _____ (g) Instruction in study habits should begin in the elementary school.
   _____ (h) Poor readers use various standards to evaluate their comprehension.

SUGGESTED ACTIVITIES

1. Read something that is difficult for you to understand. For each breakdown, identify the source from Figure 6-3 and a remedy from Figure 6-4.
2. Examine your own study reading. Can it be improved? If not, tell what you do and why it works. If so, develop a new procedure and practice it for two weeks.
3. If you are currently teaching, make note of each time you encourage students to make their own metacognitive decisions. Is this sufficient or do you think that they need more encouragement? How could you add metacognitive decision making to other parts of your curriculum?
4. Study Figure 1-1 (p. 6). For each subprocess, describe a situation in which a reader might choose to use that subprocess more than the others.

REFERENCES

Anderson, T. H. (1978). *Another look at the self-questioning study technique* (Reading Education Report No. 6). Urbana-Champaign: Center for the Study of Reading, University of Illinois.

Anderson, T. H. (1980). Study strategies and adjunct aids. In R. J. Spiro, B. C. Bruce, & W. F. Brewer (Eds.), *Theoretical issues in reading comprehension*. Hillsdale, N.J.: Lawrence Erlbaum.

André, M. E. D., & Anderson, T. H. (1978–79). The development and evaluation of a self-questioning study technique. *Reading Research Quarterly, 14*, 605–623.

Baker, L. (1984). Spontaneous vs. instructed use of multiple standards for evaluating comprehension: Effects of age, reading proficiency, and type of standard. *Journal of Experimental Child Psychology, 38*, 289–311.

Baker, L. (1985). Differences in the standards used by college students to evaluate their comprehension of expository prose. *Reading Research Quarterly, 20,* 297–313.

Baker, L., & Brown, A. L. (1980). *Metacognitive skill and reading.* (Technical Report No. 188). Urbana-Champaign: Center for the Study of Reading, University of Illinois.

Bransford, J. D. (1979). *Human cognition: Learning, understanding, and remembering.* Belmont, Calif.: Wadsworth.

Casazza, M. (1988) The effects of direct macroprocessing instruction on college students' comprehension monitoring strategies. Unpublished Ph.D. dissertation, Loyola University of Chicago.

Collins, A., & Smith, E. E. (1980). *Teaching the process of reading comprehension* (Technical Report No. 182). Urbana-Champaign: Center for the Study of Reading, University of Illinois.

Davey, B., & Porter, S. M. (1982). Comprehension-rating: A procedure to assist poor comprehenders. *Journal of Reading, 26,* 197–202.

DiVesta, F. J., Hayward, K. G., & Orlando, V. P. (1979). Developmental trends in monitoring text for comprehension. *Child Development, 50,* 97–105.

Gambrell, L. B., & Boles, R. J. (1986). Mental imagery and the comprehension-monitoring performance of fourth- and fifth-grade poor readers. *Reading Research Quarterly, 21,* 454–464.

Garner, R. (1987). *Metacognition and reading comprehension.* Norwood, N.J.: Ablex.

Garner, R. (1980). Monitoring of understanding: An investigation of good and poor readers' awareness of induced miscomprehension of text. *Journal of Reading Behavior, 12,* 55–63.

Garner, R., Hare, V. C., Alexander, P., Haynes, J., & Winograd, P. (1984). Inducing use of a text lookback strategy among unsuccessful readers. *American Educational Research Journal, 21,* 789–798.

Garner, R., Macready, G. B., & Wagoner, S. (1984). Readers' acquisition of the components of the text-lookback strategy. *Journal of Educational Psychology, 76,* 300–309.

Garner, R., & Reis, R. (1981). Monitoring and resolving comprehension obstacles: An investigation of spontaneous lookbacks among upper-grade good and poor comprehenders. *Reading Research Quarterly, 16,* 569–582.

Heller, M. F. (1986). How do you know what you know? Metacognitive modeling in the content areas. *Journal of Reading, 29,* 415–422.

Jacobs, J. E., & Paris, S. G. (1987). Children's metacognition about reading: Issues in definition, measurement, and instruction. *Educational Psychologist, 22,* 255–278.

Paris, S. G., & Winograd, P. (1989). How metacognition can promote academic learning and instruction. In B. F. Jones & L. Idol, (Eds.), *Dimensions of Thinking and Cognitive Instruction* (Vol. 1). Hillsdale, NJ: Lawrence Erlbaum.

Pauk, W. (1974). *How to study in college* (3rd ed.). Boston: Houghton Mifflin.

Reis, R., & Leone, P. E. (1985). Teaching text lookbacks to mildly handicapped students. *Journal of Reading, 28,* 416–420.

Robinson, F. P. (1961). Study skills for superior students in the secondary school. *Reading Teacher, 25,* 29–33.

Smith, R. J., & Dauer, V. L. (1984). A comprehension-monitoring strategy for reading content area materials. *Journal of Reading, 28,* 144–147.

Taylor, B. M. (1982). A summarizing strategy to improve middle grade students' reading and writing skills. *Reading Teacher, 36,* 202–205.

Taylor, K. K. (1983). Can college students summarize? *Journal of Reading, 26,* 524–529.

Thomas, E. L., & Robinson, H. A. (1977). *Improving reading in every class* (2nd ed.). Boston: Allyn and Bacon.

Wixson, K., Bosky, A. B., Yochum, M. N., & Alvermann, D. (1984). An interview for assessing students' perceptions of classroom reading tasks. *Reading Teacher, 37,* 346–352.

7

INDIVIDUAL READER CONTEXTS: WHO IS READING?

You will remember from Chapter One that the "comprehension context" can be divided into three sets of influences: the reader-related context, the text-related context, and the situational context. An easy way to remember these contexts is always to think in terms of the five W's: who, what, where, when, and why. The "who" is the reader and his and her individual characteristics that affect what he or she will comprehend; the "what" is the reading material itself and its individual characteristics that will affect what is comprehended; the "where," "when," and "why" are the situational characteristics that affect what is comprehended. The next three chapters include discussions of each of these contexts. Because they all affect what is comprehended, they have important implications for how you teach.

You may also remember from Chapter One that the characteristics of the individual reader affect what is comprehended, because the reader actively interprets the cues on the printed pages in the light of what he or she brings to it. This includes his or her prior knowledge about the topic, emotional attitudes relative to the topic and the assignment, and reading skills. Thus, all comprehension instruction must begin with an assessment of *who* will be "constructing a set of meanings" (see Chapter One, p. 9) in terms of these individual characteristics.

PRIOR KNOWLEDGE

Comprehension has been defined as "building bridges between the new and the known" (Pearson & Johnson, 1978, p. 24). This definition, like the one used in this book, stresses the active nature of the process and the importance of prior knowledge. Comprehension simply cannot occur when nothing is already "known" because then there is nothing to which the reader can link the "new." That readers remember more when they are familiar with the topic has been extensively substantiated by research (Chiesi, Spilich, & Voss, 1978; Spilich, Vesonder, Chiesi, & Voss, 1979; and others). Presumably, this is because the knowledgeable readers can link the incoming information to what they already know.

Indeed, prior knowledge is so necessary for comprehension that some speculate that it can often account for a large portion of the difference between successful and unsuccessful comprehenders. Taylor (1979) found that poor readers seem to be more vulnerable to the effects of topic familiarity in terms of the amount recalled than are good readers. Johnston and Pearson (1982) found that manipulating topic familiarity affected comprehension even when differences associated with standardized test scores were partialed out. Moreover, in their study, scores on prior-knowledge questions were significant predictors of scores on all the other types of questions!

One can easily trace how prior-knowledge influences all of the comprehension processes discussed in Chapters Three through Six in this book. One example of the effects of prior knowledge on microprocessing is provided by Anderson, Reynolds, Schallert, and Goetz (1977) (see Chapter One, page 7). This was the study in which the music students thought a passage was about a rehearsal whereas the physical education students thought it was about a card game. The reader's prior knowledge also affects the ability to make integrative inferences (Pearson, Hansen, & Gordon, 1979; Wilson & Hammill, 1982). Hildyard (1979) found that although such inferential ability seems to develop with age, younger students do make these inferences when they have adequate prior knowledge. Similarly, macroprocessing ability seems to depend on prior knowledge of the content area: good readers recall more when the passage is organized according to expected patterns. Obviously, elaborative processing, which includes integration with prior knowledge, predictions based on prior knowledge, and so on, requires that the reader have some prior knowledge. Finally, remedying comprehension failures and selecting material for rehearsal require that students have prior knowledge about alternative sources of information and about what information is most likely to be important.

Facilitating Prior-Knowledge Usage

Students can directly be told to use their prior knowledge when necessary for various comprehension processes. For instance, when teaching students to make connective inferences, teachers will want to remind students to think of what they already know about the events and then to determine how they might be related. As part of comprehension monitoring, students can learn to identify the comprehension failures that result from not having the background knowledge assumed by the author.

Another excellent way to teach students to use their prior knowledge actively while reading is to use the modeling approach suggested for many other processes in this text. As you read to students, pause and share your thinking processes. Show them how you are using your prior knowledge for all the processes needed for comprehending. Ask them to do the same. Figure 5-4 (Chapter Five) gives an example of a teacher doing this to teach prior-knowledge elaboration. A similar procedure could be used to show students how prior knowledge helps with the other processes.

Previewing an assignment provides an excellent opportunity to review prior knowledge. As students preview, have them discuss what they already know. Write key concepts on the board and have students speculate about what they expect in the reading, given what they already know about the topic. The process of prethinking about prior knowledge when previewing an assignment at home can also be modeled for the students by the teacher or by one of the other students. Finally, the following three activities have also been suggested for encouraging prethinking about prior knowledge.

K-W-L   (Ogle, 1986). First, have students brainstorm what they already know about the topic about which they will be reading. Have them write this information on a K-W-L worksheet (see Figure 7-1) in the first column: K—What I Know. Have them try to categorize the information and list these categories at the bottom of this column. Then encourage students to generate questions about the reading. They can list these in the second column: W—What I Want to Know. This can be done section by section, and questions can be added while they are reading. Finally, new information can be entered in the third column: L—What I Learned. An example of a student's K-W-L worksheet is provided in Figure 7-1. Note that the information in the last column has been categorized. This is to facilitate two added steps suggested by Carr and Ogle (1987): mapping of the material and then using the map to write a summary. Note that this activity could have been included in many sections of this book: comprehension monitoring, studying, organizing, and summarizing. It is included here because it begins with an emphasis on the students' prior knowledge.

Personal meaning guide.   Macklin (1978) has suggested that students' prior attitudes can also be activated to help them connect with the material being read. He suggests constructing a prereading guide by writing several statements about the material with which students can agree or disagree. A sample of such a guide is provided in Figure 7-2. Divide the students into groups to discuss their opinions. Then have them read the material and follow this with a discussion of how their opinions have changed.

A similar procedure could be used for trade books that students are reading for pleasure. Prereading guides could be kept in an envelope in the back of the book. Students could then mark the guide before and after reading, and discuss the changes

FIGURE 7-1   Ninth-grade Disabled Reader's K-W-L Worksheet on Killer Whales

K (Know)	W (Want to know)	L (Learned)
They live in oceans. They are vicious. They eat each other. They are mammals.	Why do they attack people? How fast can they swim? What kind of fish do they eat? What is their description? How long do they live? How do they breathe?	D—They are the biggest member of the dolphin family. D—They weigh 10,000 pounds and get 30 feet long. F—They eat squids, seals, and other dolphins. A—They have good vision underwater. F—They are carnivorous (meat eaters). A—They are the second smartest animal on earth. D—They breathe through blow holes. A—They do not attack unless they are hungry. D—Warm blooded. A—They have echo-location (sonar).
Description Food Location		L—They are found in the oceans.

Final category designations developed for column L, information learned about killer whales: A = abilities, D = description, F = food, L = location.

Source: E. Carr, and D. M. Ogle, "K-W-L Plus: A strategy for comprehension and summarization," *Journal of Reading, 30* (1987), p. 628. Reprinted with permission of the International Reading Association.

FIGURE 7-2   Personal Meaning Guide

DIRECTIONS: Here are seven statements that deal with the concept of change. Place a "+" by those you agree with and a "–" by those you don't agree with. Leave blank those statements that affect you neither way. Feel free to add your own statements about change and how you feel about them. Be prepared to discuss the reasons for your choices.

___ 1. It takes time for change to be felt.
___ 2. The effects of change are often felt by those not directly involved in change.
___ 3. Change is generally hard to stop.
___ 4. Change needs the support of the majority in order to occur.
___ 5. Fortune smiles on those who change.
___ 6. The greater the degree of change, the more resistance there is to that change.
___ 7. Change guarantees growth.
___ 8. _____

Source: M. Macklin, "Content Area Reading Is a Process for Finding Personal Meaning," *Journal of Reading, 22* (1978), 214. Reprinted with permission of Michael D. Macklin and the International Reading Association.

in their opinions in their response journals, literature discussion groups, or individual conferences with the teacher.

PreP (Prereading Plan).   Langer (1981) has suggested that teachers guide students to think about their prior knowledge in three stages. First the teacher should select key words, phrases, or pictures from the text, and use them to stimulate initial associations with the concept (for example, "Tell me anything that comes to your mind when you hear the word feudalism"). The teacher records all the responses and then moves to the second stage, reflection on the initial associations. Questions like "What made you think of...?" or "Can you tell me more about..." or "What does this have to do with that?" can lead to a sharing of ideas. Finally, the teacher leads students to reformulate their prior knowledge (for example, "Before we read the assignment, and based on this discussion, do you have any new ideas about...?"). After writing their ideas on the board, the teacher helps the students to set purpose questions. They then read and finally share the answers to their questions.

Langer (1981) also points out that such an activity actually helps the teacher to diagnose the students' prior knowledge. She suggests that students can be divided into three categories: those with much prior knowledge can supply definitions, analogies and superordinate concepts. Those with some prior knowledge can supply examples, attributes, and major characteristics. Those with little prior knowledge may only supply things like words that sound like the stimulus word or irrelevant personal experiences. Students in the latter category will probably need help with reading the text with understanding.

Schema Theory

Many recent researchers discuss "prior knowledge" as being organized into "schemata" (singular, "schema"), so it is probably important for you to have a basic understanding of this term (Anderson, Spiro, & Anderson, 1977; Rumelhart, 1981; and others). Put simply, a schema is a knowledge structure. It can be a concept or it can be a set of related concepts and it can be about objects, ideas, or phenomena (see Pearson & Spiro, 1980). For instance, you probably have a schema for a desk that includes the characteristics of desks and a mental image of a typical desk. Similarly, you also probably have a schema for going to a movie that includes buying a ticket, smelling popcorn, and so on.

Based on cues in the text, we select the schema to be used for comprehension. Then, as we read, we fill in the details required by that schema, sometimes from explicit information and sometimes with slot-filling inferences. For instance, suppose we are reading about Johnny going to a movie and mention is made of something white and crunchy on the floor. Our movie schema would probably enable us to determine the source of this unknown substance. If the story mentioned that he tripped when looking for a seat, most readers would infer that this was because it was dark in the theatre. Popcorn and darkness in the theatre are probably parts of a typical movie schema, and such inferences would also help to explain the upcoming facts about his going to buy something and then accidentally returning to the wrong seat. Note, however, that a student who has no movie schema might not know what he bought, why he bought it, or why he could not find his seat. Moreover, a student who was using a classroom schema might have inferred that there was a paper on the floor, that someone tripped him, that he went to buy a pencil, and so on.

A schema can also determine what prior knowledge elaborations are made. If nothing to the contrary is said in the text, good readers using a movie schema will probably infer that Johnny enjoyed the movie. This is because the movie schema says that this is true by "default" (Rumelhart, 1981)—that is, if nothing is said to the contrary. Again, students without a developed schema might not elaborate in this way, and students using a classroom schema might elaborate with totally different assumptions about the purpose of the movie.

Finally, schemata also help students to select important information. Anderson, Spiro, and Anderson (1977) wrote two similar passages containing mention of the same eighteen foods. One was about a restaurant visit and the other was about a grocery trip. They found that readers of the restaurant version were more likely to remember who got what food than were readers of the grocery version. This was, presumably, because "who gets what food has significance within a restaurant schema whereas it matters not in a supermarket who throws the brussel sprouts in the shopping cart" (Anderson, 1977, p. 12). Thus, the schema selected can determine what students choose to remember as well as what slot-filling inferences and prior-knowledge elaborations they make as they read.

In terms of schema theory, then, teachers need to make sure that students have the appropriate schema, that they select the appropriate schema to use for interpreting while reading, that they maintain an awareness of the relevant schema for as long as is necessary, and that they not over- or underrely on their schema for interpretation. These strategies have been called "schema availability," "schema selection," "schema maintenance," and "control mode reliance" (Pearson & Spiro, 1980).

Pearson and Spiro (1980) have made several instructional suggestions for the teacher attempting to teach students to use schema-related strategies. Techniques for helping students to select the right schema and making that schema available in their short-term memory are similar to the preceding ones for facilitating prior-knowledge usage. For instance, have them brainstorm and discuss what they already know about the topic. Schema maintenance, or keeping the appropriate prior knowledge in mind while reading, however, is something that teachers often take for granted. According to Pearson and Spiro (1980), "some students begin appropriately but somewhere along the way forget what they are reading about" (p. 82). Again, creating an ongoing visual representation such as a map or other organizational chart (see Chapter Four) while reading may help with this.

Finally, *control-mode reliance* refers to relying on text cues and prior knowledge. The good reader uses both of these in a balanced approach, but some poor readers overrely on one or the other. Students who overrely on text cues need to be encouraged to see reading as a meaning-oriented activity. Using listening and reading tasks, embed anomalous statements and have the students find the statements that do not make sense. You can also try this: provide students with multiple answers to questions. One answer can be text based, another schema based, and the rest wrong. Have them select the two best answers and tell which is from the text and which is from what they know. The opposite and somewhat less common problem is the problem of the student who overrelies on schemata. For these students, the multiple-answer activity may help. Also, activities that focus on details and precise meaning may be necessary for them.

The question of the flexible use of schema-based and text-based processing strategies has also been addressed by Tierney and Pearson (1981): In different situations, different patterns are appropriate. For instance, when reading lab directions, one would need to be more text based than when reading a novel for pleasure. Teachers can alert students to these approaches especially when text-based interpretations are necessary. Also teachers can provide study guides that encourage text- or schema-based approaches when necessary.

It also seems that the tendency to rely on schema- or text-based processes may be related to individual characteristics of the reader. Spiro and Tirre (1979) found that college students who were more "stimulus bound" on an embedded figures task were also more "text bound" on a reading comprehension task. As Spiro (1979) points out, however, for good readers, this tendency to rely on one or the other is used only when the situation permits, whereas poor readers may overrely on one even when it has negative effects on comprehension. Also, for poor readers, an overreliance on one style can be an attempt to compensate for a weakness: using prior knowledge to avoid decoding, and vice versa. Remediation must be based on a clear assessment of the cause of the inappropriate style.

Finally, it has also been suggested that schema theory gives us a useful way to understand students' wrong answers. In examining these answers, one might discover that they have been caused by one of the following (Strange, 1980):

1. No schema exists.
2. Schema is naîve.
3. No new information exists in story, so details are forgotten.
4. Story has insufficient cues for schema development.
5. Inappropriate schema is used.
6. Schema-based response is not sufficiently related to the text.
7. Text-based response is not sufficiently related to schema.

If you are able to determine that one student habitually falls into one or two of these errors, then the problem can be remedied by addressing the cause.

Building Prior Knowledge

Perhaps the major teaching implication of prior-knowledge and schema theory is that teachers must make sure that students have the necessary background knowledge before reading. If a schema pretest or prereading discussion reveals that students have insufficient background knowledge, then comprehension will be poor unless the teacher or the students find some way to fill in the important gaps in their background. Lectures and activities that build background may be useful. Such things as field trips, movies, and guest speakers build motivation as well as background knowledge. Using reading to build background is a strategy that is often overlooked, although Crafton (1983) found that students who read two passages on the same topic made more inferences, used more prior knowledge, became more personally involved, and recalled more than did students reading passages on different topics. Library books, magazines, and even lower-level textbooks can be used to help students acquire the necessary background knowledge. This will also give them a strategy for acquiring background information on their own when there is no teacher there to provide it for them. Finally, many of the prereading activities mentioned earlier for encouraging prior-knowledge usage and schema availability will also naturally lead to building students' background through discussion. Two other examples of techniques for building prior knowledge are the Guided Reading Strategy and The Coming Attraction.

Guided reading strategy (Bean & Pardi, 1979). Have students survey an assigned section of a text chapter looking for titles, graphs, charts, vocabulary, and guide questions. Have them close their books and list this information on the board. Then have them check their books to fill in added information. During this discussion you can have them check the glossary for vocabulary definitions, and you can fill in other information that they should know before reading. Then organize the information into a topical outline on the board for them to use as they read the text.

Coming attraction. Graves, Prenne, and Cooke (1985) have suggested that students needing a great deal of support may benefit from being given a preview of fictional works they are about to read. This preview should consist of rhetorical questions to arouse the students' interest and to build a bridge between their prior knowledge and the topic of the story, questions focusing on the story's theme, and descriptions of the characters, setting, and plot up to the climax. Take a few minutes to discuss the questions in the preview before asking them to read. In classrooms where students are reading self-selected materials, such previews could be written by students for each other. They could be kept in a file or on the inside cover of the book.

Vocabulary Development

In practice, it is difficult to separate a knowledge of relevant background information from a knowledge of relevant word meanings. Expanding students' meaning vocabulary is a critical part of making sure that they have adequate background knowledge, and because word meanings are learned best when learned in terms of their associations with other concepts, it is probably best to think of expanding prior knowledge and building vocabulary simultaneously. Indeed, McNeil (1984) has suggested that one hypothesis explaining the strong correlation between vocabulary knowledge and comprehension ability is that "a person who knows a word well knows other words and ideas related to it. It is this network of ideas that enhances comprehension" (pp. 96–97). Indeed, McKeown, Beck, Omanson, and Poole (1985) found that "rich" instruction in which students had experiences beyond the definition, experiences like relating the word to other words, responding affectively, and applying words to various contexts, was more effective for improving comprehension than instruction in which students were just given definitions.

One problem with the way vocabulary is often taught has been pointed out by Herber (1970). There is evidence that words must be used "many times in many situations" (p. 160) before they are really known. Traditional memorization of definitions and brief prereading discussions are insufficient. "Students develop vocabulary when they use words in situations that have meaning, in conversations and animated discussion" (p. 162). Similarly, Shank (1982) hypothesizes that "to teach new words one must allow them to be used immediately and orally" (p. 164). McKeown et al. (1985) also found that more encounters (twelve as opposed to four) with a word resulted in better word knowledge, more fluent access to word meanings, and improved comprehension. Moreover, rich instruction in which students were also encouraged to use the words beyond the classroom setting (see "word wizard" later) was the most effective type of instruction in their study. Thus, vocabulary teaching methods that require students to *use* the words in meaningful ways, orally and in writing, as well as in nonschool settings, are more likely to result in learning than is decontextualized memorization.

Carr and Wixson (1986) also suggest that effective vocabulary instruction "should provide for active student involvement in learning new vocabulary" (p. 590) and "should develop students' strategies for acquiring new vocabulary independently" (p. 591). These require that the classroom atmosphere be one that fosters a love of words. Vocabulary activities should be interesting and useful, and, whenever possible, they could be student directed. Students can be actively involved with selecting words to learn, determining the best definition of the word, and identifying their own best word-learning strategy. This will be more likely to produce independent word learners than will strategies in which the teacher picks the words and directs the learning. (See the vocabulary self-selection strategy later, for example.)

Finally, as Pearson and Johnson (1978) point out, "One of the axioms of instruction for concept development is that there is no substitute for direct experience" (p. 34). If there is no way to relate the new word meaning to the direct experience of the students, then it should be associated with something they have experienced. Concrete examples, role-playing simulations, pictures, and other aids that provide some direct experience are likely to be more useful than abstract definitions. All vocabulary discussions should involve prior knowledge.

To summarize, teachers may wish to (1) teach vocabulary word meanings in terms of their connections to the other key background concepts needed for comprehension of the material, (2) encourage and facilitate repeated use of these words in meaningful oral and written situations before and after reading, (3) facilitate active student involvement and independent word-learning strategies, and (4) find links between the meanings of the new words and the prior experience of the students.

At this point, you may have noticed that if vocabulary instruction is to be done well, the teacher (or student) will have to limit the number of words to be introduced. Herber (1970) recommends that teachers consider choosing only key terms, and that the number of these to be taught reflect the relative importance to the unit and the background and abilities of the students. If students are choosing the words to be learned, they also should be encouraged to keep the number manageable.

Of course, all words are not of equal difficulty, depending on the prior knowledge of the student. Nagy, Anderson, and Herman (1987) found that the most instruction was probably needed when the words were high in "conceptual difficulty" because these words were the least likely to be learned from reading in context. They defined four levels of conceptual difficulty as follows (p. 250):

1. Reader already knows the concept and knows a one-word synonym.
2. Reader already knows the concept, but there is not a one-word synonym.
3. Concept is not known but can be learned on the basis of experiences and information already available to the reader.
4. Concept is not known, and learning it requires new factual information or learning a related system of concepts.

Graves and Prenn (1986) similarly distinguish between vocabulary teaching methods necessary when students already know the concept and those appropriate when the students need to learn the concept as well as the word. The latter require more time and effort, and the sample activities that follow are probably most appropriate for these situations. Numerous other vocabulary teaching suggestions can be found in Johnson and Pearson (1978), McNiel (1984), and other reading methods texts.

Activities for Teaching Vocabulary Related to Reading

In most cases, you will probably wish to teach vocabulary words prior to reading as part of building the students' prior knowledge. In the content areas, you will also be introducing new concepts at the beginning of units. Moreover, in some cases, you may decide to let students try to learn the words from context during reading, and then you may wish to follow reading with a discussion of critical vocabulary. If students are reading independently, then you will probably rely on independent word-learning strategies (see page 143). Whenever you decide to teach vocabulary, the following ideas may be helpful.

FIGURE 7-3   Class-constructed Semantic Map for "Natural Resource"

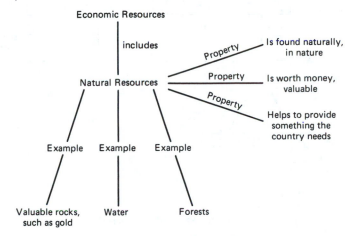

Brainstormed terms: Valuable
                    Rocks
                    Trees
                    Nature
                    Water

Map:

Semantic mapping.   To teach students to see how new concepts can be defined and related to other concepts, a class-constructed semantic map may be useful (see Hanf, 1971; McNiel, 1984; Pearson & Johnson, 1978; and others). For mapping the meaning of an individual concept, you may wish to include words telling properties, categories, and examples. Begin by having students list any related terms that come to mind. Then, assemble them into a diagram in which the relations of property, category, or example are indicated. Figure 7-3 shows a possible prereading map for the concept "natural resource." A similar procedure can be used to link together all the new words in a unit. Simply lead the students through a map of the whole assignment, inserting the new words where they belong. Figure 7-4 shows a postreading map that places the new concept of natural resources in a general network with the other new concepts in the chapter.

Frayer model.   The Frayer model of concept development (Frayer, Frederick, & Klausmeir, 1969) provides an outline for defining words so that students understand the concepts rather than memorizing the definitions. This model suggests that defining words should proceed through the following steps:

1. Name relevant attributes.
2. Eliminate irrelevant attributes.
3. Give examples.

FIGURE 7-4   Post-reading Semantic Map for Social Studies Chapter

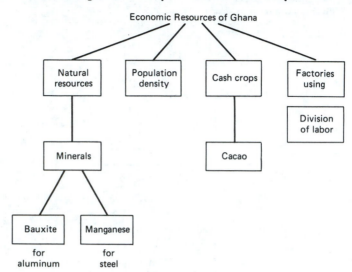

4. Give nonexamples (examples of what it is not).
5. Give subordinate terms.
6. Give superordinate terms.
7. Give coordinate terms.

For instance, to define the term "natural resource," a teacher might say,

1. A natural resource is anything occurring naturally in the environment that has monetary value.
2. It doesn't matter whether it is liquid, gas, or solid.
3. Gold, oil, forests, rich soil, and coal are examples.
4. In contrast, cars and wheat crops are *not* natural resources. They do not occur naturally but require human intervention.
5. Natural energy resources such as coal are one type of natural resource.
6. Natural resources are part of a country's economic resources.
7. Crops and factories are other economic resources.

Involving the students in each of these steps would probably be better than having the teacher supply all the information. Indeed, it might be useful to make sure that students always define words in these ways. A definition form in which these categories are listed can be made available to students who are learning words independently. An example of one such form is provided in Figure 7-5, a "word map"

FIGURE 7-5 Word Map

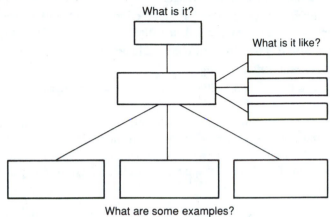

Source: R. M. Schwartz, and T. Raphael, "Concept of Definition: A key to improving students' vocabulary," *Reading Teacher, 39* (1985), p. 201. Reprinted with permission of Robert M. Schwartz and the International Reading Association.

as suggested by Schwartz and Raphael (1985). This could be expanded to include other Frayer categories as well.

Word wizard.   In the McKeown et al. (1985) study, students could earn points toward becoming a "word wizard" by bringing evidence that they had heard, seen or used the new vocabulary words independently. The points were prominently displayed on a chart in the classroom. This technique could involve writing as well as reading, and encouraged the children to use the words at home and in various contexts.

Direct instruction.   Eeds and Cochrum (1985) have recommended a four-step approach for teaching vocabulary that they found to be more effective than dictionary work or reading in context. These steps were as follows:

1. Activate the students' prior knowledge (for example, "Have you experi-enced...?").
2. Have them write about an experience that illustrates the concept being taught.
3. Have them write a nonexample.
4. Have them write the definitions in their own words.

You will wish to have students share their writing between each of these steps.
   Blanchowicz (1986) has recommended a similar five-step procedure as fol-lows:

1. Activate the students' prior knowledge.
2. Have the students make "preliminary, predictive connections between words or between words and the topic and structure of the selection" (p. 644).
3. Read the text so that the words can be read in context.
4. Refine the meaning after reading.
5. Use the words in writing activities and in additional readings.

For Step 1, she recommends brainstorming, but for reluctant readers, Blanchowicz (1986) suggests "exclusion brainstorming." Place a list of related words on the board along with some words that do *not* fit the topic. Ask students to select the words that will probably not appear in the text and ask them to justify their answer.

Knowledge rating.   One useful technique for promoting the students' metacognitive awareness of their knowledge of words is the "knowledge rating" procedure (Blanchowicz, 1986). Using the knowledge rating sheet provided in Figure 7-6, have students analyze their own familiarity with the words to be studied. After discussing what they know about the words, they can decide which words they want to focus on during their reading. In some cases these will be the new words in the last column; however, if many words are in the second or third column, it might be more appropriate to learn those first. Moreover, students can decide what level of knowledge they want after reading. For instance, they may just want to "know something about" some of the words. Other words may be important enough to define completely. After discussion and reading, have the students review the same sheet to assess how their knowledge has changed.

FIGURE 7-6   Knowledge Rating Sheet

Word	Can easily define	Know something about	Have heard or seen	Have never heard or seen

Directions: Before reading, place a ✓ in the appropriate column next to each new word. After reading, place a ✗ in the appropriate column.

Source: Adapted from C. Blanchowicz, "Making Connections: Alternatives to the Vocabulary Notebook," *Journal of Reading, 29* (1986), 645.

Development of Word-Learning Independence

Many words learned during the school years are not learned from teacher-directed instruction. Indeed, some children may learn as many as three thousand words per year, with only about three hundred of them attributable to instruction (Nagy, Anderson, & Herman, 1987). Nagy, Herman, and Anderson (1985) found that eighth-grade students with average or above-average ability did learn a small but statistically significant amount of word knowledge from context. Thus, Nagy, Anderson, and Herman (1987) conclude that the most effective way to increase a student's vocabulary may be to involve that student in a lots of reading. (One problem with this has been suggested by the research of McKeown [1985] in which poor readers had difficulty with acquiring meaning from context.)

Although little research exists about how to help students learn words in the context, some students may benefit by teaching them about context clues and word parts to help them in this process. Students also need to be encouraged to develop their own vocabularies actively with directed study, and the vocabulary self-selection strategy is described later to help with this process.

Teaching context clues.   Dulin (1970) has recommended teaching students about the six types of context clues provided in Table 7-1. You can teach them directly, but it would probably be essential to reinforce these clues whenever new words are being introduced. Give students experience with defining words from their reading on the basis of the context. Ask them to tell how they figured out the meaning. Tell them that this important strategy is one that good readers use to increase their vocabulary.

Teaching word parts.   You will probably also want to encourage students to figure out the meanings of new words using word parts (prefixes and suffixes) whenever possible. Lindsay (1984) has recommended that students make a personal "affixionary." For each page, they write a word part at the top along with its usual definition. For instance, one page might say "un—not" or another might say "tri—three." They can then keep a record of words they find with those word parts. You may wish to ask them to also include sample sentences. Even if you choose not to do anything formal, the emphasis on word parts during other vocabulary discussions is probably useful.

Vocabulary self-selection strategy.   Students need to learn to select their own vocabulary words. Moreover, if given the opportunity to select words they are interested in, they will be much more likely to learn them. For these reasons, Haggard (1982) has suggested that each week students can be asked to bring to class one or two words they would like to learn. These can be words they have encountered either orally or in their independent reading. They each place their words on the board, telling what they mean and why they would like to learn them. The class can then

TABLE 7-1   Types of Context Clues

---

1. Linked Synonyms and Appositives—almost like little dictionary definitions supplied by the author. For example:
   "*Democracy,* rule by the people, was developed by the Greeks."
   Clues: *commas, dashes*—usually in pairs
2. Contrast—to tell you what it *is,* the author tells you what it *is not.* For example:
   "Instead of his usual happy demeanor, today he seemed quite dejected."
   Clues: *instead of, unlike, rather than,* etc.
3. Direct Description—the author actually creates a picture for you. For example:
   "The *gargoyle* on the corner of the church, with its ugly face, flapping wings, and extended claws, was a frightening piece of sculpture indeed."
   Clues: *that is, in short, in summary, thus,* etc.
4. Cause-Effect—the author explains the reason for or result of the word. For example:
   "Because she wanted to impress all her dinner guests with the food she served, she carefully studied the necessary *culinary* arts.
   Clues: *because, since, therefore, thus, so,* etc.
5. Language Experience—the reader uses prior knowledge to figure out the meaning. For instance:
   "She walked away from her closet and quickly slipped a *jersey* over her head. She smoothed it into place over her hips, added a belt, glanced at the mirror, and left for work."
   Clues: *The reader* is the clue, using his or her prior knowledge.
6. Combination Methods—students use several strategies to figure out the word. For instance:
   "The balloon sank lower and lower. The flyer nodded his head toward the edge of the basket. *Jettison* everything we don't need! Get rid of the heaviest stuff first. We will float better if the basket is lighter."
   Clues: *the reader* and his or her experience and prior knowledge, *direct description,* and *cause-effect.*

Source: Adapted from K. Dulin, "Using Context Clues in Word Recognition and Comprehension," *Reading Teacher,* 23 (1970), 440–445, 449.

narrow the list down to a manageable number of words to be learned that week. These words can be discussed, recorded, and used throughout the week. Another alternative is to ask each student to be responsible for his or her own words and some selected others.

AFFECTIVE FACTORS

When considering the act of comprehending, it is essential to consider the affective characteristics of the reader as well as the cognitive ones. How motivated is the student? Is the material interesting to the student? What are the student's expectations? Is the student an active participant in "constructing a set of meanings" that he or she feels is "useful" (see Chapter One)?

Motivation and Interest

Students can read with greater comprehension when they are motivated (see Fass & Schumacher, 1979). Interest in the material leads to more motivation, and students read interesting material with greater comprehension than uninteresting material, even when the readability level is the same for each (Asher, Hymel & Wigfield, 1978; Bernstein, 1955). Moreover, when investigating metacognitive approaches used by remedial high school students, Ngandu (1977) found that "motivation provided by interesting material usually led to the use of appropriate behaviors" (p. 233). Thus, teachers can probably improve their students' comprehension by making sure that they are motivated and interested.

One good model for the teacher concerned with promoting motivation has been suggested by Dulin (1978). This model can be stated as follows:

$$\text{Motivation} = \frac{\text{expected reward}}{\text{expected effort}}$$

According to this ratio, motivation can be increased by increasing the expected reward *or* by decreasing the expected effort. The greatest amount of motivation would result from doing both of these things. You can probably think of many ways to do this. Some example suggestions are provided in Table 7-2. Space is left so that you can include some of your own.

One thing you should notice in studying Table 7-2 is that the teacher behaviors listed as "decreasing expected effort" are strategies suggested in other parts of this book. When you are adequately preparing students to read for comprehension, you are decreasing the amount of effort needed to comprehend. An automatic side result is that you will also be increasing motivation.

Although a thorough treatment of the topic of motivation is beyond the scope of this book, several basic considerations should be stressed within the context of a developing comprehension pedagogy. Motivation should always be a prime consideration when giving students reading assignments. When students have ownership of the assignment through choice (see Chapter Two), they are more likely to be motivated. Never present reading as a chore or punishment. Make all reading

TABLE 7-2 Selected Sample Procedures for Increasing Motivation

INCREASING EXPECTED REWARD	DECREASING EXPECTED EFFORT
Provide regular praise.	Provide background information.
Provide interesting activities.	Give specific purpose.
Write fair tests.	Preview assignment.
Provide high-success tasks.	Preview vocabulary.
Involve students in purpose setting.	Discuss reading strategies.
Involve students in questioning.	Use high-success materials.
Use meaningful reading tasks.	Divide long chapters into shorter assignments.
Give students choices.	
_____	_____
_____	_____

assignments relevant and meaningful to students by suggesting interesting purposes for reading (see Chapter Nine). When possible, use materials that are related to the students' interests and show them how the material learned can be used by them in the future. Make sure that each student has a chance to succeed, and help students to develop a positive attitude toward reading in general.

Self-concept related to reading. Another affective factor influencing a student's ability to apply the strategies described in this book successfully is his or her self-concept related to reading. Does the student expect to succeed? Does the student view himself or herself as an active participant in the reading process? Johnston and Winograd (1985) have described a learning problem that they call "passive failure in reading...It is our thesis that many of the problems evidenced by poor readers stem from, or are compounded by, the fact that they are passive, helpless participants in what is fundamentally an interactive process-reading" (p. 279). They describe passive failure as a complex of characteristics involving, among other factors, a belief that one has low ability and that this cannot be changed, low expectations for success, attribution of success to factors beyond their control, low self-esteem, apathy, and a tendency to make negative affective statements while performing reading tasks. They suggest that it is best to view this as a temporary learning problem that can be prevented and remediated.

Perhaps the best remedial technique for passive responses to reading tasks is to set up situations in which negative self-assessments are unnecessary. These would be contexts that are noncompetitive and task involving (Winograd & Niquette, 1988). (Nichols [1983] distinguishes between situations that are ego involving where the focus is on competition with others and those that are task involving in which the focus is on the task for its own sake.) These students need to experience reading to fulfill their own purposes. They need experiences with reading for pleasure in supportive, nonthreatening environments. They need experiences with aesthetic reading (see Chapter Five). (See Winograd & Niquette, 1988; Winograd & Smith, 1987.) Unfortunately, as Winograd and Niquette (1988) point out, these are often the children who are put in the intensely ego-involving situation of being evaluated on their ability to complete meaningless skill sheets, thus further distorting their view of successful reading as an active, meaningful task.

CULTURAL DIFFERENCES

Students in the public schools in the United States come from various cultural backgrounds. These differences are likely to have a strong influence on comprehension, though, in this author's opinion, remarkably little research has been done in this area. Perhaps it is because these differences can be largely subsumed under the previous two categories, prior knowledge and motivation and interest.

For instance, students from divergent subcultures may have different vocabularies and different schemata, and this is likely to interfere with comprehension (see Obah, 1983; Steffensen, 1986). In the movie example on page 133, a migrant worker who had never seen a movie theater would be unable to make any of the necessary slot-filling inferences or prior-knowledge elaborations. Moreover, culturally different students may also have different text structure expectations (Kintsch & Greene, 1978). They may have different attitudes toward language (Bernstein, 1971; Torrey, 1970; and others), different approaches to school tasks (Houston, 1973), and they may find it difficult to be interested in materials that appear to exclude their cultural group (see Elasser & John-Steiner, 1977). Ignoring these differences perpetuates low achievement for these divergent cultural groups. Teachers wishing to teach comprehension to all children must assess how cultural differences are influencing the prior knowledge, motivation, and interest level of the children in their classrooms. Materials that reflect the important contributions of the children's cultural heritages should be made part of the classroom library (see Simonson & Walker, 1988).

Moreover, when we remember that our society is composed of a dominant and various subordinate cultures when viewed from a standpoint of power and access to resources, we can see that in the schools, we are trying to teach the linguistic practices of the dominant culture (Giroux, 1981). (Indeed, this book is about the cognitive practices of the dominant culture.) Needless to say, this pedagogy can be alienating to children whose ways of thinking are being labeled "incorrect." Taking the opposite position and saying that it is cultural imperialism to teach these processes would have an effect similar to that found by educators in the 1970s who abandoned teaching standard English; it did not get anybody anywhere. Being able to comprehend in these ways is useful in a society in which this is the dominant mode. Teachers must help culturally divergent students see that their own thinking patterns have value and are not necessarily inferior. Simultaneously, they can teach the students these new ways of comprehending as a means of social mobility and self-understanding. Researchers should begin to examine the cognitive processes of divergent cultural groups so that "incorrect" answers can be viewed in terms of the cultural values and schemata they may reflect.

DECODING FLUENCY

Finally, although word identification is not the topic at hand, a chapter on individual differences in comprehension would be seriously remiss if decoding (word identification) were not mentioned. Just as the comprehension processes all interact with each other, they also interact with word identification processes.

Readers who are having to devote attention to identifying words will not simultaneously have attention available for comprehension processes (LaBerge & Samuels, 1974; and others). Imagine yourself having to read a passage in which many of the key words were written backward. Each time you had to stop to figure out the word, you would forget the point of the sentence. This is similar to what happens when students try to read materials with too many words they must work to identify. Indeed, in their theory of automaticity in reading, LaBerge and Samuels (1974) suggest that word identification processes must be *automatic* for comprehension processes to proceed fluently. The implication of this theory is that intensive reading with easy materials or repeated reading of the same material to develop decoding automaticity may also have a facilitative effect on comprehension skills (see Samuels & LaBerge, 1983; Dowhower, 1987; and others). Even if you do not choose to develop students' decoding automaticity, it will be useful to remember that decoding automaticity may be an individual difference affecting how well your students comprehend, and all students will be more successful comprehenders when they are given materials they can decode fluently. Although this is often done for reading instruction, teachers need to consider matching students to materials in the content areas as well (see Chapter Eight).

SUMMARY

All of the comprehension processes require that the students have the requisite prior knowledge (schemata). Teachers must begin by assessing whether or not this is true, by providing background information and vocabulary instruction when necessary, and by helping students to select what information they will need to apply and when to apply it. Some students overrely or underrely on schema-based processes and need to be shown how to use an appropriately balanced approach. Moreover, inaccurate student answers can often be interpreted in light of what they reveal about defects in the students' prior knowledge and their ability to use it.

Comprehension is also improved when students are motivated and interested. To some extent, teachers facilitate motivation each time they make the task easier by making sure that students have the requisite skills and schemata. Moreover, poor readers' motivation is often depressed by their low expectations for success. They often adopt a passive approach to reading as a result of their low expectations, low self-esteem related to reading, and belief in their own low ability. Meaningful, noncompetitive activities may help them to overcome these difficulties.

Teachers should also be aware of how cultural differences influence the comprehension of individual students. Cultural differences can be related to differences in prior knowledge, vocabulary, and interest. Moreover, teachers must be careful to recognize the validity of the thinking strategies of culturally different students, even when trying to teach standard ones.

Finally, students cannot be expected to comprehend passages when they are devoting large amounts of attention to identifying individual words. They must be given material they can decode fluently if they are to develop their comprehension processing abilities.

SELF-CHECK TEST

1. Define the following terms:

schema

schema availability

schema selection

schema maintenance

control mode reliance

conceptual difficulty

motivation ratio

decoding automaticity

semantic mapping

passive failure

ego involving

task involving

2. Answer true or false:

____ (a) Prior knowledge is not important for microprocessing.

____ (b) Providing background knowledge is not worth the time.

____ (c) Once you give the students the prior knowledge, they will know how to apply it.

____ (d) All readers use the same combination of schema- and text-based processes.

____ (e)
$$M = \frac{\text{expected effort}}{\text{expected reward}}$$

____ (f) Comprehension and decoding processes operate independently.

3. List five procedures for assessing and building prior knowledge.

4. List the seven comprehension problems related to schema usage.

5. List the four major reader-related comprehension contexts.

6. Describe five ways to teach vocabulary.

7. How can you help students to become independent vocabulary learners?

8. How can you build motivation and interest?

9. How can you help students overcome passive failure?

SUGGESTED ACTIVITIES

1. While carefully reading a content-area or reading assignment, write down what prior knowledge is necessary. Can you assume that all students have this prior knowledge?

2. Design a lesson for preteaching the new vocabulary in a specific reading assignment. Be sure to link concepts, provide opportunities for use, and relate the concepts to students' direct experience. Be selective in determining which words to teach.

3. Try using the K-W-L format for some of your own reading. Does it help? Why or why not?

4. Add twenty items to Table 7-2.
5. If you are a college student, monitor your own reading motivation for a week. What factors increase and decrease your motivation?
6. What factors in schools today lead to poor motivation and passive failure? How can these be changed?

REFERENCES

Anderson, R. C. (1977). *Schema-directed processes in language comprehension* (Technical Report No. 50). Urbana-Champaign: Center for the Study of Reading, University of Illinois.

Anderson, R. C., Reynolds, R. E., Schallert, D. L., & Goetz, E. T. (1977). Framework for comprehending discourse. *American Educational Research Journal, 14,* 367–381.

Anderson, R. C., Spiro, R. J., & Anderson, M. C. (1977). *Schemata as scaffolding for the representation of information in connected discourse* (Technical Report No. 21). Urbana-Champaign: Center for the Study of Reading, University of Illinois.

Asher, S. R., Hymel, S., & Wigfield, A. (1978). Influence of topic interest on children's reading comprehension. *Journal of Reading Behavior, 10,* 35–47.

Bean, T., & Pardi, R. (1979). Guided reading strategy. *Journal of Reading, 23,* 144–147.

Bernstein, B. (1971). *Class, codes, and control* (Vol. 1). London: Routledge & Kegan Paul.

Bernstein, M. R. (1955). Relationship between interest and reading comprehension. *Journal of Educational Research, 49,* 283–288.

Blanchowicz, C. (1986). Making connections: Alternatives to the vocabulary notebook. *Journal of Reading, 29,* 643–649.

Carr, E., & Ogle, D. M. (1987). K-W-L Plus: A strategy for comprehension and summarization. *Journal of Reading, 30,* 626–631.

Carr, E., & Wixson, K. (1986). Guidelines for evaluating vocabulary instruction. *Journal of Reading, 29,* 588–595.

Chiesi, H. L., Spilich, G. J., & Voss, J. F. (1979). Acquisition of domain-related information in relation to high and low domain knowledge. *Journal of Verbal Learning and Verbal Behavior, 18,* 257–273.

Crafton, L. K. (1983). Learning from reading: What happens when students generate their own background information? *Journal of Reading, 26,* 586–593.

Dowhower, S. L. (1987). Effects of repeated reading on second-grade transitional readers' fluency and comprehension. *Reading Research Quarterly, 22,* 389–406.

Dulin, K. (1970). Using context clues in word recognition and comprehension. *Reading Teacher, 23,* 440–445, 449.

Dulin, K. (1978). Reading and the affective domain. In S. Pflaum-Connor (Ed.), *Aspects of reading education.* Berkeley, Calif.: McCutcheon Publishing.

Eeds, M., & Cochrum, W. A. (1985) Teaching word meanings by expanding schemata vs. dictionary work vs. reading in context. *Journal of Reading, 28,* 492–502.

Elasser, N., & John-Steiner, V. P. (1977). An interactionist approach to advancing literacy. *Harvard Educational Review, 47*, 355–369.

Fass, W., & Schumacher, G. M. (1978). Effects of motivation, subject activity, and readability on the retention of prose materials. *Journal of Educational Psychology, 70*, 803–807.

Feather, N. T. (1982). *Expectations and actions: Expectancy-program for cognitive modifiability*. Baltimore, Md.: University Park Press.

Frayer, D. A., Frederick, W. C., & Klausmeir, H. J. (1969). *A schema for testing the level of concept mastery* (Working Paper No. 16). Madison: Wisconsin Research and Development Center for Cognitive Learning, University of Wisconsin.

Giroux, H. (1981). Literacy, ideology, and the politics of schooling. *Humanities in Society, 4*, 335–361.

Graves, M., & Prenn, M. (1986). Costs and benefits of various methods of teaching vocabulary. *Journal of Reading, 29*, 596–602.

Graves, M., Prenn, M., & Cooke, C. L. (1985). The coming attraction: Previewing short stories. *Journal of Reading, 28*, 594–598.

Haggard, M. R. (1982). The vocabulary self-collection strategy: Using student interest and world knowledge to enhance vocabulary growth. *Journal of Reading, 29*, 634–642.

Hanf, M. B. (1971). Mapping: A technique for translating reading into thinking. *Journal of Reading, 14*, 225–230, 270.

Herber, H. (1970). *Teaching reading in the content areas*. Englewood Cliffs, N.J.: Prentice-Hall.

Hildyard, A. (1979). Children's production of inferences from oral texts. *Discourse Processes, 2*, 33–56.

Houston, S. (1973, March). Black English. *Psychology Today*, pp. 45–48.

Johnson, D. D., & Pearson, P. D. (1978). *Teaching reading vocabulary*. New York: Holt, Rinehart and Winston.

Johnston, P., & Pearson, P. D. (1982). *Prior knowledge, connectivity, and the assessment of reading comprehension* (Technical Report No. 245). Urbana-Champaign: Center for the Study of Reading, University of Illinois.

Johnston, P. H., & Winograd, P. N. (1985). Passive failure in reading. *Journal of Reading Behavior, 17*, 279–299.

Kintsch, W., & Greene, E. (1978). The role of culture-specific schemata in the comprehension and recall of stories. *Discourse Processes, 1*, 1–13.

LaBerge, D., & Samuels, S. J. (1974). Toward a theory of automatic information processing in reading. *Cognitive Psychology, 6*, 293–323.

Langer, J. (1981). From theory to practice: A prereading plan. *Journal of Reading, 24*, 152–156.

Lindsay, T. (1984). The affixionary: Personalizing prefixes and suffixes. *Reading Teacher, 38*, 247–248.

Macklin, M. (1978). Content area reading is a process for finding personal meaning. *Journal of Reading, 22*, 212–215.

MacNiel, J. (1984). *Reading comprehension: New directions for classroom practice*. Glenview, Ill.: Scott, Foresman.

McKeown, M. G. (1985). The acquisition of work meaning from context by children of high and low ability. *Reading Research Quarterly, 20,* 482–496.

McKeown, M. G., Beck, I. L., Omanson, R. C., & Pople, M. T. (1985). Some effects of the nature and frequency of vocabulary instruction on the knowledge and use of words. *Reading Research Quarterly, 20,* 522–535.

Moore, D. W., & Arthur, S. V. (1981). Possible sentences. In E. K. Dishner, T. W. Bean, & J. E. Readence (Eds.), *Reading in the content areas: Improving classroom instruction.* Dubuque: Kendall/Hunt.

Nagy, W. E., Anderson, R. C., & Herman, P. A. (1987). Learning word meanings from context during normal reading. *American Educational Research Journal, 24,* 237–270.

Nagy, W., Herman, P. A., & Anderson, R. C. (1985). Learning words from context. *Reading Research Quarterly, 20,* 233–253.

Ngandu, K. (1977). What do remedial high school students do when they read? *Journal of Reading, 21,* 231–234.

Nichols, J. G. (1983). Conceptions of ability and achievement motivation: A theory and its implications for education. In S. Paris, G. Olson, & H. Stevenson (Eds.), *Learning and motivation in the classroom.* Hillsdale, N.J.: Lawrence Erlbaum.

Obah, T. V. (1983). Prior knowledge and the quest for new knowledge: The Third World dilemma. *Journal of Reading, 27,* 129–133.

Ogle, D. M. (1986). K-W-L: A teaching model that develops active reading of expository text. *Reading Teacher, 39,* 564–570.

Paris, S. G., & Winograd, P. (1989). How metacognition can promote academic learning and instruction. In B. F. Jones, & L. Idol, (Eds.), *Dimensions of thinking and cognitive instruction* (Vol. 1). Hillsdale, NJ: Lawrence Erlbaum Associates.

Pearson, P. D., Hansen, J., & Gordon, C. (1979). The effect of background knowledge on young children's comprehension of explicit and implicit information. *Journal of Reading Behavior, 11,* 201–210.

Pearson, P. D., & Johnson, D. D. (1978). *Teaching reading comprehension.* New York: Holt, Rinehart and Winston.

Pearson, P. D., & Spiro, R. J. (1980). Toward a theory of reading comprehension instruction. *Topics of Language Disorders, 1,* 71–88.

Rumelhart, D. E. (1981). Schemata: The building blocks of cognition. In J. T. Guthrie (Ed.), *Comprehension and teaching: Research reviews.* Newark, Del.: International Reading Association.

Samuels, S. J., & LaBerge, D. (1983). Critique of a theory of automaticity in reading: Looking back. A retrospective analysis of the LaBerge-Samuels reading model. In L. Gentile, M. Kamil, and J. Blanchard (Eds.), *Reading research revisited.* Columbus: Charles E. Merrill.

Schank, R. C. (1982). *Reading and understanding: Teaching from the perspective of artificial intelligence.* Hillsdale, N.J.: Lawrence Erlbaum.

Schwartz, R. M., & Raphael, T. (1985). Concept of definition: A key to improving students' vocabulary. *Reading Teacher, 39,* 198–205.

Simonson, R., & Walker, S. (1988). *Multi-cultural Literacy.* Saint Paul, Minn.: Greywolf Press.

Spilich, G. J., Vesonder, G. T., Chiesi, H. L., & Voss, J. F. (1979). Text processing of domain-related information for individuals with high and low domain knowledge. *Journal of Verbal Learning and Verbal Behavior, 18*, 275–290.

Spiro, R. J. (1979). *Etiology of reading comprehension style* (Technical Report No. 124). Urbana-Champaign: Center for the Study of Reading, University of Illinois.

Spiro, R. J., & Tirre, W. C. (1979). *Individual differences in schema utilization during discourse processing* (Technical Report No. 111). Urbana-Champaign: Center for the Study of Reading, University of Illinois.

Steffensen, M. (1986). Register, cohesion, and cross-cultural reading comprehension. *Applied Linguistics, 7*, 71–85.

Strange, M. (1980). Instructional implications of a conceptual theory of reading instruction. *Reading Teacher, 33*, 391–397.

Taylor, B. M. (1979). Good and poor readers' recall of familiar and unfamiliar text. *Journal of Reading Behavior, 11*, 375–380.

Tierney, R. J., & Pearson, P. D. (1981). *Learning to learn from text: A framework for improving classroom practice* (Reading Education Report No. 30). Urbana-Champaign: Center for the Study of Reading, University of Illinois.

Torrey, J. W. (1970). Illiteracy in the ghetto. *Harvard Educational Review, 40*, 253–259.

Wilson, C. R., & Hammill, C. (1982). Inferencing and comprehension in ninth graders reading geography textbooks. *Journal of Reading, 25*, 424–427.

Winograd, P., & Niquette, G. (1988). Assessing learned helplessness in poor readers. *Topics in Language Disorders, 8*, 38–55.

Winograd, P., & Smith, L. (1987). Improving the climate for reading comprehension instruction. *Reading Teacher, 40*, 304–310.

8

TEXT CONTEXTS: WHAT IS BEING READ?

In Chapter Seven it was suggested that it is important to prepare students for reading comprehension by assessing and developing their schemata related to the topic. It was also suggested that motivation and interest should be developed prior to reading. Is there anything else you can do to ensure that students will understand when they read?

Just as comprehension depends on a match between your students' prior knowledge and the prior knowledge required by the text, successful comprehension also depends on a match between your students' reading abilities and the abilities required to read the material. If the material is reasonably "readable" for this group of students, then you can preteach strategies that you think need emphasis. To do that, you must understand the strategic demands of the text.

Traditionally, "readability" has been measured by formulas that attempt to determine the grade level for which a piece of reading material is appropriate. Unfortunately, these formulas, though useful, are not 100 percent accurate, cannot be used to rewrite materials, fail to consider many important factors, and give the teacher little information about what strategies to preteach to promote comprehension with difficult materials.

The purpose of this chapter, therefore, is to help you become more skillful at detecting possible sources of difficulty in reading materials. Then, you can make effective choices about what materials to use, and you can predict what reading strategies the students will need to read with success. When necessary, you can provide prereading instruction to help the students deal with potential text difficulties.

READABILITY FORMULAS

Many readability formulas are available, and the results often vary from one to the next (see Daines, 1982, pp. 48, 50). (For descriptions of frequently used formulas, see any general reading methods text.) Most of these formulas attempt to measure semantic ("meaning") complexity by assessing the number or percentage of "hard words." ("Hard words" are usually defined as unfamiliar words or words with several syllables.) The other factor that most formulas measure is syntactic complexity. This is usually measured by counting the average number of words per sentence. These measures are then correlated with comprehension scores of students of varying ability levels to determine a predictive formula.

As you know, correlations do *not* indicate causality. This means, then, that although readability scores tend to correlate with successful or unsuccessful comprehension scores, the factors that they measure are not necessarily the *causes* of those scores. Thus, simply rewriting materials by taking out unfamiliar and long words and shortening sentences will *not* necessarily make the material easier to comprehend. Unfortunately, it seems that textbook writers sometimes do this to make their textbooks fit into the desired readability levels. Examples 8a and 8b demonstrate the difference between an original version and one that has been rewritten to lower the readability level according to a readability formula based on sentence length. Study these passages. Note the number of inferences necessary to understand the passage with the "lower" readability score.

Example 8a: Original Version[1]

In the 1800s, Hawaii was an independent republic. The Hawaiians had settled there from all over the world, but most of them spoke English. Because of this, Hawaiians wanted to become part of the United States. In 1900, Hawaii was make a U.S. territory. This resulted in increased trade with the United States, and this brought great prosperity.

Example 8b: Rewritten Version[2]

In the 1800s, Hawaii was an independent republic. English was the dominant language. In 1900, Hawaii was officially made a territory. Increased trade with America brought prosperity.

In a study examining original and revised versions of school materials, Davison, Kantor, Hannah, Hermon, Lutz, and Salzillo (1980) found that the revised

[1,2]From p. 6, Moe, A. J. & Irwin, J. W. Cohension, coherence, and comprehension. In Irwin, J. W. *Understanding and Teaching Cohesion Comprehension*, International Reading Assn. (1986).

versions were less coherent, especially in the area of intersentential connectives. Similar results were found by Anderson, Armbruster, and Kantor (1980). Thus, teachers cannot be content with simply accepting the readability scores given for their textbooks. It may be that the original text was actually more understandable than the poorly adapted version rewritten artificially to fit formula restrictions.

Another problem you have probably already noticed is that these formulas do not consider many important factors. Formulas consider only word difficulty and the syntactic complexity of individual sentences. Stop and think about the processes described in Part One of this book. What are some other text factors that might affect how easily your students can understand something? Write down as many as you can and then go on to the next section.

ASSESSMENT OF "PROCESSABILITY"

As you probably already figured out, to assess the "processability" of your reading materials, you need to examine what cues are available to the reader for micro-, integrative, macro-, elaborative, and metacognitive processing, as well as what reader-related characteristics are assumed. Once you understand the text demands in each of these areas, you can begin to decide if the book or article is appropriate for your students, and which strategies you might wish to teach to the whole class or to those students who are having problems with the assignment.

Microprocessing Factors

Microprocessing factors are the ones best assessed by readability formulas. (Indeed, readability formulas measure *only* microprocessing factors!) Word familiarity, concept difficulty, and within-sentence syntactic complexity all affect the students' comprehension (see Chall, 1984). Sentence length may affect the students' ability to connect these phrases and to extract the most important facts. If the sentences are too long, unskilled readers who cannot select as they go along may be unable to deal with the sentences as unified wholes. If students are having trouble understanding individual sentences in a text, you might wish to analyze the microprocessing demands of the text with questions like the following:

1. Was the vocabulary load appropriate or were understandable context clues provided for difficult words?
2. Were the sentences short enough to be read with understanding?
3. Were the syntactic patterns ones with which the students were familiar?
4. Was the figurative language understandable?
5. Was the importance of critical information made clear?

Integrative Processing Factors

Integrative processing considerations provide interesting examples of how readability formulas can be misused to rewrite materials. When sentences are rewritten to make them shorter, important information is often made implicit (see Examples 8a and 8b). For instance, a typical readability adjustment is illustrated in the change from 8c to 8d.

8c. Because Mexico allowed slavery, many Americans and their slaves moved there.

8d. Mexico allowed slavery. Many Americans moved there.

The sentences in 8d are shorter, but important intersentential information has been deleted. Now, the reader must infer that the Americans had slaves, and that, because they wanted to keep them, they had to move to Mexico. With all the integrative inferences required by 8d, we would probably predict that it would be more difficult to understand than 8c, even though it is at a lower readability level. Moreover, implicit connectives such as these seem to be as common in lower-level books as they are in higher-level books (Irwin, 1983). In Chapter Three of this book, you had some practice with identifying explicit and implicit integrative information. Just remember that implicit integrative information requires the reader to make inferences; and, in general, the more inferences required, the more difficult comprehension will be (Irwin & Pulver, 1984; Kintsch & Vipond, 1977; and others). Thus, in assessing the processability of a story or content passage, you may also wish to ask yourself questions like the following:

1. Are important cause-effect relationships made clear enough?
2. Will the sequence of events be clear to these students?
3. Are the connections between events sufficiently explained?
4. Are the pronoun referents clear?

Macroprocessing Factors

A similar principle applies to macroprocessing. If main ideas are implicit or difficult to find, processing will be inhibited (Christie & Schumacher, 1978; Fishman, 1978; and others). At larger levels, if the main points of whole sections and chapters are unclear, or if the organizational pattern is unfamiliar, macrocomprehension will be more difficult to achieve (Kintsch, 1977; Stein & Nezworski, 1978; and others). Also, the presence of too many irrelevant details can make it difficult for students to perform summarizing processes, probably because the details obscure the main points (Bruning, 1970; Thorndyke, 1979). To assess macroprocessing factors in narrative materials, you may want to ask yourself questions like the following:

1. Does the story use a typical story pattern that will be clear to the students?
2. Is the setting clear?

3. Are the characters' motivations, responses, and reactions made clear?
4. Are events sufficiently explained?

To assess macroprocessing factors in expository materials, you may be thinking about the following:

1. Is the organizational pattern clear and one with which the students are familiar?
2. Are the main ideas clearly stated?
3. Do introductions and summaries highlight the important information?

Elaborative Factors

A text can encourage prior-knowledge elaboration by explicitly linking new material to what the students already know. The text itself can provide elaboration in the form of numerous examples of new concepts (Klausmeir & Feldman, 1975). If the examples and definitions are concrete, then mental imagery can be encouraged. Finally, prereading questions can encourage prediction and postreading questions can encourage elaborations of all types, including higher-level thinking responses, and elaborations facilitate recall (Reder, 1978). To assess elaborative factors, you will probably be thinking about questions like the following:

1. Are there ways that students can connect the story or content to their own lives?
2. Are there clues that can help the reader predict events and/or upcoming content?
3. Are there characters or events with which the reader can identify?
4. Are there vivid descriptions which can help the reader form vivid mental images?

Metacognitive Factors

For metacognitive factors, you will probably want to examine your materials in terms of how easy they are to study. You may wish to think about the following questions:

1. Do they provide opportunities for practice and review?
2. Are there opportunities for students to check their own comprehension (see Anderson, 1980)?
3. Is the material broken into manageable units for note taking?
4. How easy is it to preview?

Reader-Related Factors

An analysis of reading material would be incomplete without an assessment of the match with the students in terms of their conceptual, vocabulary, and experiential backgrounds (see Kintsch & Miller, 1984). Also, you will probably want to assess how motivational the material is (Klare, 1976). Such qualities as format, pictures, print size, and style will affect comprehension if they affect motivation. To assess reader-related factors, you will probably be thinking about questions like the following:

1. Will my students have the prior knowledge necessary for reading this material?
2. Is this material motivating for my students?
3. Will my students be able to decode the words fluently?
4. Is the topic one that will interest my students?
5. Is the material presented in an interesting fashion?
6. Will readers want to become actively engaged in making sense of this material for purposes that are meaningful to them?
7. Does this material provide positive and motivating role models for both boys and girls, and for my students from divergent cultural backgrounds?

THE READABILITY CHECKLIST

The point of all of this is that if you can assess the strengths and weaknesses of your reading materials, you can provide prereading activities, study guides, and other activities that take advantage of the strengths and compensate for the weaknesses. You can assess the readability in such a way that you have information about how best to facilitate comprehension. You can also use your knowledge of comprehensibility factors to select readable materials and to create readable materials of your own.

In Figure 8-1, a checklist is provided to help you structure an analysis of content area materials that you want to examine in depth. Take a moment to look it over. You should note that you are asked to rate this material in relation to an ideal, not in relation to the "even worse" book you used last year. Also, note that the checklist is provided in its original format, in which these factors were divided into those that affect "understandability" (immediate recall) and those that affect "learnability" (long-term recall). As you look over the checklist, you will probably see how these factors all are related to the processes and contexts presented in this book.

The biggest advantage of using this checklist is that once you have used it to analyze your materials, you can provide instruction that helps students to comprehend. For instance, if the main ideas or organizational patterns are found to be unclear, they can be given to students in the form of a study guide. If the vocabulary is difficult, it can be presented first. If there are many implicit connectives, this can be discussed as part of the assignment. If no introduction is given, you can provide one. You can also teach students to use the assets of the material. For instance, you

FIGURE 8-1   Readability Checklist

This checklist is designed to help you evaluate the readability of your classroom texts. It can be used best if you rate your text while you are thinking of a specific class. Be sure to compare the textbook to a fictional ideal rather than to another text. Your goal is to find out what aspects of the text are or are not less than ideal. Finally, consider supplementary workbooks part of the textbook and rate them together. Have fun!
Rate the questions below using the following rating system:

5   Excellent
4   Good
3   Adequate
2   Poor
1   Unacceptable
NA Not applicable

Textbook title: _____
Publisher: _____

Copyright date: _____

UNDERSTANDABILITY
A. ____ Are the assumptions about students' vocabulary knowledge appropriate?
B. ____ Are the assumptions about students' prior knowledge of this content area appropriate?
C. ____ Are the assumptions about students' general experiential backgrounds appropriate?
D. ____ Does the teacher's manual provide the teacher with ways to develop and review the students' conceptual and experiential backgrounds?
E. ____ Are new concepts explicitly linked to the students' prior knowledge or to their experiential backgrounds?
F. ____ Does the text introduce abstract concepts by accompanying them with many concrete examples?
G. ____ Does the text introduce new concepts one at a time with a sufficient number of examples for each one?
H. ____ Is each definition understandable and at a lower level of abstraction than the concept being defined?
I. ____ Is the level of sentence complexity appropriate for the students?
J. ____ Are the main ideas of paragraphs, chapters, and subsections clearly stated?
K. ____ Does the text avoid irrelevant details?
L. ____ Does the text explicitly state important complex relationships (e.g., causality and conditionality) rather than always expecting the reader to infer them from the context?
M. ____ Does the teacher's manual provide lists of accessible resources containing alternative readings for the very poor and the very advanced readers?
N. ____ Is the readability level appropriate (according to a readability formula)?

LEARNABILITY
Organization
A. ____ Is an introduction provided for each chapter?

B. ____ Is there a clear and simple organizational pattern relating the chapters to each other?
C. ____ Does each chapter have a clear, explicit, and simple organizational structure?
D. ____ Does the text include such resources as an index, a glossary, and a table of contents?
E. ____ Do questions and activities draw attention to the organizational pattern of the material (e.g., chronological, cause and effect, spatial, and topical)?
F. ____ Do consumable materials interrelate well with the textbook?

Reinforcement
A. ____ Does the text provide opportunities for students to practice using new concepts?
B. ____ Are there summaries at appropriate intervals in the text?
C. ____ Does the text provide adequate iconic aids, such as maps, graphs, and illustrations, to reinforce concepts?
D. ____ Are there adequate suggestions for usable supplementary activities?
E. ____ Do these activities provide for a broad range of ability levels?
F. ____ Are there literal recall questions provided for the students' self-review?
G. ____ Do some of the questions encourage the students to draw inferences?
H. ____ Are there discussions that encourage creative thinking?
I. ____ Are questions clearly worded?

Motivation
A. ____ Does the teacher's manual provide introductory activities that will capture students' interest?
B. ____ Are chapter titles and subheadings concrete, meaningful, or interesting?
C. ____ Is the written style of the text appealing to the students?
D. ____ Are the activities motivating? Will they make the student want to pursue the topic further?
E. ____ Does the book show clearly how the knowledge being learned might be used by the learner in the future?
F. ____ Are the cover, format, print size and pictures appealing to the students?
G. ____ Does the text provide positive and motivating models for both sexes as well as for many racial, ethnic, and socioeconomic groups?

READABILITY ANALYSIS
Weaknesses
A. On which items was the book rated the lowest?
B. Did these items tend to fall in certain categories? Which?
C. Summarize the weaknesses of this text.
D. What can you do in class to compensate for the weaknesses of this text?
Assets
A. On which items was the book rated the highest?
B. Did these items fall in certain categories? Which?
C. Summarize the assets of this text.
D. What can you do in class to take advantage of the assets of this text?

Source: J. W. Irwin and C. J. Davis, "Assessing Readability: The Checklist Approach," *Journal of Reading,* 24 (1980), 124–130. Reprinted with permission of the International Reading Association.

can show the students how an author has made the organization clear. You can encourage them to use graphic aids, subheadings, and study questions for self-review. You can make sure they know how to use appendices, glossaries, indexes, and so on. A careful analysis of the materials can clearly help you to select useful instructional strategies.

Finally, to assess the processability of literary materials, you may wish to use the assessment questions provided in the "processability" section of this chapter. Remember, negative answers to these questions do *not* mean that you should not use the materials. Many excellent authors purposely make some points unclear so that readers can make discoveries for themselves, use their imagination, or be held in suspense. You may wish to use a piece because it involves a particular theme or literary style or because you know the children love it. The point is to be aware of processing demands so that you can be of assistance when necessary.

MATCHING STUDENTS WITH MATERIALS

A limit to what students can read still exists, even with good teaching assistance. It is common practice to divide students into reading groups in which students are given materials at their reading levels, and some teachers teach reading using individualized reading selections appropriate for each student's level. It is much less common, however, for students to be given material at their level in the content areas, especially at the secondary level. Perhaps that is because teachers think that the large-group, lecture-discussion, one-textbook approach is the only way to teach those subjects.

That is, of course, untrue. When an extreme gap exists between the level of the material and the ability level of a student or students, a multitext approach can be used. Simply find textbooks on the same subject from two or three different levels. You can do this by salvaging old texts from other grade levels when those classes move into a new text, and you may find that you can order a few multilevel books when the ones you normally use need to be replaced. The numbers and levels you need will be determined by the needs of children in your classroom and will vary from school to school.

Once you have some multilevel textbooks, you will need to make up assignments for each topic in each text. This need not take large amounts of time, especially if you phase in only one textbook a year and do it for just a few units at a time. The reward in terms of giving every student something that he or she can read and comprehend will be well worth it!

For example, suppose you are teaching a unit on weather in a seventh-grade classroom. Several of your students are unable to read the text. You suggest that they read a different assignment from the text you have stored at the back of the room. (It happens to be at the fourth-grade level.) It contains information about types of clouds not contained in the regular seventh-grade text. Their responsibility will be to read this section, answer the questions in the text, and report the information back to the whole class, which will be held responsible for knowing it. You can use a similar procedure for your gifted students, who read a special assignment on acid rain and give a report to the class. The "average" students read the regular text and report the information to the whole class, thereby reviewing and simultaneously teaching the other students any information they missed by reading the alternative assignments. All students are held responsible for reporting something to the class. All students have been given assignments at which they can succeed. This should increase motivation because students expect a reward (successful classroom recitation), and the expected effort is realistic (the material is at their level). Finally, all students are held responsible for all the material discussed in class, so no student misses important content because of having done an alternative assignment.

A short-term alternative is to use multilevel reference books for a specific unit. You can have students write individual or small-group reports using reference books that are at their level. The librarian can be a valuable aide in gathering books at a variety of reading levels, and you may be able to store the multilevel reference books in your room while the students are working on their reports. Finally, you may wish to use a contract system rather than specific reports when your students are working in multilevel reference books.

Giving students reading material they can comprehend is absolutely fundamental for developing comprehension abilities. Berliner (1981) has defined "academic learning time" as "the time a student is engaged with academic materials or activities that yield a high success rate" (p. 211). In the Beginning Teacher Evaluation Study he reports, academic learning time was found to be consistently associated with student achievement, but considerable variance across classrooms in terms of this variable (from four to fifty-two minutes per day) was also found. Teachers can increase the amount of academic learning time related to comprehension by preparing students to read in terms of the reader-related variables discussed in Chapter Seven and by providing them with materials at an acceptable difficulty level. Each teacher must carefully consider the advantages and disadvantages of providing multilevel materials in his or her classroom.

STUDENT ASSESSMENT OF TEXT DEMANDS

Finally, the teacher is not the only one who should be aware of text differences. If students are to be actively in control of their own learning, then they must be given opportunities to select their own materials. Hansen (1987) reports that children can learn to select books at an appropriate level of difficulty. Moreover, she recommends giving students the opportunity to read books at various levels. She describes a classroom in which students are involved with reading "challenge books," the "books I'm workin' on," and "easy books" (p. 31). Labeling books in this way can begin to develop metacognitive awareness. Encouraging students to determine what makes the challenge book difficult or, conversely, what makes the simple book easy can begin to sensitize students to text demands so that they can become independent readers who can select their own reading material.

SUMMARY

The "readability" of the reading material affects whether or not it will be comprehended. Formulas that assess readability give the teacher one clue about the possible level of the material, but they do not consider many factors. A good teacher will assess the "processability" of the material by critically examining the microprocessing, integrative processing, macroprocessing, elaborative processing and metacognitive processing cues provided by the author. Also, prior-knowledge and motivational factors must be examined. A "readability checklist" is provided in this chapter to help the teacher assess these factors in content-area texts. It can help the teacher prepare prereading presentations and study guides that encourage students to use the cues that are present and help them to compensate for the cues that are missing. When an extreme mismatch occurs between the levels of the students and the materials, the teacher can provide alternative materials for the students to read. The goal is to increase the amount of time students spend engaged in successful comprehension tasks. Finally, students should be encouraged to select appropriate materials for themselves.

SELF-CHECK TEST

1. Define the following terms.

   academic learning time   multilevel textbook approach
   readability formulas   multilevel references
   readability checklist   challenge books

2. List twenty factors you would examine when assessing the "processability" of your materials.

3. Answer true or false.

   ____ (a) Readability formulas assess only microprocessing and integrative factors.

   ____ (b) The readability checklist should be used instead of a formula.

   ____ (c) If you find difficulties in a text, do not use it.

   ____ (d) You would rate a text the same regardless of what group of students is going to use it.

_____ (e) The readability checklist is primarily designed to help content-area teachers know how to teach with the reading materials at hand.

_____ (f) All students should read the same text.

SUGGESTED ACTIVITIES

1. Assess the processing demands of a content-area textbook or other expository assignment using the readability checklist, or assess the demands of narrative materials using the questions provided in the "processability" section of this chapter. What are the difficulties students might encounter as they use these materials? How can you help them? What are the strengths of these materials in terms of comprehensibility? How can you help students take advantage of these strengths?

2. Write your own "readability checklist" using any of the items suggested in this chapter and/or adding ones that are appropriate to your teaching situation.

3. After assessing the characteristics of a particular piece of reading material, write a prereading lesson that will help the students to comprehend better.

4. Find alternative materials for a specific unit in your regular content-area textbook. Make up parallel assignments and a list of concepts to be emphasized in the class discussion.

REFERENCES

Anderson, T. H. (1980). Student strategies and adjunct aids. In R. J. Spiro, B. C. Bruce, and W. F. Brewer (Eds.), *Theoretical issues in reading comprehension*. Hillsdale, N.J.: Lawrence Erlbaum.

Anderson, T. H., Armbruster, B. B., & Kantor, R. N. (1980). *How clearly written are children's textbooks? Or, of bladderworts and alfa* (Reading Education Report No. 16). Urbana-Champaign: Center for the Study of Reading, University of Illinois.

Berliner, D. C. (1981). Academic learning time and reading achievement. In J. T. Guthrie (Ed.), *Comprehension and teaching: Research reviews*. Newark, Del.: International Reading Association.

Bruning, R. H. (1970). Short-term retention of specific factual information in prior contexts of varying organization and relevance. *Journal of Educational Psychology, 61,* 186–192.

Chall, J. S. (1984). Readability and prose comprehension: Continuities and discontinuities. In J. Flood (Ed.), *Understanding reading comprehension*. Newark, Del.: International Reading Association.

Christie, D. G., & Schumacher, G. M. (1978). Memory for prose: Development of mnemonic strategies and use of higher order relations. *Journal of Reading Behavior, 10,* 337–344.

Daines, D. (1982). *Reading in the Content Areas: Strategies for Teachers*. Glenview, Ill.: Scott, Foresman.

Davison, A., Kantor, R. N., Hannah, J., Hermon, G., Lutz, R., & Salzillo, R. (1980). *Limitations of readability formulas in guiding adaptations of texts* (Technical Report No. 162). Urbana-Champaign: Center for the Study of Reading, University of Illinois.

Fishman, A. S. (1978). The effect of anaphoric references and noun phrase organization on paragraph comprehension. *Journal of Reading Behavior, 10*, 159–170.

Hansen, J. (1987). *When writers read*. Portsmouth, N.H.: Heineman.

Irwin, J. W. (1983). Coherence factors in children's textbooks. *Reading Psychology, 4*, 11–23.

Irwin, J. W., & Davis, C. (1980). Assessing readability: The checklist approach. *Journal of Reading, 24*, 124–130.

Irwin, J. W., & Pulver, C. (1984). The effects of explicitness, clause order, and reversibility on children's comprehension of causal relationships. *Journal of Educational Psychology, 76*, 399–407.

Kintsch, W. (1977). On comprehending stories. In M. A. Just and P. A. Carpenters (Eds.), *Cognitive processes in comprehension*. Hillsdale, N.J.: Lawrence Erlbaum.

Kintsch, W., & Miller, J. R. (1984). Readability: A view from cognitive psychology. In J. Flood (Ed.), *Understanding reading comprehension*. Newark, Del.: International Reading Association.

Kintsch, W., & Vipond, D. (June, 1977). Reading comprehension and readability in educational practice and psychological theory. Paper presented at the Conference on Memory, University of Uppsala, Sweden.

Klare, G. R. (1976). A second look at the validity of readability formulas. *Journal of Reading Behavior, 8*, 129–252.

Klausmeir, H., & Feldman, K. (1975). The effects of a definition and a varying number of examples and nonexamples on concept attainment. *Journal of Educational Psychology, 67*, 174–178.

Reder, L. (1978). *Comprehension and retention of prose: A literature review* (Technical Report No. 108). Urbana-Champaign: Center for the Study of Reading, University of Illinois.

Stein, N. L., & Nezworski, T. (1978). The effects of organization and instructional set on story memory. *Discourse Processes, 1*, 177–193.

Thorndyke, P. W. (1979). Knowledge acquisition from newspaper stories. *Discourse Processes, 2*, 95–112.

9

SITUATIONAL CONTEXTS: WHY, WHEN, AND WHERE ARE THEY READING?

Suppose you have prepared students to read in terms of strategies, prior knowledge, and motivation. You have examined the reading material and feel confident that no serious difficulties exist with its processability. Yet your students still cannot answer any of your postreading questions. What has gone wrong?

The answer is that you still must consider many other aspects of the situation. Did the students understand the purpose for reading, and did they know how to read for that purpose? Did your questions reflect the purpose? Were the questions understandable? Were the social, emotional, and physical environments during reading and testing ones in which they could perform their best? All of these "situational contexts" affect student performance and should be considered when giving assignments and when assessing comprehension. In addition, when students are involved in self-directed reading tasks, they need to know how to control these situational factors for themselves.

THE COMPREHENSION TASK

As discussed in Chapter Six, students can adjust their reading strategies according to the purpose for reading. Research seems to indicate that when students know the objectives of their assignment, they do better (Duchastel, 1979). Many students seem to read differently when they are expecting a test (Christie & Schumacher, 1978; Graesser, Higgenbotham, Robertson, & Smith, 1978), and they may process differently according to what type of test or task they are expecting (Fredericksen, 1975;

Mayer, 1975). All this indicates that having a clear purpose and an appropriate method are important components of successful comprehension tasks.

Reading Purposes

A reading "purpose" can be defined as either the new behavior the student expects to exhibit as a result of reading or the aesthetic experience he or she has during reading. Examples include the following:

1. After reading, the student will be able to describe the major parts of a cell.
2. After reading, students will be able to discuss their opinions on the morality of the issue.
3. During reading, the student will enjoy the story. (After reading, he or she will tell us if this was so and why.)
4. After reading, the student will understand why Johnny decided to steal the bread.

If the students are reading literature, you may wish to help them to use their own predictions to determine purposes like number 4 in the preceding list. Their purpose will probably also be to enjoy the story. Thus, they may wish to focus on the characters and events in the story for their own sake. If they are also involved in writing their own stories, they may wish to read to see how the author made the story enjoyable. You can probably think of other examples of purposes students choose for reading literary materials.

If the students are reading content-area materials, you may wish to clarify the purpose for them. You can give prereading questions with the direction to "read to find the answers to these questions." (You will want to make sure that these questions require processing the information rather than just rote recall—see Chapter Ten.) You can preview with them, telling them what they should learn from each section. Moreover, they will probably want to know what will be asked of them after reading. Will you be giving a test? Will they be doing an application activity?

Another alternative, however, is involving the students in setting their own content-area reading purposes. Ask them to preview the chapter or reading selection, and list some points they hope to learn. The K-W-L strategy presented in Chapter Seven provides a specific structure for this approach. As discussed in Chapter Two, comprehension is enhanced when readers are actively involved, and it is reasonable to assume that setting one's own purpose may increase the amount of active involvement.

Reading Strategies

The next step is finding a reading method appropriate for the intended purpose. Indeed, a reading "method" can be defined as the strategy selected to achieve the intended goal. Choosing an appropriate method is a metacognitive process. (See Chapter One for the definition of metacognitive processes.) This includes choices about reading rate (which may vary throughout the selection), study strategies (see Chapter Six), and the flexible use of various comprehension processes (for instance, if the purpose was to be able to diagram a cell, a student might wish to be sure to use mental imagery while reading, whereas if the purpose was to summarize an editorial, a student might make extra use of macroprocesses). Examples of methods specific students might select for specific purposes are given in Table 9-1. Study this chart and try to fill in three more of your own.

In studying Table 9-1, you probably noticed that, as mentioned in Chapter Six, to select an appropriate reading method, students must also consider the difficulty of the material in relation to their own skills and prior knowledge. The eighth-grade student with no background in current events had to study vocabulary and background with the help of resource people. A good reader with extensive background in current events could probably read quickly, jotting down a few key ideas for discussion.

Moreover, students vary in terms of their ability to be flexible in their approach to reading tasks. Thus, it would probably be useful to explain the concept of varying methods for varying purposes. Model your own procedure for choosing strategies. Eventually encourage them to choose their own strategies before reading. These discussions will increase metacognitive awareness as well as the ability to make metacognitive choices.

The Assessment Task

Finally, another component of many comprehension tasks in your classroom is the assessment method itself. Sometimes students understand the assignment but not the test. The method you choose to assess whether students have understood what they read should not introduce extraneous skills that do not have anything to do with comprehension. Make sure questions and directions are clear. For instance, if you are asking students to fill in a chart and they cannot do it, two possible reasons are: (1) they did not understand the material, or (2) they did not understand the chart.

Moreover, your assessment task should reflect the stated purpose. If you tell students to read for details and then give an essay test, they will be justifiably frustrated. The best procedure is to be consistent in purpose setting, discussing, and testing in terms of the mix of types of information requested. (See Chapter Ten for a taxonomy of questions based on the type of information requested.)

THE SOCIAL CONTEXT

Another major component of the situation in which comprehension is occurring is the social context. The relationship between the student and teacher or other listener,

TABLE 9-1 Examples of Typical School Reading Situations and Effective Reading Strategies

TYPE OF READER	TYPE OF READING MATERIAL	PURPOSE	STRATEGY
Kindergarten student	Picture book	For enjoyment	Look at the best picture. Make up a fun story.
First-grade student, average reading group, wants to succeed	Basal reader	To please teacher; to read aloud with perfect accuracy	Read slowly and carefully. Focus on every word; sound out unknown words.
Second-grade student, good reader, knows a lot about horses	Trade book about horses from school library; looks like easy reading	To give an oral report to the class about the book	Skip the boring parts. Read especially about the pictures so they can be shown. Read quickly, since most information is known already.
Third-grade student, interested only in baseball	First science textbook, section on the planets	To answer questions in the textbook	Look over the questions first. Read the section slowly, noting the subheadings. Use those to help locate the answers.
Fourth-grade student, average reader, generally does all right in math	Math text, section on multiplying fractions	Missed school; must read to do the homework problems	Read very slowly, making sure each sentence is completely understood. Study the examples in the text, step by step. Try practice problems when they are suggested.
Fifth-grade student, below average reader, little interest in history	Social studies textbook on American history, chapter on Constitutional Congress	To pass test	Take each section separately. Use the context to figure out the vocabulary. For each section, write down the key idea. Find someone to listen while you tell him or her what the chapter was about.

TABLE 9-1   (cont.)

TYPE OF READER	TYPE OF READING MATERIAL	PURPOSE	STRATEGY
Sixth-grade student, above-average reader, loves science, has chemistry set at home	Laboratory activity in science text on melting	To do lab the next day	Read each step while visualizing the activity. Make note of special warnings. Try to predict places where things could go wrong. Try to predict the results of each step.
Seventh-grade student, poor reader but very interested in this book	Adolescent novel	For enjoyment and for book report	Read straight through at your own pace in fairly long sittings. Let yourself "get into it"; worry about book report later.
Eighth-grade student, average reader but has little background in current events	Newspaper	To be able to discuss current events in social studies class the next day	Make a list of names, places, and vocabulary words that are causing you trouble. Get help with them from parents, friends, or the teacher the next day. For each major news item, make sure you understand the title and the first two paragraphs. Make a list of these as well. When possible, get background information from adults or older siblings.
Ninth-grade student, upper-level track, college-bound	*Moby Dick,* Chapter 1	To be able to discuss possible symbolism and potential themes	Read slowly circling figurative language and recurring images. Think about common themes in the images. What do they have to do with the action?

TABLE 9-1 (cont.)

TYPE OF READER	TYPE OF READING MATERIAL	PURPOSE	STRATEGY
Tenth-grade student, lower-level track	*Auto Mechanics* magazine	To find new things to do with recently pur- chased "antique" car	Look at the ads and the titles of the arti- cles. If anything seems "do–able," read carefully, picturing yourself doing it.
Eleventh-grade stu- dent, average reader, "C" student, not moti- vated in general	Chemistry textbook, a whole chapter	To understand what's going on in class	Use a systematic study system. Take notes, at least gen- eral ones. Keep a list of new vocabulary words. Find a friend to review the chapter with you. This may keep your interest up.
Twelfth-grade stu- dent, average reader, *no* interest in Shakespeare	Shakespearean play, one scene	For quiz	Read aloud, trying to use intonation. Try to visualize the action. If you can't tell what they are saying, think about what they might be saying and *then* see if that is right. Try to make it interesting by think- ing about how it would be today.

the classroom environment including the students' reading group if applicable, and community beliefs about schooling may all have an influence on how each student chooses to comprehend a text.

Teacher-Student Interactions

Mosenthal (1984) has suggested that

> while reading researchers have tended to define reading comprehension primarily in terms of text, task, and subject contexts, the most important context influencing reading comprehension in classroom lessons may be the interaction between the teacher and the students. (p. 17)

An example is provided by Mosenthal (1979). He found that the way students resolved contradictions in the text was different when the audience was second-graders from when it was the teacher. Moreover, this difference was different for third-grade readers and sixth-grade readers. Third-graders minimized text restructuring for the teacher as contrasted to when their audience consisted of second-graders; sixth-graders maximized it for the teacher as contrasted to when their audience consisted of second-graders.

Mosenthal and Na (1980b) divided students into three groups in terms of how they verbally interacted with the teacher: (1) imitative—students who generally added no information to teacher's utterances—(2)noncontingent response—students who would identify a new topic, often having little relation to the topic discussed by the teacher—and (3) contingent response—students who added new information that clarified or added to what the teacher said. The interesting finding was that differences also existed among these groups in terms of their recall in a normal reading lesson. The imitative group tended to recall stories literally; the noncontingent response group tended to elaborate and sometimes even to distort; and the contingent response group tended to include text-based inferences. Mosenthal (1984) concludes that "these findings emphasize the importance the interaction between the Audience and Reader Contexts plays in how students comprehend during reading lessons" (p. 23).

Finally, in a study comparing student recall in normal reading lessons, assumed to be low-risk situations, and testing situations, assumed to be high-risk situations, Mosenthal and Na (1980a) found that though responses in the low-risk situation tended to be related to the social interaction patterns described earlier, differences in performance in the testing situation appeared to be related to ability: average- and low-ability students tended simply to reproduce the text, whereas high-ability students used both reproductions and elaborations. Mosenthal and Na speculate that these differences reflect the poor- and average-ability students' desire to minimize risk in the testing situation and the high-ability students' desire to process the text fully.

The point of all this is that student comprehension will be affected by the social context in which it is occurring. This context includes the audience, the teacher-student relationship, and the purpose of the assessment interaction: Recall will be different with you from what it is with peers. For each individual, recall for you may be related to the way he or she usually relates to you. Moreover, students will report their recall differently in formal and informal situations.

The Reading Group

Finally, another social context to consider is the reading group. Evidence exists that teachers interact differently with different reading groups. Cazden (1981) reviews research that indicates that there may be a contrast between the foci of high and low reading groups: for the poorer readers, the focus is on decoding, whereas for the high group, the focus is on meaning. For instance, Allington (1978) found that the cues provided by the teacher to help students decode were different according to group. For the poorer readers, these tended to be letter-sound relationships; however, for the better readers, these tended to be semantic or syntactic cues. All this is cause for concern when viewed in light of the study by Anderson, Mason, and Shirey (1983) that found that a focus on meaning was more effective: their data support the conclusion "that a meaning emphasis gets better results than a word identification emphasis with poor readers as well as good readers" (p. 71).

Moreover, Cairney and Langbien (1989) have also summarized the results of research comparing the instruction received by high- and low-ability readers into several unfortunate differences: Poor readers are interrupted two to five times more, and often in the middle of sentences, whereas good readers are usually only corrected at the end of the sentence (Allington, 1980; Hoffman, et al., 1984). Poor readers are given less time to correct themselves (Pflaum, Pascarella, Bostwick, & Auer, 1980); read fewer words each day (Allington, 1977); do mostly oral reading (whereas good readers do mostly silent reading (Allington, 1983)); are given a decoding focus (see earlier); and are often given materials that are too difficult for them (Gambrell, Wilson, & Gantt, 1981). Each teacher who decides to use reading groups must monitor his or her attitudes toward individual groups. Do you expect these students to be able to comprehend? Are you encouraging it? Are you teaching with a meaning emphasis with all groups? Is grouping the best way to organize instruction for these children?

Classroom Environment

In the larger sense, the entire classroom environment can be considered part of the situational context. Recent research on environments conducive to learning indicates that such things as academic learning time (see Chapter Eight), academic focus, and teacher encouragement and direction seem to be related to achievement gains on tests (see Rosenshine, 1978). Even time of day has been shown to affect comprehension styles (Folkard, 1979). In Chapter Two of this text, it was pointed out that the degree of student control over the learning task, the amount and variety of printed material available to the students, and the degree to which diversity is respected are all examples of classroom factors that are likely to affect the amount of active involvement in comprehension. Although a thorough discussion of effective classroom environments is not possible here, it is important to note that the quality of the classroom environment in all of its academic, emotional, physical, and social aspects is likely to affect a student's comprehension performance.

The School and Community

It is impossible to understand the classroom environment without viewing it in the context of the school and the community. Such factors as school size, teacher characteristics, teacher morale, student body characteristics, administrative organization, flexibility of the programs, administrator-teacher rapport, and community-school relationships all contribute to the general school climate, which in turn affects the classroom environment (see Anderson, 1982).

Moreover, the type of community in which the school is situated is likely to have a powerful effect on students' concepts about reading. For instance, Heath (1983) found that in one working-class community children were praised for reading, whereas in another they were not. Anyon (1981) observed schools in four different types of communities, defined in her study as working class, middle class, affluent professional, and executive elite. She found that the definitions of school knowledge seemed to vary from one community to another: In the working-class school, emphasis was on rote learning of facts; in the middle-class school there was some recognition of general concepts and student creation of knowledge, although the emphasis was still on learning content. In the affluent professional school, however, the emphasis was on creative and critical thought; in the executive elite school, the emphasis was on reasoning and problem solving along with rigorous academics. These sorts of implicit community beliefs about education may be inhibiting good comprehension instruction in some communities, and all teachers would probably benefit from examining the beliefs about knowledge and literacy prevalent in the community in which they teach.

SUMMARY

Even if your students have the necessary abilities, schemata, and motivation for the assignment, comprehension problems may be present. These may arise if the purpose for reading is unclear, if students do not know how to read for the intended purpose, if the assessment introduces extraneous factors, if the assessment is unrelated to the original purpose, or if students are unable to perform well because of problems in the classroom environment. Moreover, the entire social context must be considered: the student's usual social patterns will affect what he or she will report in terms of recall, and this can be be affected by whether it is a formal (testing) or an informal setting. The students will comprehend better if some emphasis is on meaning, and teachers may wish to make this emphasis similar for all reading-ability levels. Finally, teachers should be aware of the definitions of literacy and the home literacy environments common in their students' communities, and they must be careful to ensure that all students are expected and encouraged to become active comprehenders.

SELF-CHECK TEST

1. What are the two major situational contexts described in this chapter? What are the components of each?

2. Answer true or false.

_____ (a) Most teachers treat all reading groups the same.

_____ (b) Poor readers should be taught decoding, not comprehension.

_____ (c) Testing brings out poor readers' ability to elaborate.

_____ (d) Purposes should be reflected in assessment tasks.

_____ (e) There are only three or four different ways to read.

_____ (f) Most students already know how to read for the stated purpose.

_____ (g) All U.S. communities probably define literacy the same.

3. To review Part Two, fill in the following outline.

  I. Reader Contexts
    A.
    B.
    C.
    D.
  II. Text Contexts
    A.
    B.
    C.
    D.
    E.
    F.
 III. Situational Contexts
    A.
      1.
      2.
      3.
    B.
      1.
      2.
      3.
      4.

SUGGESTED ACTIVITIES

1. Observe a teacher working with high- and low-ability reading groups. What are the differences between these groups in terms of what goes on in these sessions? How should these differences be minimized?

2. Observe a classroom teacher for an extended period. For each assignment, answer the following questions: Was the purpose made clear? Did the assessment match the purpose?

3. Observe a classroom teacher for an extended period of time. Describe the classroom environment from a social viewpoint. What is the relationship between the teacher and the students? How does this facilitate or hinder comprehension? What are the relationships among the students? How does this facilitate or hinder comprehension? What are the social uses of reading in the classroom? How is literacy defined in this classroom? You may wish to repeat this with another classroom to get a sense of how these factors differ in various classrooms.

4. If you are a classroom teacher, do Activity 1 by observing yourself.

5. If you are a classroom teacher, do Activity 2 by observing yourself.

6. If you are a classroom teacher, do Activity 3 by observing yourself and your students. Write in a journal every day for at least a week before coming to any conclusions.

REFERENCES

Allington, E. L. (1978, March). Are good and poor readers taught differently? Is that why poor readers are poor readers? Paper presented at the annual meeting of the American Education Research Association, Toronto.

Allington, R. L. (1977). If they don't read much, how they ever gonna get good? *Journal of Reading, 21*, 57–61.

Allington, R. L. (1980). Teacher interruption behaviors during primary grade oral reading. *Journal of Educational Psychology, 72*, 371–377.

Allington, R. L. (1983). The reading instruction provided readers of differing reading abilities. *Elementary School Journal, 83*, 548–559.

Anderson, C. (1982). The search for school climate: A review of the research. *Review of Educational Research, 52*, 368–420.

Anderson, R. C., Mason, J., & Shirey, L. (1983). *The reading group: An experimental investigation of a labyrinth* (Technical Report No. 271). Urbana-Champaign: Center for the Study of Reading, University of Illinois.

Anyon, J. (1981). Social class and school knowledge. *Curriculum Inquiry, 11*, 4–42.

Cairney, T. H., & Langbien, S. (1989). Building a community of readers and writers. *Reading Teacher, 42*, 560–567.

Cazden, C. B. (1981). Social context of learning to read. In J. T. Guthrie (Ed.), *Comprehension and teaching: Research reviews*. Newark, Del.: International Reading Association.

Christie, Daniel J., & Schumacher, Gary M. (1978). Memory for prose: Development of mnemonic strategies and use of higher order relations. *Journal of Reading Behavior, 10*, 337–344.

Duchastel, P. (1979). Learning objectives and the organization of prose. *Journal of Educational Psychology, 71*, 100–106.

Folkard, S. (1979). Time of day and level of processing. *Memory and Cognition, 7*, 247–252.

Frederiksen, C. H. (1975). Effects of context-induced processing operations on semantic information acquired from discourse. *Cognitive Psychology, 7,* 139–166.

Gambrell, L. B., Wilson, R. M., & Gantt, W. N., (1981). An analysis of task attending behaviors of good and poor readers. In Wilson, R. M. (ed.), *Diagnostic and remedial reading.* Columbus, Ohio: Charles E. Merrill.

Graesser, A. C., Higgenbotham, M. W., Robertson, S. P., & Smith, W. R. (1978). A natural inquiry into the national enquirer: Self-induced versus task-induced reading comprehension. *Discourse Processes, 1,* 355–372.

Heath, S. B. (1983). *Ways with words: Language, life, and work in communities and classrooms.* New York: Cambridge University Press.

Hoffman, J., O'Neal, S., Kastler, L., Clements, R., Segal, K., & Nash, M. (1984). Guided oral reading and miscue focussed verbal feedback in second-grade classrooms. *Reading Research Quarterly, 16,* 14–20.

Mayer, R. E. (1975). Forward transfer of different reading strategies evoked by testlike events in mathematics text. *Journal of Educational Psychology, 67,* 165–169.

Mosenthal, P. (1979). Children's strategy preference for resolving contradictory story information under two social conditions. *Journal of Experimental Child Psychology, 28,* 323–443.

Mosenthal, P. (1984). Reading comprehension research from a classroom perspective. In J. Flood (Ed.), *Promoting reading comprehension.* Newark, Del.: International Reading Association.

Mosenthal, P., & NA, T. J. (1980a). Quality of children's recall under two classroom testing tasks: Toward a socio-psycholinguistic model of reading comprehension. *Reading Research Quarterly, 15,* 501–528.

Mosenthal, P., & NA, T. J. (1980b). Quality of text recall as a function of children's classroom competence. *Journal of Experimental Child Psychology, 30,* 1–21.

Pflaum, S., Pascarella, E., Bostwick, M., & Auer, C. (1980). The influence of pupil behaviors and pupil status factors on teacher behaviors during oral reading lessons. *Journal of Education Research, 74,* 99–105.

Rosenshine, B. V. (1978). Academic engaged time, content covered, and direct instruction. *Journal of Education, 160,* 38–66.

10

ASKING QUESTIONS

In Part One of this book, you learned about specific processes involved in comprehension and some ways to help students to use those processes more effectively.
Chapter Two of that section provided some general teaching suggestions that were
exemplified throughout the other chapters. In Part Two, the factors that influence
how students will comprehend a specific assignment, and some related teacher
behaviors that can promote successful comprehension, were presented. Now it is
time to "put it all together" by looking at the application of these ideas to questioning,
assessment, and actual classroom situations.

One of the commonest ways to teach comprehension has been to ask questions
before, during, or after reading. Although the use of questions as the only way to
teach comprehension is currently being criticized, the use of questions as one part
of teaching comprehension still seems viable. As Pearson and Johnson (1978) have
said, "The issue is not whether or not to use questions, but how, when, and where
they ought to be used" (p. 154).

One of the problems with teacher questioning in the past is that many teachers
tended to ask trivial, literal recall questions most of the time (Guszak, 1967). Recent
research (Gambrell, 1987) indicates that, at least in basal reading lessons, teachers
rarely ask questions that require more than a word or phrase for a response. Because
many students tend to display the level of thinking required by the questions asked
(Hunkins, 1970), these are questionable procedures at best. The purpose of this
chapter is to suggest ways for teachers to plan and use questions that facilitate all
comprehension processes by actively involving the readers in constructing meaning.
(Questions are defined in this chapter rather broadly as "any intellectual exercise

calling for a response; this would include both problems and projects" as well as questions (Sanders, 1968, p. 2).

QUESTIONING TAXONOMIES

To improve teacher-made questions, several questioning taxonomies have been designed (Barrett, 1979; Sanders, 1968; and others). These taxonomies are useful for helping teachers to ask various types of questions. The categories listed in these taxonomies include such things as literal recognition or recall, inference, evaluation, and appreciation (Barrett, 1979) and memory, translation, interpretation, application, analysis, synthesis, and evaluation (Sanders, 1968). Note how these include higher-level thinking processes (see Chapter Five), though they are not strictly based on a complete cognitive model of the comprehension process itself.

A Question-Answer Relationship (QAR) Taxonomy

One possible exception to this is the taxonomy suggested by Pearson and Johnson (1978). In this taxonomy, questions are classified according to the relationship between the question and the source of the answer given, thus reflecting the process involved in going from text to response. This QAR taxonomy classifies questions according to whether the answer is taken from

1. Textually explicit information (TE)—that is, information that was directly stated in the text.
2. Textually implicit information (TI)—that is, information that was implied in the text.
3. Scriptally implicit information (SI)—that is, information already in the mind of the reader. (A script in this case is roughly equivalent to a schema, or prior knowledge of the reader.)

Examples of these types of QARs are provided in Figure 10-1. Study this example before reading further. Try classifying the last three QARs. The answers are at the end of the chapter. Note that you must know the answer before you can classify the question.

This taxonomy is easy to use and helps teachers remember that many questions that appear to be at a fairly low level still require inferences of textually implicit information. For instance, questions that require students to infer implicit connective concepts (such as question 2 in Figure 10-1) require a different process from those requesting explanations of explicitly stated connectives.

Unfortunately, though this taxonomy is appealing in its simplicity, this simplicity may limit its utility in helping you to write more diversified questions. For instance, this taxonomy makes no distinction between such things as connectives and main ideas. Thus, you might forget to ask about one or the other.

FIGURE 10-1   Examples of Questions Classified According to the QAR Taxonomy

Sally was very eager to get her birthday present. It was going to change her life. The present was 26 inches high and went fast. It meant she could get to school and to baseball practice in half the time. It was not an ugly red like John's. It was a beautiful yellow like daffodils and sunlight, which she loved. Yes, yellow was her favorite color anyway. It made her feel happy.

QUESTION	ANSWER	CATEGORY
1. How high was her present?	26 inches	TE
2. Why was she eager to get her present?	Because it was going to change her life	TI
	Because it was a bike and everyone loves bikes	SI
3. What is her present?	A bike	SI
4. Does John have a bike?	Yes, an ugly red one	TI
5. What was her favorite color?	Yellow	
6. Do you think Sally would like buttercups?	Yes, because they are yellow	
7. Why was yellow her favorite color?	Because it made her feel happy	

An Expanded QAR Taxonomy

A similar but more specific way to structure your questions is suggested by the subprocess model described in this book. You could probably write this taxonomy yourself. Just think about the QAR categories and how they relate to the processes described herein. Think about what kind of information can be textually explicit. Microlevel details, explicit connectives, and explicit main ideas and summaries would be examples that should come to mind. Now think about the processes you have studied in terms of what kinds of information can be textually implicit. What comes to mind? You will probably think of implicit connectives immediately, which should remind you of anaphora and slot-filling inferences. Then you may think of implicit main ideas and summaries. (Also, at the microlevel, figurative language often contains implicit information.) Finally, what process draws on scriptally implicit information? Right! Elaboration. Simple. Right?

In case you are getting a little confused, all of this is diagrammed for you in Figure 10-2. A category called "prereading prior knowledge" has also been added to remind you that you need to ask these kinds of questions as well. Take a minute to experiment with this new taxonomy, called EX-QAR because it expands on the original QAR taxonomy. Try writing questions for a story with which you are familiar. Do not worry if you think of a great question that cannot be easily classified. The purpose of this taxonomy is to stimulate teacher questions, not eliminate them. It could very well be a good question. Keep it. Also, remember that you cannot really

FIGURE 10-2 EX-QAR Taxonomy

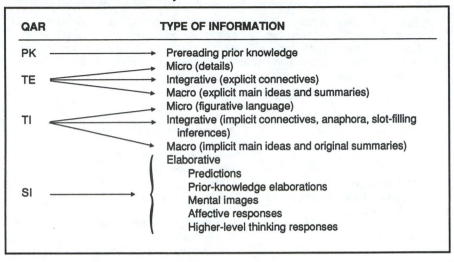

QAR	TYPE OF INFORMATION
PK ──────────────▶	Prereading prior knowledge
	──▶ Micro (details)
TE ◀══════════════▶	Integrative (explicit connectives)
	──▶ Macro (explicit main ideas and summaries)
	──▶ Micro (figurative language)
TI ◀══════════════▶	Integrative (implicit connectives, anaphora, slot-filling inferences)
	──▶ Macro (implicit main ideas and original summaries)
	Elaborative
	Predictions
SI ──────────────▶	Prior-knowledge elaborations
	Mental images
	Affective responses
	Higher-level thinking responses

finally classify your questions until you have the students' responses. Different students can answer the same question with different kinds of processes.

It would be unreasonable for you to ask all kinds of questions all the time. Just try to make sure that you ask those important for the specific reading situation and that, overall, you achieve a balance among the types of information and between the explicit and implicit categories. In other words, you need ask none of the types all of the time, but you should ask all the types some of the time!

The question also often arises as to which of the QARs are easier or for younger students and which are more difficult or are to be reserved for older students. Comprehension processes interact. *All students can be asked all types of questions.* Relative difficulty is more likely to be related to the actual content of the question and difficulty of the reading material than it is to question category. The important thing is to have prereading, study guide, postreading, and testing questions, when used, cover the same kinds of categories. If you ask microquestions in class and macroquestions on the test, you will be preparing your students for failure. (See Chapter Nine for a discussion of matching purpose and assessment.)

Now let us look at a seventh-grade teacher's actual questions planned according to the Ex-QAR taxonomy along with the students' answers (see Figures 10-3 and 10-4.) For the purposes of this example, more questions have been included than would probably be asked for such a short passage. Can you think of others? (You will note that this particular passage lent itself particularly well to TI-integrative QARs. Another passage might require more QARs in another category. This varies from passage to passage and from subject to subject.) Try to classify the last three questions in Figure 10-4 yourself. The answers are provided at the end of the chapter.

FIGURE 10-3   Possible EX-QAR Questions for Brief History Passage

This is what the students read:

England's religious problems. The people of England had long been members of the Roman Catholic Church, which was the only Christian church in western Europe. Englishmen, like other Roman Catholics, recognized the Pope as head of the church.

Then, in the 1530s, King Henry VIII led the people of England to break away from the Roman Catholic Church. He set up a church for England completely separate from the Roman Catholic Church. The church founded by King Henry VIII was called the Church of England, or the Anglican Church. The king was the head of the Church of England, as well as the head of the government of England.

Englishmen were not required to belong to the Church of England. But every Englishman had to pay taxes to help support it. And the government did not allow Englishmen to be members of any other church.

Yet many Englishmen did not like the Church of England. One group—the group that angered King James I—wanted to change the Church of England. These people were called *Puritans* because they wanted to "purify" the church. They wanted to change the way the church was organized under bishops. They also thought that certain church customs, such as kneeling, were wrong.

Another group did not stop at asking for changes. Unlike the Puritans, they wanted to separate from the Church of England and set up their own churches. These people were called *Separatists.*

The Pilgrims. Among the Separatists was a small group of people who lived in the English village of Scrooby. It was a pleasant little village where everyone knew everyone else. On Sunday, most of the villagers met at church to worship together. But the Separatists met by themselves and had their own kind of service.

The other people of Scrooby did not like this. Neither did the English government. Time and again, officials tried to make the Separatists of Scrooby worship according to the rules of the Church of England. The Separatists always refused. Finally, the officials acted. Some of the Separatists were put in prison and others had "their houses beset [surrounded] and watched day and night."

The Separatists of Scrooby made plans to leave England and go to the Netherlands. There the government was more tolerant, and the people could worship more freely. So in 1607–1608—just about the time the settlement of Jamestown was getting started—small groups from Scrooby left for the Netherlands.

Religious life in the Netherlands was better. But there were still problems. It was hard to live among foreign people and learn foreign ways. The Separatists were still Englishmen. It worried them to see their children growing up among the people of the Netherlands (called Dutchmen or the Dutch) and speaking the Dutch language.

The Pilgrims crossed the Atlantic. After 12 years in the Netherlands, the Separatists decided to go to America. There they could have their own church and still be Englishmen. They had to borrow money to buy supplies and get a ship. They got permission from the London Company to settle in its territories north of Jamestown.

A number of Englishmen who were not Separatists asked if they, too, might go along to start a new life in America. The leaders agreed. Since so many of the group were willing to go on a long journey for religious reasons—like a pilgrimage to a holy place—the whole group became known as the Pilgrims.

Source: Excerpt from AMERICA: ITS PEOPLE AND VALUES, Second Edition Revised, by Leonard C. Wood, Ralph H. Gabriel, and Edward L. Biller, copyright © 1979 by Harcourt Brace Jovanovich, Inc. Reprinted by permission of the publisher.

FIGURE 10-4   EX-QAR Questions and Answers for Brief History Passage

EX-QAR TYPE	QUESTION	ANSWER
TE—micro	Who lead the break from the Roman Catholic Church?	King Henry VIII.
SI—elaborative	Why do you think he wanted his own Church?	Because he wanted to have things his own way.
TI—macro	What groups did not like the Church of England, and what did they want?	The Puritans wanted to purify the Church and the Separatists wanted to have a church of their own.
TI—integrative	Why did the people of Scrooby not like the Separatists' meetings?	Because the Separatists met by themselves.
TI—integrative	Why were some Separatists put in jail?	Because they refused to worship according to the rules of the Church of England.
TI—integrative	Why did the Separatists go to the Netherlands?	Because that government was more tolerant.
	Why did they leave the Netherlands for America?	It worried them seeing their children growing up among the Dutch.
	Summarize the story of how the Pilgrims came to America.	They wanted to worship in their own way, but the people in their town would not let them. The Pilgrims moved to the Netherlands, but they were unhappy living among "foreigners" so they moved to America.
	What kind of people do you think the Pilgrims were?	They remind me of my friends last year…

When reading through these questions you probably got a sense of what it means to require students to use their "prior experience and the writer's cues to construct a set of meanings…" (see Chapter One). Certainly, students will have to be active comprehenders to answer these questions. Something could still be added to this lesson, however. The teacher has effectively assessed the product of the students' comprehension processes, but has comprehension been taught? Do the students know what processes to use to get from text and prior knowledge to the right answer? Have the questions reflected all the comprehension processes?

A Taxonomy for Process Questions

The answer, of course, is no. You probably noticed that none of these questions dealt with metacognitive processes. The reason they were left off the EX-QAR taxonomy is that they are so important that they deserve a taxonomy of their own. Metacognitive questions ask students about *how* they processed the information. Because they ask about comprehension processes, I introduced them in Chapter Two by calling them *process questions*. You could also call them metacognitive questions if you like.

Durkin (1981) has made a distinction between product and process questions. This distinction provides an important criticism of the Ex-QAR taxonomy and others like it. Product questions ask students to report the product of their comprehension process, for example, "Why didn't he cross the Delaware?" In contrast, process questions direct attention to the process used to answer the question, for example, "What do you need to know to understand how these sentences fit together?"

Situations may occur in which you would like to focus the students' attention on the processes they are using to arrive at their answers. This will especially be the case when they don't know the answers. A simple process questioning taxonomy can be used for these situations. Table 10-1 provides examples of process questions for each category. Study this table. Can you think of other process questions?

Let us look at our history lesson again, this time adding process questions (see Figures 10-5 and 10-6). Note the quality of comprehension instruction that can emerge when product and process questions are interleaved (a process-product processing procedure!?). Also note that when initial student answers are not quite accurate, the teacher can guide the students so they can see other ways of answering the question. In Chapter Two, this was discussed in terms of scaffolding and substantive feedback. (Refer back to that chapter if you do not remember these terms.)

In these examples, the teacher is asking questions that are directed toward teaching the students *how* to read for comprehension and recall. When you are first trying to teach a strategy using process questions, you may need to schedule extra time for class discussion, but the goal of these discussions as modeled here is to move

TABLE 10-1   Examples of Questions Categorized According to the Process Taxonomy

CATEGORY	SAMPLE QUESTIONS
Micro	1. What word is being used in a new way? 2. What else do you need to know to understand this sentence?
Integrative	1. How did you know what caused it to happen? 2. How did you know who "he" was?
Macro	1. How can you decide which sentence contains the main idea? 2. How should we go about writing a summary of this article?
Elaborative	1. What did you already know that led you to predict that this would happen? 2. What part painted a picture in your mind? How did it do this?
Metacognitive	1. What part made this hard for you to understand? 2. How might you go about reading this in order to achieve your goal?

FIGURE 10-5   Questioning Elaborative Processes

QAR TYPE	TEACHER	STUDENT
TE—Micro	Who led the break from the Roman Catholic Church?	The king.
SI—Elaborative	Why did he do this?	Because he was angry.
Elaborative—process	What makes you say that?	Because when my parents changed churches, it was because they were angry.
Substantive feedback, scaffolding	Very good! You have taken what you already know and applied it to this situation.	
	Let's look to see if there is anything in the passage that tells you if you are right. Everyone, read the second paragraph again.	I think it was because he wanted to be head of it.
Elaborative-process	What do you know that makes you say that?	Well, it says he was the head of it. He was probably one of those people who like to be the head of everything. I know a lot of people like that.
	I do, too. That's why that was the inference I made as well.	

the students toward independence. In the second example, for instance, we would hypothesize that the students would eventually move toward writing their own summaries. Then, discussion would consist of reviewing the important content and comparing summaries.

The point of all this is to show you how you can ask both product and process questions based on the model presented in this book. You will ask strictly product questions when you are trying to assess, review, or practice what students have learned, and you will mix in process questions when you are trying to teach a comprehension process as well. You will probably wish to follow some process questions with substantive feedback and scaffolding as needed (see Chapter Two). Both kinds of questions can be used in all types of classes.

PLANNING FOR QUESTIONING

You should probably do some planning for questioning as often as possible. Indeed, the purpose of a taxonomy as complex as the EX-QAR is to help you write good questions. Even if you do not get a chance to use all your questions, the thought processes that went into writing them will make you a better discussion leader. The point is not to ask all the questions you plan in some prespecified order. That would

FIGURE 10-6   Questioning Macroprocesses

QAR TYPE	TEACHER	STUDENT
Macroprocess	OK, then, how can we summarize this section?	Select the main things and combine the rest into general statements.
TE—Macro	What is the main idea of this section?	"Then, in the 1530s, King Henry VIII led the people of England to break away from the Roman Catholic Church."
Substantive feedback, scaffolding, and macro—process	Good—the break was the first main event. But that sentence has some details in it. Let's write an easier sentence for your notes. How can we simplify it?	How about using the next sentence, "The King of England started a church for England completely separate from the Roman Catholic Church?"
Substantive feedback, macro—process	Good—yes, that sentence seems to be more general and still captures all the main points. I like the way you substituted "the King of England" for "he." Is this better than saying "Henry VIII"?	I think so.
Macro—process	Why?	Because Henry VIII is a specific name. We want the general point.
	Very good! OK. I'll write the first sentence on the board while you write it in your notes.	
TE or TI—Macro	Now, what other main ideas do we need in our summary?	

lead to a stilted, boring discussion. You will need to be prepared to be flexible and to use teachable moments as they occur. However, having a stash of good questions will be a valuable resource.

For instance, you will probably want to plan to ask some prior-knowledge questions and some purpose-setting questions before reading. Cunningham (1981) points out that prior-knowledge questions must be simple and straightforward and free of technical terminology. The terminology can be checked, too, but if you try to separate concepts and vocabulary when possible, you will get a more accurate picture of what the students already know. For purpose-setting questions, it is important that you avoid focusing student attention too narrowly. Specific questions asked before reading are good for helping students retain specific information but are probably not the best if general recall is required (Singer & Donlan, 1980, p. 55).

It is possible to ask questions during reading using a study guide or a group reading strategy (see Chapter Two). These may be process or product questions, and, again, they should not be so specific as to actually reduce comprehension. Questions asked after reading should be of a variety of types and should encourage synthesis and review, depending on the purpose of the assignment.

Always consider your purpose for questioning. If you are trying to teach a reading strategy, you will ask more process questions. If you are trying to assess and review content, you will ask more product questions. If you want students to remember specific facts, you will ask more micro- and integrative questions than in other situations. If you are interested in encouraging creative applications, you will ask more elaborative questions than usual. Just remember that all comprehension processes interact. It makes no sense to say, "I'm only interested in elaboration. Their microlevel comprehension isn't important." Specific facts *are* the building blocks of elaborations! Similarly, it makes no sense to say, "I'm only interested in making sure they have the facts. I won't encourage elaboration and summarizing at all." Elaborations and summaries promote retention of specific facts.

INVOLVING STUDENTS IN QUESTIONING

Research seems to indicate that it may be useful to make students aware of whether the question is requiring that they use explicit, implicit, or prior-knowledge information (Raphael, 1981; Raphael & Wonnacott, 1981; Raphael & Pearson, 1982). Raphael (1981) taught students three question-answering strategies based on the Pearson and Johnson (1978) QAR questioning taxonomy: "Right There" (textually explicit), "Think and Search" (textually implicit), and "On My Own" (scriptally implicit). Results generally indicated that children from grades four to eight can learn these simple classifications and that this may improve their ability to answer questions.

In an update of her work in this area, Raphael (1986) has suggested several modifications. First, very young readers may learn better when a two-category distinction is introduced first—"In the Book" and "In My Head." In general, however, students find that this can be expanded into four categories (see Figure 10-7). In addition to "Right There" and "Think and Search," the "In My Head" category has been divided into the questions that require reference to something in the piece, "Author and You," and questions that can be answered without referring to the story, "On Your Own." The key to distinguising between these is helping the students determine if the question would make sense without reading the story. If so, then it is an "On Your Own" question. If not, then it is an "Author and You" question. When teaching these four question types to students, it is important to emphasize that the goal is *not* to classify questions but, rather, to determine what *strategy* the reader wants to use to answer it. (It is probably for this reason that, as

FIGURE 10-7   Relationships among Four Types of Question-Answer Relationships

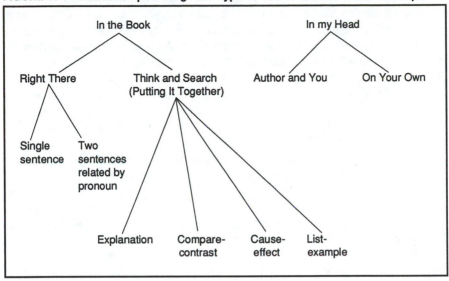

*Source:*T. E. Raphael, "Teaching Question-Answer Relationships Revisited," *Reading Teacher,* 40 (1986), p. 517. Reprinted with permission of Taffy E. Raphael and the International Reading Association.

you may have noticed, anaphora questions have been put in the "Right There" category in this new system.)

Another possibility that has not yet been researched is that of teaching students to identify questions according to whether they request micro-, integrative, macro-, or elaborative information. Smith (personal communication, 1983) reports that this has facilitated both comprehension and writing strategies with high-ability seventh-graders. If you have been directly explaining and modeling comprehension processes to your students as recommended in Chapter Two, then teaching them to identify questions in this way may follow naturally. You will need to simplify the terminology to "detail," "connection," "summary," and "elaboration." The point is to help students identify the *strategy* needed.

Related to teaching students to identify question types is teaching students to ask the questions. Kitagawa (1982) reports success with involving fourth-and fifth-grade students with asking the questions used for discussion. As Rycik (1982) points out, teacher questioning makes the focus of control for the reader's task external rather than internal. Involving students in asking questions can get them more actively involved in their own learning. The following activities are among those that can be suggested.

Reciprocal teaching.   One of the most successful remedial techniques involving students in asking questions has been *reciprocal teaching* (Palincsar & Brown, 1989). The purpose of this procedure is to teach children to regulate their own reading in ways used by good readers. First, the teacher models and then the children take turns leading discussions of brief portions of the text. The discussion leader (the teacher and then the students) begins by *asking questions* about what was read. The group answers the questions, and others may also suggest questions. Then, the discussion leader *summarizes* the portion read, and members of the groups can also offer contributions. At this point, if anything is unclear, then the group works on *clarifying* the ambiguity. Finally, the students *make predictions* about the next segment to be read. Over time, the teacher's role in the discussion shifts from modeling and leading the discussions to coaching only when needed.

The goal of reciprocal teaching is the internalization of the use of these strategies. You may note that these steps will include all the of processes described in this book if students are actively processing the text. The questioning and clarifying steps will often include discussions of micro- and integrative information. Summarizing is, of course, macroprocessing. Clarifying will encourage metacognition, and comprehension monitoring in particular. Finally, prediction is a form of elaboration.

The ReQuest procedure. Manzo (1969) has recommended a similar procedure of shared questioning in which the students and the teacher take turns asking and answering the questions. This "ReQuest procedure," as it is called, is suitable for all grades and types of texts. After each sentence is read, the books are closed and the students ask the teacher questions. When the students are done, the teacher asks the students questions. This procedure gives the teacher an opportunity to praise good questions and to model question-answering strategies as well as to ask questions. When the students can predict what will be in the rest of the selection, they can read to see if they are right.

Write your own test.   The test-writing activity mentioned in Chapter Three for teaching selection can also be used to involve students in writing questions. If you teach your students the categories of detail, connection, summary and elaboration, you can ask them to write test questions for each category. You can then construct the test with the students' questions. (You may wish to eliminate the "connection" category, because the text is generally necessary for identifying the distinction between it and the detail category.)

Study sessions.   After teaching the QAR question classification system, ask students to prepare three questions for each category while they are reading the assignment. Tell them that these questions will be used for study and review. After reading, divide the students into pairs. They can then take turns asking and answering questions.

A FINAL REMINDER

As you are working through these and other taxonomies, you will find that some questions are difficult to classify, or that you and someone else, or you and your students, disagree on the classification. This is true even for the taxonomies herein that take the question-answer relationship into account. One reason may be that any taxonomy that is usable is inevitably going to be incomplete. It should not be a point of concern, however, because the purpose of the taxonomies is to provide a stimulus for writing a variety of teacher questions (Ex-QAR) and ideas for student question-answering strategies (Raphael's (1986) QAR, for instance).

SUMMARY

Because teachers have had a tendency to ask mostly literal-level, short-answer questions, taxonomies for writing various types of questions have been developed. The QAR taxonomy designed by Pearson and Johnson (1978) represents the first such taxonomy to focus on the relationship between the text and the answer. Because this taxonomy does not include mention of the processes discussed in this book, a similar but expanded taxonomy that includes process categories has been presented. This taxonomy should be useful for writing questions that assess and guide student comprehension. For directly teaching specific comprehension processes, a process questioning taxonomy was also suggested. In addition, some procedures for involving students in classifying and asking questions were given. Involving students in this way again encourages them to become actively involved in their own learning.

SELF-CHECK TEST

First, answer the following questions. Then, classify them according to the taxonomies presented in this chapter.[1]

a. What is the difference between a product question and a process question?

b. What should you do to find out what kind of question deals with anaphora?

c. What were the main points of the chapter?

d. How can you go about answering question (c)?

e. How do these new taxonomies compare to Bloom's or some other taxonomy you have already studied?

f. What are the advantages and disadvantages of the QAR taxonomy?

---

[1]See discussion in "A Final Note" regarding ambiguities in this exercise.

g. What are the best ways to learn to use the taxonomies presented in this chapter?

h. In general, what is the ReQuest procedure?

SUGGESTED ACTIVITIES

1. Classify a group of the questions used in the basal reader or in a content-area text you do or might use. What other kinds of questions would you like to ask? Write a sample lesson in which *you* write the questions!

2. Conduct a small-group discussion in which you use both product and process questions. Keep track of whether students answered the questions in the QAR that you predicted.

3. Write a set of questions for a short reading task using the QAR taxonomy. Then classify those questions according to the Ex-QAR taxonomy. Fill in other questions suggested by the expanded taxonomy.

ANSWERS TO FIGURE 10-1:

5. TE.

6. SI.

7. TI.

ANSWERS TO FIGURE 10-4:

TI—integrative (implicit connective).

TI—macro (implicit summary).

SI—elaboration (higher-level thinking).

REFERENCES

Allington, R. L. (1983). A commentary on Nicholson's critique of Thorndike's Reading as reasoning—A study of mistakes in paragraph reading. In L. Gentile, M. Kamil, & J. Blanchard (Eds.), *Reading research revisited*. Columbus, Ohio: Charles E. Merrill.

Barrett, T. (1979). Taxonomy of reading comprehension. In R. Smith & T. C. Barrett (Eds.), *Teaching reading in the middle grades*. Reading, Mass.: Addison-Wesley.

Cunningham, J. W. (1981). How to ask questions before, during, and after reading. In E. K. Dishner, T. W. Bean, & J. E. Readence (Eds.), *Reading in the content areas: Improving classroom instruction*. Dubuque: Kendall/Hunt.

Durkin, D. (1981). Reading comprehension instruction in five basal reader series. *Reading Research Quarterly, 16,* 515–544.

Gambrell, L. (1987). Children's oral language during teacher directed reading instruction. In J. E. Readance & R. S. Baldwin (Eds.), *Research in literacy: Merging perspectives* (36th Yearbook, pp. 195–200). National Reading Conference.

Guszak, F. J. (1967). Teacher questioning and reading. *Reading Teacher, 21,* 227–234.

Hunkins, F. P. (1970). Analysis and evaluation questions: Their effects upon critical thinking. *Educational Leadership, 3,* 699–705.

Kitagawa, M. M. (1982). Improving discussions or how to get the students to ask the questions. *Reading Teacher, 36,* 42–45.

MacGinite, W. H. (1983). A critique of "What classroom observations reveal about reading comprehension instruction" and "Reading comprehension instruction in five basal reader series": Durkin's contribution to our understanding of current practices. In L. Gentile, M. Kamil, & J. Blanchard (Eds.), *Reading research revisited.* Columbus, Ohio: Charles E. Merrill.

Manzo, A. V. (1969). ReQuest: A method for improving reading comprehension through reciprocal questioning. *Journal of Reading, 12,* 123–126, 163.

Palincsar, A. S., & Brown, A. L. (1989). Classroom dialogues to promote self-regulated comprehension. In S. Brophy (Ed.), *Teaching for understanding and self-regulated learning* (Vol. 1,). JAI Press.

Pearson, P. D., & Johnson, D. D. (1978). *Teaching reading comprehension.* New York: Holt, Rinehart and Winston.

Raphael, T. E. (1981, April). The effect of metacognitive training on children's question-answering behavior. Paper presented at the annual meeting of the American Educational Research Association, Los Angeles.

Raphael, T. E. (1986). Teaching question-answer relationships revisited. *Reading Teacher, 40,* 516–522.

Raphael, T. E., & Pearson, P. D. (1982). *The effect of metacognitive awareness training on children's question-answering behavior* (Technical Report No. 238). Urbana-Champaign: Center for the Study of Reading, University of Illinois.

Raphael, T. E., & Wonnacott, C. A. (1981, December). The effect of metacognitive awareness training on question-answering behavior: Implementation in a fourth grade developmental reading program. Paper presented at the annual meeting of the National Reading Conference, Dallas, Texas.

Rycik, J. A. (1982). What, no questions? *Journal of Reading, 26,* 211–213.

Sanders, N. (1968). *Classroom questions: What kinds?* New York: Harper & Row.

Singer, H., & Donlan, D. (1980). *Reading and learning from text.* Boston: Little, Brown.

11

INFORMAL COMPREHENSION ASSESSMENT

Traditional measures of comprehension ability provide general indications of how well students can comprehend as compared to their peers. Unfortunately, however, knowing how well a student comprehends on a test tells you little about what sort of instruction to provide. It also gives you no situation-specific information: Can the student understand fiction better than nonfiction? Was prior knowledge a problem? Is his or her comprehension improved when the purpose is stated? and so forth.

This chapter presents some informal assessment ideas that can be used to supplement the information gained from traditional tests of comprehension ability. A multiple-context approach using observations of natural reading tasks is recommended. Teachers are urged to be observant but cautious in their conclusions.

TRADITIONAL MEASURES OF COMPREHENSION ABILITY

In most traditional tests of comprehension, including diagnostic tests, group standardized tests, and informal reading inventories, comprehension is measured by a cloze task (students fill in blanks where words have been omitted), multiple-choice questions, or short-answer questions. Cloze has the problem of measuring primarily lower-level skills (McCan, 1983; Shanahan, Kamil, & Tobin, 1982), and it is not really a natural reading task. Multiple-choice questions usually test recognition comprehension only, and short-answer questions lack the reliability of more objective formats. Thus no one testing format is ideal.

Moreover, these standardized testing procedures must be interpreted in light of several other serious limitations. First, because of time restraints, only short passages are generally used; this limits the degree of macroprocessing that can occur. Second, for similar reasons, all different types of passages are usually mixed together, so it is difficult to assess text-specific effects. Finally, prior knowledge is not generally assessed or controlled, so it is reasonable to assume that the students' final scores are heavily loaded on this factor (see Johnston, 1984; Royer & Cunningham, 1981).

Recently, several states have attempted to overcome these limitations by designing their own tests to measure reading ability. The Michigan Educational Assessment Program has undergone an extensive revision in which test items are designed to measure background knowledge ("topic familiarity"), "constructing meaning," "knowledge about reading," and "attitudes and self-perceptions." Also, the reading selections on these tests are full-length examples of real classroom materials (Wixson & Peters, 1987; Wixson, Peters, Weber, & Roeber, 1987). Similar efforts are under way in Illinois (see Valencia & Pearson, 1987). These tests are still the exception, however, and you will probably still find it useful to supplement these standardized test scores with informal observations of your students' comprehension strategies.

INFORMAL ASSESSMENT FOR THE CLASSROOM TEACHER

The classroom teacher has the chance to observe each student in a variety of situations. This allows the teacher to draw conclusions about student performance relative to type of material, task characteristics, and so on. For instance, you may discover that although Johnny scores poorly on standardized tests, he can read materials at grade level when he is highly motivated; Janice does very well in the basal reader but has trouble with content-area materials, probably because of a lack of background knowledge; Sam does very poorly on tests, probably because of anxiety, but he can answer comprehension questions in informal or one-to-one situations; and so on. This *multiple-context approach* can help you to begin to consider a student's comprehension ability in terms of the total context involved in each task. Research indicates that students do perform differently according to a combination of factors such as task and passage type (Hunter, Kendall, & Mason, 1979), and as Johnston (1987) has suggested, the skilled classroom teacher may be the best person to assess these factors.

Moreover, one problem with writing a chapter on assessment is the implication that diagnosis and instruction can or should be separated. Clearly, the best diagnostic information is gathered during teaching situations in which the students are trying to comprehend for meaningful purposes. Many of the activities suggested throughout this book for teaching comprehension will also yield important information about students' reading abilities. For instance, the reading-response journal (see Chapter

Five) will provide numerous insights into student reading strategies. Can they summarize? Are they picking out important ideas? What kinds of elaborations are they using? Involving students in mapping will give you insights into their use of organization (see Chapter Four). Macrocloze and other story structure activities will help you to assess their awareness of story structure (see Chapter Four). K-W-L will give you insights into their prior knowledge (see Chapter Seven). Reciprocal teaching will give you insights into the strategies they use for predicting, summarizing, and clarifying. Indeed, most of the activities you might use will give you useful assessment information.

If you wish to focus your attention on a specific child, you may want to use "ethnographic notetaking" (Smith, 1988). Smith (1988) defines this as "a system of taking repeated and detailed notes about a subject or subjects in a single environment, for a specified time" (p. 171). These detailed notes can be supplemented by video and audio taping if this is not intrusive. As the collection of observations continues, the teacher can hypothesize about the student's attitudes and abilities and then revise and refine these hypotheses as more situations are observed. My own experience with teachers taking such notes is that it is essential to write as much as possible as often as possible. Then, when you are away from the pressures of the classroom, you can read and reflect on your notes.

It is absolutely necessary to exercise great caution in coming to any diagnostic conclusions because many factors affect performance. A student who appears to remember nothing may simply be shy. A student who remembers only details may have concentrated attention on those only because he or she thought that was what you wanted. A student who misses literal questions may have a vocabulary problem, not a microprocessing one per se. The safest approach probably is to avoid all definite conclusions about any child and to teach all aspects of comprehension to all students as much as possible using materials at their level as determined by a combination of testing results and your observations. Of course, occasionally, specific instructional needs of specific students will become so obvious that you would be remiss in not giving those students strategy-specific instruction. This is as it should be. Quite simply, it is recommended that individualized assessment and individualized sub-process instruction not be adopted as a general classroom procedure until we know more about testing and teaching than we know now.

THE COMPREHENSION ASSESSMENT CHECKLIST

One format that has been used to help remedial and classroom teachers to summarize their observations of student abilities is given in Figure 11-1. This "Comprehension Assessment Checklist" is designed to remind you to consider all the comprehension contexts that may be affecting performance. It begins by encouraging you to assess the specific text and situation that are affecting the student's performance. Only then can you assess the student's responses in relation to these. Take a minute to study

FIGURE 11-1   Comprehension Assessment Checklist

Name or Group _____

Assignment _____
_____

Date _____

Directions: For each item, rate your student(s) according to the scale below. A rating of 3 or lower indicates a need for remediation. Remember, you are trying to understand why there have been problems in a specific situation, so be sure to answer in terms of the specific student(s) reading the specific material(s) in the specific situation.

Student(s) has(have)...

    5   No problems in this area.
    4   Only a few problems in this area.
    3   Some problems in this area.
    2   Many problems in this area.
    1   Very serious problems in this area.
N/A   not applicable (for instance, several items cannot be answered if the student read silently).

SITUATION-RELATED FACTORS

____ 1. Was the *physical environment* during reading quiet, well lighted, comfortable, etc.?

____ 2. Was the *teacher-student relationship* one in which the student felt comfortable?

____ 3. Was the situation one in which the *anxiety* level was at a minimum?

____ 4. Was the *purpose* for reading clearly stated?

____ 5. Did the *teacher expect* the student to be able to understand the material?

____ 6. Was the *teacher prepared* to assess the student's comprehension (e.g., familiar with passage, questions ready)?

____ 7. Was the student able to answer in the *format* for assessment (multiple choice, analogy, free recall, written short answer, etc.) that you provided?
        Consider the following:
        (a) Did the student have prior experience with the format?
        (b) Was there an extraneous skill being tested (e.g., talking in front of a group, writing ability, reasoning beyond the passage, using new equipment) that the student has not mastered?

____ 8. Were the questions and/or directions in the *assessment* themselves *understandable?*
        Consider the following:
        (a) Did the student understand exactly what was expected in the questions and/or directions?
        (b) Did the questions and/or directions meet the criteria in the text-related factors section? (see following)

TEXT-RELATED FACTORS

____ 1. Was the *readability* level appropriate for the student?

____ 2. Was the *vocabulary* in the passage sufficiently concrete and familiar for the student?

____ 3. Were any *sentences* unreasonably lengthy?

____ 4. Were the *relationships* between individual sentences stated explicitly?

____ 5. Was the *organizational pattern* sufficiently simple and explicit?

____ 6. If *new concepts* were introduced, was there a sufficient description and/or a sufficient number of examples provided for each?

____ 7. Was the *amount of material* to be remembered manageable (e.g., was the length of the passage appropriate)?

READER-RELATED FACTORS
Was the student...
____ 1. *healthy* and well rested?
____ 2. able to read the individual *words* accurately and easily?
____ 3. able to group the words into meaningful *phrases* and read with proper *intonation?*
____ 4. able to draw on adequate *prior knowledge* of this topic including a knowledge of the general and specialized vocabulary?
____ 5. able to identify *main ideas* whether they were stated explicitly or not?
____ 6. able to *summarize?*
____ 7. able to recall the *sequence* of important events?
____ 8. able to explain important *cause-effect relationships* whether they were stated explicitly or not?
____ 9. more likely to recall *important details* than unimportant details?
____ 10. able to identify *pronoun* referents?
____ 11. able to understand the *figurative language* in the passage?
____ 12. able to make *text-based inferences?*
____ 13. able to make *predictions* and/or draw *conclusions?*
____ 14. able to limit *elaboration* to those helpful in understanding and recalling the author's message?
____ 15. able to *adjust* his or her reading *strategies* according to the purpose selected?
____ 16. able to read at an appropriate *rate?*
____ 17. able to *attend* to such a task for the required amount of time?
____ 18. aware when he or she had *not* understood something?
____ 19. *expecting* to be able to understand the material?
____ 20. *interested* in the material?
____ 21. *motivated* to try to understand and recall?
____ 22. free from *emotional* problems that might have interfered with concentration?

SUMMARY
Now, in general, what situation-related factors (if any) were causing problems?

Now, in general, what text-related factors (if any) were causing problems?

Now, in general, what reader-related factors (if any) were causing problems?

What can you do to alleviate these problems?

Source: J. W. Irwin, C. Pulver, and K. Koch, "A New Technique for Improving Reading Teachers' Diagnoses," Unpublished manuscript, (Chicago: Loyola University of Chicago, 1983). Reprinted by permission.

the checklist. Like many of the other aids provided in this book, it follows naturally from the process approach, and, if you have read the previous chapters, you would probably have written something similar yourself.

This checklist seems to be particularly useful for working with a new or a particularly puzzling student. There are so many things to consider that it is all too easy to forget some of them! We have also found that this checklist can be a useful exercise in training yourself to be a better diagnostician. Try using it to teach yourself to think of these things automatically. Finally, this checklist can be useful in helping you plan instruction for an individual or for a whole class. Checklist results often help to point out that if you provide certain kinds of assistance, such as background knowledge or clearly stated purposes, then students will be able to comprehend better.

OBSERVATION IN REMEDIAL SITUATIONS

In a remedial or one-to-one situation, you can gather situation-specific information by planning and administering student-specific assessment activities in which you try to observe the student's ability to use the various comprehension processes in various realistic situations.

The first step in planning your observation is selecting a variety of contexts in which you would like to observe the student's reading behavior. You will need to consider (1) relevant aspects of texts such as content area, difficulty level, and organization; (2) different purposes relevant for that student's goals; and (3) reader characteristics (prior knowledge, motivation, decoding ability) relative to (1) and (2). The use of various natural tasks with passages long enough for macroprocessing will provide information not available on standardized tests.

For instance, suppose you have been asked to tutor Sally, a sixth-grade student who, on a recently administered standardized test, scored on grade level for decoding ability but at the low fourth-grade level for comprehension ability. What tasks would you like to give Sally to do so that you can observe her comprehension abilities? Well, you may want to use a fourth-grade–level story about something in which she is interested to see if she can read for fun. You may want to have her read an assignment in her classroom social studies textbook, one that she needs to read for class. You may want also to try an easier content-area book, a story she isn't interested in, or a piece of nonfiction about a familiar topic. You may wish to have something read aloud so you can listen to her intonation and fluency and so you can ask questions at selected points.

For each task you choose, you will want to prepare ways to assess the effectiveness of her processing abilities. You will want to assess prior knowledge directly. You may wish to use free recall (discussion in the next section) or to design questions according to the product and process questioning taxonomies presented in Chapter Ten. You may wish to ask the student for self-reported information about strategies, prior knowledge, motivation, and expectations. The comprehension assessment checklist (see Figure 11-1) has been used by remedial teachers as an aid for planning such informal assessment procedures.

While the student is engaged in the natural reading tasks you have provided, keep notes of your observations. Establish rapport. Make sure your directions are clear. Involve the student in his or her diagnosis. Tape-record free recall. Keep a record of reading times. Use the comprehension assessment checklist (see Figure 11-1) to structure your data summary.

ANALYSIS OF FREE RECALL

Of course, asking questions can be an effective way of assessing student comprehension. Another way of examining what a student has comprehended is to ask the student to tell you in his or her own words what was said in the passage. Students should be told ahead of time that they will be asked to retell the content of the passage, and you will probably want to tape-record the student's recall for later analysis.

For a long passage, listening to a student's recall would give you insight into the student's macroprocessing abilities, especially his or her ability to summarize. For shorter passages, you can examine the student's ability to select important details. The theory is that what the student says in this unprompted situation is what he or she has encoded into memory, but it is important to remember that what the student says may also be affected by what he or she thinks you want to hear. Students may report only facts because they think that that is what is appropriate in a testing situation. Remember to consider the text and the total situation before drawing conclusions about the reader!

Irwin and Mitchell (1983) have recommended using a holistic approach to evaluate the "richness of retellings" (p. 394). They believe that each retelling is too individualistic to conform to predetermined systems that delineate exactly what ideas the student should recall. Their system is described in Figures 11-2 and 11-3. Each retelling can be assigned a level according to these criteria. In this system, the student is given credit for including summarizing statements and other relevant "generalizations beyond text" (elaborations) and "supplementations" (inferences).

Finally, another way to examine a student's free recall is to answer the questions given in Figure 11-4. These questions direct you to try to infer what you can about the student's processing abilities. As with the aforementioned procedures, your answers will be subjective and situation specific and should *not* be used as a test score. Rather, they should help you hypothesize about instructional procedures that might help the student. Other suggestions for using retellings as a diagnostic tool can be found in Morrow (1988).

FIGURE 11-2   Judging of Richness of Retellings

LEVEL	CRITERIA FOR ESTABLISHING LEVEL
5	Student generalizes beyond text; includes thesis (summarizing statement), all major points, and appropriate supporting details; includes relevant supplementations; show high degree of coherence, completeness, comprehensibility.
4	Student includes thesis (summarizing statement), all major points, and appropriate supporting details; includes relevant supplementations; shows high degree of coherence, completeness, comprehensibility.
3	Student relates major ideas; includes appropriate supporting details and relevant supplementations; shows adequate coherence, completeness, comprehensibility.
2	Student relates a few major ideas and some supporting details; includes irrelevant supplementations; shows some degree of coherence; some completeness; the whole is somewhat comprehensible.
1	Student relates details only; irrelevant supplementations or none; low degree of coherence; incomplete; incomprehensible.

5 = highest level, 1 = lowest level.

Source: P. A. Irwin and J. N. Mitchell, "A Procedure for Assessing the Richness of Retellings," *Journal of Reading,* 26 (1983), 394. Reprinted by permission of the authors and the International Reading Association.

FIGURE 11-3   Checklist for Judging of Richness of Retellings

	5	4	3	2	1
Generalizes beyond text	X				
Thesis (summarizing) statement	X	X			
Major points	X	X	X	?	?
Supporting details	X	X	X	X	?
Supplementations	Relevant	Relevant	Relevant	Irrelevant	Irrelevant
Coherence	High	Good	Adequate	Some	Poor
Completeness	High	Good	Adequate	Some	Poor
Comprehensibility	High	Good	Adequate	Some	Poor

The matrix describes the evaluation of retellings in a holistic fashion on the basis of criteria, similar to a procedure used to grade written compositions. This technique is an alternative to questioning for assessment of student comprehension of both narrative and expository text.

Source: P. A. Irwin and J. N. Mitchell, "A Procedure for Assessing the Richness of Retellings," *Journal of Reading,* 26 (1983), 395. Reprinted by permission of the authors and the International Reading Association.

THINK-ALOUD PROCEDURE

One potentially diagnostic reading activity that has not been mentioned previously in this text is the "think-aloud" procedure. In this activity, the student is asked to voice his or her thoughts periodically during reading. This "thinking aloud" could

FIGURE 11-4   Free Recall Processing Checklist

Answer each of these questions according to the following scale:

    5   Yes, very well
    4   Yes, more than adequately
    3   Yes, adequately
    2   No, not too well
    1   No, poorly
    NA Not applicable or can't tell

1. _____ Did the student recall a sufficient number of ideas?
2. _____ Did the student recall the ideas accurately?
3. _____ Did the student select the most important details to recall?
4. _____ Did the student understand explicit pronouns and connectives?
5. _____ Did the student infer important implicitly stated information?
6. _____ Did the student include the explicitly stated main points?
7. _____ Did the student create any new summarizing statements?
8. _____ Did the student use the organizational pattern used by the author?
9. _____ Did the student elaborate appropriately?
10. _____ Did the student know how to adjust strategies to the purpose given?

What effective comprehension processes were evident in the student's recall?

What comprehension processes were not evident, or seemed to be causing problems?

To what extent was the student's performance as just described affected by each of the following?

1. Limited prior knowledge or vocabulary.
2. Limited motivation or interest.
3. Cultural differences.
4. Decoding problems.
5. Difficulties in the text.
6. Social context.
7. Discomfort with the task.
8. Other environmental influences.

occur after every sentence or every paragraph. It is helpful for the teacher to model the procedure first. Myers and Lytle (1986) suggest that this is an important part of "process assessment." Teachers can gain useful insights into their students' processing strategies by carefully listening to what they say during this procedure. Figure 11-5 shows the kinds of observations that can be made, although for diagnosis you would probably be working with one student at a time.

Lytle (1982) has suggested that there are six categories of statements made during this procedure: (1) monitoring of doubts (e.g. "I don't understand..."); (2) signaling understanding (e.g. "now, I know..."); (3) analyzing text features (e.g. "I see how this text is organized..."); (4) elaboration of the text (e.g. "this makes me think of..."); (5) judgments of the text (e.g. "I like this part..."); and (6) reasoning (e.g. "I can figure this out by..."). In her study, she found that secondary-level readers had specific "styles" of verbalized strategies that remained fairly consistent across

FIGURE 11-5   Example of Group Think-Aloud

> (See story in Figure 4-1. Parts read are in italics.)
> Teacher: "*Once there was a very tall girl named Alice.* Well, we really don't know much from that except that she is tall."
> Observation: This teacher has begun by using microselection to highlight what was important in the first sentence.
> Student 1: "*Alice was the tallest girl in her class.* They certainly are making a big thing about her being tall. I think something is going to happen because of it."
> Observation: This student is analyzing the text (higher-level thinking) and predicting.
> Student 2: "*All of her classmates made fun of her.* That makes me think of when we teased Sally because she was tall in the first grade. Now she isn't any taller than anyone else. Maybe that will happen to Alice."
> Observation: This student is using prior-knowledge elaborations to make a prediction.
> Student 3: "*This made her feel bad.* Of course. I really don't like this story. So far it isn't very happy."
> Observation: This student is reacting affectively.
> Student 4: "*She even tried walking with her knees bent.* That must have really looked funny."
> Observation: This student is probably getting a mental image.

different texts. In Figure 11-5, the teacher is monitoring doubt and signaling understanding. Student 1 is analyzing the text and elaborating. Student 3 is making a judgment of the text, and students 2 and 4 are elaborating.

It should be noted that think-aloud activities can also be recommended as classroom teaching procedures (Brown & Lytle, 1988). Several procedures discussed earlier in the book, like modeling (Chapter Two) and reciprocal teaching (Chapter Six) also involve some kinds of thinking aloud. When students think aloud or hear others think aloud, their metacognitive awareness of options for responding to text increases. It can also help them to become aware of how much thinking goes into comprehending a text. Students can take turns talking after each sentence is read until they are so involved in the reading that they would like to finish silently. Predictions and other elaborations that are shared in this way then become a part of the meaning that is being created in a shared comprehension activity. Figure 11-5 gives a simple example of what might be said in a think-aloud activity. Even in this simple example, the active thinking that this procedure stimulates is apparent.

PORTFOLIO ASSESSMENT

One of the most exciting recent developments in assessment procedures is portfolio assessment (see Winograd & Paris, 1988). In portfolio assessment, examples of student work are assembled into a portfolio that can be examined periodically to make instructional decisions throughout the school year. Portfolios can contain reading-response journals and other reading-related writing or drawing projects, lists of books read, lists of topics in which the student is interested, checklists designed to measure reading attitude and behavior, results of retellings, and audio and video tapes in which the students are reading. Many teachers have found that when students' written reading responses, lists of books read, and audio tapes are compared from different times of the year, striking differences in reading ability are often apparent. Such qualitative comparisons can be helpful for deciding on student placement or for conferencing with parents, for instance, and they provide a useful alternative to reporting test scores for these purposes.

STUDENT SELF-ASSESSMENT

One of the many benefits of portfolio assessment is that it provides a way to involve the student in self-assessment. As Johnston (1987) says, "process oriented evaluation strongly emphasizes the development of continual self evaluation so that learners may be responsible for and direct their own learning" (p. 747). Students can be involved in periodic reviews of their portfolios as well as decisions about what the contents of these portfolios might be. They can be directed to self-assessment with a checklist of questions like the following: Have I been reading more books than I used to? Am I enjoying reading more than I used to? Are my reading responses more interesting than they used to be? In what way? Have my reading interests changed? Does my oral reading show that I can read with expression? What would I like to improve about my reading? Teachers can model this self-assessment by talking about how their own reading has changed.

SUMMARY

Although standardized tests and reading inventories provide general measures of student comprehension abilities, they provide little situation- or process-specific information that can give clues about how best to help these students comprehend better. A classroom teacher can get additional information by observing students in a variety of settings in the classroom itself. Indeed, many teaching activities, including the think-aloud procedure, can be used to gather data about specific students' reading strategies. For intensive diagnosis of one student, this data can be gathered systematically with ethnographic note taking. A remedial teacher can also select various natural tasks in which to observe the student's strategies through observation, questioning, and free recall. All teachers are urged to exercise caution in drawing conclusions from informal observation, but if used with care, the comprehension assessment checklist provided in this chapter can be used to structure the planning and summarizing of observations. This should result in useful instructional information because it encourages the teacher to look at all the comprehension processes and contexts. Finally, portfolio assessment offers a useful qualitative alternative to testing. Moreover, students can study their own portfolios to become more aware of their own strengths and weaknesses, and to be actively involved in setting their own reading goals.

SELF-CHECK TEST

1. Why do you need to supplement the information gained in standardized tests and informal inventories?
2. Define the following.

   multiple-context approach
   think-aloud procedure
   comprehension assessment procedure
   free recall
   portfolio assessment
   ethnographic note taking
   richness of retellings
3. Answer true or false.
   ____ (a) The comprehension assessment checklist should be used to prescribe specific process instruction for each student in every class.
   ____ (b) The comprehension assessment checklist can be used to provide additional clues as to possible instructional procedures for classes and specific students.
   ____ (c) Only short passages should be used for assessment.
   ____ (d) Only long passages should be used for assessment.
   ____ (e) Only content-area assignments should be used for assessment.
   ____ (f) Only basal stories should be used for assessment.
   ____ (g) Only motivational materials should be used for assessment.

SUGGESTED ACTIVITIES

1. For a specific student, plan three assessment sessions using natural tasks. Plan your questions and procedure for each.
2. Administer your planned informal multiple-context assessment (see Activity 1). Take careful notes. Summarize your data using the comprehension assessment checklist.
3. If you are currently teaching, use the comprehension assessment checklist for a specific student. What have you learned? Can you plan some instruction as a result? What needs to be done next?

4. For one specific student, practice ethnographic note taking. As often as possible, take time to observe that student involved in natural classroom tasks. Jot down your observations in an informal journal. Do this for a couple of weeks. What hypotheses are starting to develop?

5. With one student, or with a small group of students, try the think-aloud procedure. What happens? Are they learning from this experience? What are you learning about them? How could you keep a record of your observations?

6. Begin reading portfolios for your students. What do you already have available that can be filed in these folders? What else could you collect during the rest of the year? Describe your plans.

REFERENCES

Brown, C. S., & Lytle, S. L. (1988). Merging assessment and instruction: Protocols in the classroom. In S. M. Glazer, L. W. Searfoss, & L. M. Gentile (Eds.), *Reexamining reading diagnosis: New trends and procedures*, Newark, Del.: International Reading Association. (pp. 94–102).

Hunter, W. J., Kendall, J., & Mason, J. (1979, September). *Which comprehension? Artifacts in the measurement of reading comprehension*. Paper presented at the annual convention of the American Psychological Association, New York.

Irwin, P. A., & Mitchell, J. N. (1983). A procedure for assessing the richness of retellings. *Journal of Reading, 26,* 391–396.

Irwin, J. W., Pulver, C., & Koch, K. (1983). A new technique for improving reading teachers' diagnoses. Unpublished manuscript, Loyola University of Chicago.

Johnston, P. (1984). Prior knowledge and reading comprehension test bias. *Reading Research Quarterly, 19,* 219–239.

Johnston, P. (1987). Teachers as evaluation experts. *Reading Teacher, 40,* 744–748.

Lytle, S. L. (1982). *Exploring comprehension style: A study of twelfth grade readers' transactions with text.* Doctoral dissertation, University of Pennsylvania. *Dissertation Abstracts International, 43,* 2295A.

McCan, J. (1983). *The relationship between specific processing abilities and traditional measures of comprehension skills.* Unpublished doctoral dissertation, Purdue University.

Morrow, L. M. (1988). Retelling stories as a diagnostic tool. In S. M. Glazer, L. W. Searfoss, & L. M. Gentile, (Eds.), *Reexamining reading diagnosis: New trends and procedures* (pp. 128–149). Newark, Del.: International Reading Association.

Myers, J., & Lytle, S. L. (1986). Assessment of the learning process. *Exceptional Children, 53,* 138–144.

Royer, J. M., & Cunningham, D. J. (1981). On the theory and measurement of reading comprehension. *Contemporary Educational Psychology, 6,* 187–216.

Shanahan, T., Kamil, M. L., & Tobin, A. W. (1982). Cloze as a measure of intersentential comprehension. *Reading Research Quarterly, 17,* 229–255.

Smith, G. B. (1988). Physical arrangement, grouping, and ethnographic notetaking. In S. M. Glazer, L. W. Searfoss, & L. M. Gentile (Eds.), *Reexamining reading diagnosis: New trends and procedures* (pp. 169–177). Newark, Del.: International Reading Association.

Valencia, S., & Pearson, P. D. (1987). Reading assessment: Time for a change. *Reading Teacher, 40*, 726–732.

Winograd, P., & Paris, S. G. (1988). Improving reading assessment. In *The heath transcripts*. Lexington, Mass.: D. C. Heath.

Wixson, K. K., & Peters, C. W. (1987). Comprehension assessment: Implementing an interactive view of reading. *Educational Psychologist, 22*, 333–356.

Wixson, K. K., Peters, C. W., Weber, E. M., & Roeber, E. D. (1987). New directions in statewide reading assessment. *Reading Teacher, 40*, 749–754.

12

DEVELOPMENTAL AND REMEDIAL APPLICATIONS: SOME EXAMPLES

Throughout this book, activities for encouraging students to develop specific processing strategies have been suggested. At this point, you may be wondering how all these activities can be incorporated into an effective program for teaching comprehension.

In working with teachers who have read the first part of this manuscript, I have found that they generally fall into two categories, which I will call (1) "focused subskill" lesson planners and (2) "meaningful, holistic" lesson planners. Teachers in the first category are very organized. They make up a list of specific processes that they want to teach and, for each, they make up a specific strategy lesson. When watching these talented teachers teaching these lessons, however, I have had the uneasy feeling that something is missing. Do you know what?

Teachers in the second category are fully committed to the concept of reading as a meaningful, holistic process. They arrange meaningful reading situations and then do everything necessary to teach the students how to comprehend in that situation. In particular, I have seen this procedure used with poor comprehenders in remedial one-to-one tutoring situations. Again, while watching, I have been plagued by the uneasy feeling that this is not the whole answer. I remember that when I mentioned this to one graduate student who was doing this, she threw up her arms and said, "I don't get it. So what *do* you want, anyway?" Does this express your feeling?

The tension between holistic and subskill approaches is clearly not new in discussions of reading methodology. It is theoretically resolved by saying that there are identifiable subprocesses but that they interact (the interactive hypothesis) in order for comprehension to occur. But how is it resolved operationally for teaching?

In my opinion, teachers need to be able to do both, depending on the situation. Too much subprocess instruction will result in separation of strategies from the real purposes of reading. A completely holistic program may result in overwhelming students with random advice, with little opportunity for immediate reinforcement and practice when a need is identified. A balanced approach will result in the learning of strategies that are useful to the learner. (See Chapter Two for a complete discussion of process-teaching methodology.)

This chapter begins with a review of what you have learned so far. Then, an overall approach to designing focused lessons and techniques for integrating strategy instruction into naturalistic settings will be discussed. Finally, to encourage your own creative thinking, you will consider some fictional descriptions of classroom and remedial teachers who are beginning to use what they know about comprehension to help their students become better comprehenders. These examples cover only a small part of what can be done on a day-to-day basis. They are designed to show you how easy it is to get started. The reader is encouraged to write a similar example describing plans for his or her own teaching situation.

A BRIEF REVIEW

So what have you learned so far? Before looking at the examples, you should probably review the material to be implemented. First, you learned some general considerations in teaching comprehension. These included E-M-Q-A and other basic considerations (see Chapter Two), such as creating a literate environment, using a variety of materials, helping students to make the horizontal transformation of strategies across content areas, giving students ownership of the reading activities, accepting multiple answers, using explicit strategy instruction (see Figure 12-1), scaffolding, giving substantive feedback, stressing the reading and writing connection, and using discussion to promote active strategies. Take time to review each of these concepts before reading any further. Try to complete Figure 12-1.

FIGURE 12-1   Review: Explicit Process Instruction

E:
M:
Q:
A:

FIGURE 12-2   Review: Definitions of Basic Comprehension Processes

Microprocesses

Integrative processes

Macroprocesses

Elaborative processes

Metacognitive processes

You had also learned in Chapter One about the five processes that interact whenever a reader comprehends. Can you define these in Figure 12-2? If not, review Chapter One carefully. You may also wish to refer to Chapters Three through Six.

FIGURE 12-3   Review: Teaching of Basic Comprehension Processes

NAME	SUGGESTED ACTIVITY
I. Micro	
A. ____	____
B. ____	____
II. Integrative	
A. ____	____
B. ____	____
C. ____	____
III. Macro	
A. ____	
1. ____	____
2. ____	____
B. ____	____
1. ____	
2. ____	
3. ____	
4. ____	
IV. Elaborative	
A. ____	____
B. ____	____
C. ____	____
D. ____	____
E. ____	____
1. ____	____
2. ____	____
3. ____	____
4. ____	____
V. Metacognitive	
A. ____	____
B. ____	____

FIGURE 12-4   Review: Comprehension Contexts

```
 I.  Reader related
     A.
     B.                              Thus, teachers should...
     C.
     D.
II.  Text related
     A.
     B.
     C.                              Thus, teachers should...
     D.
     E.
III. Situation related
     A.
     B.                              Thus, teachers should...
```

Then you learned about what each of these processes entails and how to teach the subprocesses either incidentally or with explicit instruction. Try to name each subprocess and a way of teaching each by completing Figure 12-3. If you have trouble, review Chapters Three through Six. You may also want to review Figure 1-1 (p. 6).

In Part Two, you learned about the comprehension contexts that influence comprehension. What were they? How can each of these factors influence the way you teach? You will find this information in Chapters Seven through Nine if you have difficulty with Figure 12-4.

Chapters Ten and Eleven gave you some specific procedures for asking questions and informally observing students' abilities. Can you list the categories in the Ex-QAR questioning taxonomy in Figure 12-5? What is the multiple-context approach to assessment? Review Chapter Eleven if you have trouble describing this.

FIGURE 12-5   Review: The EX-QAR Taxonomy

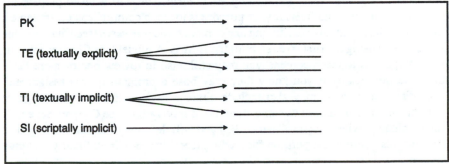

PLANNING BASAL AND CONTENT-AREA LESSONS:
THE ACTIVE READING COMPREHENSION ACTIVITY

If you are currently teaching reading with a basal reader, or if you are teaching reading in the content areas, you may have prescribed or preselected reading materials with which you are teaching. You may also have specific strategies you wish to teach. The following "active reading comprehension activity" (ARCA) is an outline of the planning steps that can be used each time you ask your students to read something specific, whether it is for a teacher-directed reading group or for another content area. Sometimes you will follow this structure when you are teaching comprehension strategies. Sometimes you will use it to facilitate comprehension of content-area materials.

Study Figure 12-6. Each lesson you conduct should include, in some way, the four stages indicated by the boxes. These correspond to (1) lesson selection, (2) before-reading activities (preparation), (3) during-reading activities, and (4) after-reading activities (comprehension development). If you have studied reading methods before, you will notice that ARCA is a form of the traditional directed reading activity. What makes ARCA new is the way the individual steps are carried out. Each step requires you to have read several chapters in this or a similar text.

Ideally, the first step is deciding on the objectives of the lesson. Are you trying to teach specific comprehension processes? Which ones? Or is your primary goal to teach content-area information? What information? What processes will need special attention to reach this goal? Once you have decided on your objectives, you can select the reading material to assign. To do this, you will also want to consider everything you know about the students' abilities (see Chapter Eleven) and the characteristics of the material (see Chapter Eight). You may not have many choices for material selection—that is, you may be required to use a certain book and to take the chapters in order. In that case, you will still want to be aware of the possible processing problems posed by the materials, you will always want to be aware of the comprehension tasks the material requires of your students (see Chapters One through Eight) for the purpose you or your students choose (see Chapter Nine), and you will want to be clear about whether your instructional purpose is to teach comprehension strategies or content-area information.

When you are giving the reading assignment, you will want to prepare the students to comprehend fully. If your purpose is to teach comprehension strategies, this will definitely involve discussing one or more basic processes (see Chapters One through Six) using the first three steps of the E-M-Q-A model (see Chapter Two). If your purpose is to teach content, you may still wish to review one or more basic processes, especially if you know they may pose a problem in this assignment. Preparing the students may also include either a review of prior knowledge or enrichment of such as well as some attention to motivation (see Chapter Seven). It may include previewing (see Chapter Six) and will definitely include either you or the students defining the purpose for reading (see Chapter Nine). Finally you may

FIGURE 12-6   Active Reading Comprehension Activity

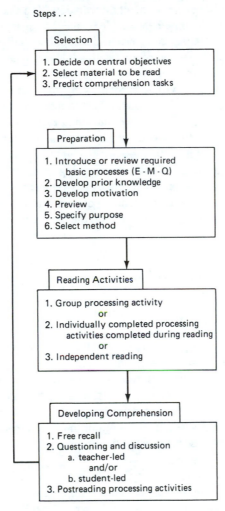

Steps . . .

Selection
1. Decide on central objectives
2. Select material to be read
3. Predict comprehension tasks

Preparation
1. Introduce or review required
   basic processes (E - M - Q)
2. Develop prior knowledge
3. Develop motivation
4. Preview
5. Specify purpose
6. Select method

Reading Activities
1. Group processing activity
   or
2. Individually completed processing
   activities completed during reading
   or
3. Independent reading

Developing Comprehension
1. Free recall
2. Questioning and discussion
   a. teacher-led
      and/or
   b. student-led
3. Postreading processing activities

choose to give the students a reading strategy or to have them select their own (see Chapter Nine).

Several options are available for procedures used during reading. If you are teaching a process, this will be the activity step of the E-M-Q-A model. You may wish to have them complete individual, guided processing activities (see Chapters One through Six and Ten), you may wish to conduct a group processing activities (see Chapter Two), or you may feel that they are ready to apply the chosen reading method independently. The latter is as important as guided reading; independence is the goal of reading instruction and should be practiced whenever students are ready.

After the material has been read, you have yet another opportunity to teach comprehension processes and/or content information. You also have an opportunity to assess what they have comprehended. To do these things, you may wish to use a free recall strategy (see Chapter Eleven), questioning—either by you or by the students (see Chapter Ten)—or other postreading activities (see Chapters One through Six). An E-M-Q-A model with process questions can be used to help students answer questions and do activities, especially for those students who are having problems (see Chapter Two), or it can be used to teach processes that were unexpectedly difficult. Finally, the arrow indicates that information gained during this stage can be used to select the next set of objectives and materials.

The point of all this is to plan lessons that get the students actively involved in reading comprehension. This includes involving them before, during, and after reading. After reading this book, you probably have enough knowledge to plan these lessons yourself based on your understanding of your students, the materials, and the goals of the curriculum. You need not rely on the basal or content-area textbook to plan your lessons.

INTEGRATION OF STRATEGY INSTRUCTION INTO NATURALISTIC SETTINGS

If you are teaching in a whole-language classroom or if you are using literature to teach reading, then you are less likely to plan focused lessons on a regular basis. If your students are reading self-selected materials at their own pace or working on individual or collaborative projects, then you are probably more likely to interact with the students during individual conferences and small-group meetings. These naturalistic settings in which students are involved in whole, meaningful, self-selected reading projects provide numerous opportunities for teachers to help students become active comprehenders through strategy lessons, conference questions and feedback, and group discussion.

For instance, when conferencing with a particular student, you may find out that this student is having trouble understanding important implicit information. You can then do explicit process instruction on the spot. Explain and model the strategy for the student as an offer of assistance for this particular reading project. You can also integrate process questions into your conference so that the student can begin to clarify for himself or herself what strategies are useful. Finally, you can ask questions that encourage active responding—those focused on story structure, elaborations of all types, and so on. These individual interactions that occur while a student is reading a book or researching a topic will have a powerful influence on the strategies the student selects.

You may also have opportunities to conduct strategy lessons during literature discussion groups or meetings of a collaborative learning group. Wait until a strategy is needed. Then explain and model the strategy using the books the students are reading. Encourage the students to discuss the strategies they are using. Model asking questions that involve all the processes. This will affect the way the students conduct their own group meetings when you are not there.

Finally, some occasions may arise when you wish to discuss a specific strategy with the whole class. Again, the strategy would be one that had caused some problems in several situations and one that you felt many of the students were ready to learn. These can be short strategy lessons conducted before students get to work on their individual projects.

The point of all this is that all of the basic considerations for teaching comprehension discussed in Chapter Two and all of the information about specific processes and contexts described in Chapters Three through Nine as well as the ideas about questioning and diagnosis in Chapters Ten and Eleven can be as useful in naturalistic student-directed settings as they are in more traditional teacher-directed programs.

TEACHING COMPREHENSION IN BASAL READING GROUPS: AN EXAMPLE

At first glance, the foregoing heading may seem absurd: of course you teach comprehension as part of your basal reading program! If you are used to working with a basal series in which many of the approaches described in this book are not used, however, you may be wondering how you can integrate these new ideas into the traditional approach with which you are familiar. The following fictional example describes a teacher who began to do this throughout the year:

Ms. Venturi taught third grade in a small town in Massachusetts. Though she tried very hard and had the reputation of being an excellent teacher, she was dissatisfied with her reading groups. It just seemed as if the students left at the end of the year with the same problems they had at the beginning.

After reading this book, Ms. Venturi realized that she could do more to teach comprehension. She didn't have time to sit down and write a whole new set of lessons, so she decided to make up specific activities throughout the year whenever she thought of them. All of these activities were designed to supplement the basal series with which she was already familiar. Here is what happened....

A few anaphora activities were already in her basal series. She always found that some students found these to be easy while others stumbled through, so she made up a series of activities using the contents of the relevant basal stories. With each reading group, she waited until the need for studying anaphora arose while reading a basal story. Then she introduced the strategy as something the students could do to understand the story better. After the children worked on a couple of her activities, she directed them to another story in the basal reader with numerous pronouns, and she conducted a group processing session so they could practice applying what they had learned. She used this procedure for several other strategies as well.

Ms. Venturi also found that the questions she asked in reading group sessions began to change. She began to ask for different kinds of information, such as connecting and slot-filling inferences. Because she used process questions, students were discussing their reasoning procedures. Several times, when they were having trouble, she modeled her own inference processes and discussed the importance of inferring while reading. She always asked students to summarize. For several lessons, she encouraged students to monitor their comprehension, and, when there were problems, they discussed remedies. With nonfiction materials, they discussed the four possible sources for an answer to a question, and students got involved in asking their own questions. She realized that everyone in her slowest group was bored with her word-attack approach, and she began to teach this group with a meaning emphasis similar to that used in the other groups.

Ms. Venturi also found that there were many independent learning center packets for comprehension that she could construct for students to work on in their free time after she had used E-M-Q-A to introduce the strategy. She designed "create your own story" activities to encourage story grammar awareness, using basal stories as the beginnings. She cut up old books from the library sale and inserted elaboration questions for the students to answer while they were reading. Indeed, while working on these packets, Ms. Venturi found that many exciting writing projects were occurring to her. She decided to experiment with having students keep a journal of reading responses (see Chapter Five), and she decided to do story writing during the reading period.

In the course of the year, Ms. Venturi began to see changes in reading group sessions. For one thing, they were more interesting. Everyone was actively involved in the process of comprehending. Moreover, Ms. Venturi found that her content-area lessons had become more interesting too. As she taught processes in reading groups, she found it easy to reinforce them in content lessons. Using EMQA and ARCA, she was helping students transform processes to improve their comprehension in social studies, science, and math, and it was making these subjects much easier to teach. Students were actually learning from the textbooks.

Ms. Venturi was really pleased with all these changes. They had not involved all that much extra work, yet she really felt as if she was teaching comprehension. It was far from perfect, but it was a start!

TEACHING COMPREHENSION IN A WHOLE-LANGUAGE CLASSROOM: AN EXAMPLE

Mr. Chung was teaching fifth grade in an inner-city environment near Chicago. Several years ago, he had become committed to the whole-language philosophy that language was learned through use in meaningful situations. He observed many teachers who were integrating subjects based on a whole-language philosophy, and he began his own program last year. All-in-all it was going pretty well. His students were much more motivated than ever, and they were doing more reading and writing than before.

Mr. Chung was now feeling frustrated, however, about two students in the class who did not seem to be progressing very well. He knew that they were reading significantly below grade level, and that they were often frustrated and confused. One had successfully persuaded a more able student to help him, but he seemed to want her to do the work for him. The other student did as little as possible and was still a discipline problem. Her parents were complaining about the "lack of structure" in the reading curriculum and blaming him for their daughter's problems.

After reading this book, Mr. Chung realized that there were some specific ways that he could help these students read better. He began to use extensive ethnographic note taking and other multiple-context procedures to assess their reading strategies. He noted that Jim liked to read books about animals but had trouble with expository structure. Susie read passively and was always sure that her opinions were "dumb." Now he was getting some specific ideas about how to help....

Mr. Chung also found that his individual conferences with other students and the literature discussion sessions that he led were also beginning to change. He felt that he better understood how to help students to become more strategic. He promoted metacognitive awareness by asking frequent process questions and by providing explicit strategy instruction when it was needed. He also encouraged elaboration by providing suggestions for new types of responses to use in their journal: They could write a new ending, illustrate the character at the end, write about something similar that happened to them, write about how they would have felt if they were one of the characters, write about why they liked the story, and so on.

Moreover, he was beginning to see how an understanding of the comprehension process would influence many of the things he said and did throughout the school day. He found himself asking a process question when a student asked him a question at recess, encouraging elaborative responses when teaching the required textbook on Illinois history, and incorporating free recall analysis into his portfolio assessment...and this was just the beginning!

TEACHING COMPREHENSION IN REMEDIAL SITUATIONS: AN EXAMPLE

If you are a remedial reading teacher or a reading clinician, your understanding of comprehension will affect how you diagnose and how you remediate. In the fictional case study that follows, a thorough understanding of comprehension was used to guide the program. Pretend that you were the remedial teacher involved. Would you have acted as described? Why or why not?

Armando was in the third grade. He was referred to you by the classroom teacher who said that he seemed to have comprehension problems. Initial tests indicated that his word recognition skills were good, even slightly above grade level.

However, on tests of comprehension, he scored at about the first-grade level. Evidently his teacher was right.

You decided to use the comprehension assessment inventory to structure your thinking about Armando (see Chapter Eleven). You noted that although Armando read words accurately, he didn't seem to use any intonation or to divide them into meaningful phrases. Although he seemed to have a good vocabulary and adequate prior knowledge when questioned, he was able to recall very little, even when prompted. He said he was interested in the topics at hand and seemed to want to do well. He also said that he considered himself to be a good reader and that he thought he had done well on the tests. When you gave him carefully selected second-grade–level short stories, you asked him to look at the pictures and guess what the story would be about. Then he read it to you. After the reading, you asked him why he had read the story. He answered, "So you could see if I could get the words."

Taken together, this all seemed to indicate to you that Armando thought of "reading" as accurate word identification. Thus, by his standards, he was a good reader, and word calling without comprehending was all right. To verify this, you asked him questions about his concept of reading and found that you were right.

You decided to begin a remedial program with very simple materials in which meaning was always the focus. With Armando at your side, you went to the library and selected books that he was interested in reading. You worked on dramatic readings together, explaining, modeling, and practicing chunking, and discussing how the characters felt and why they said what they did. You began to encourage him to write his own stories, so that he could understand how and why print was meant to be meaningful. You also asked Armando's teacher to emphasize meaning rather than individual words when working with him.

Once Armando began to see reading as meaningful, things moved fairly quickly. His teacher was reinforcing him for his answers to comprehension questions, and he was very excited about this. He seemed to be able to apply his knowledge of anaphora, and so on, from oral language to the written language. He was able to give you literal meanings for passages much more often, and, after modeling, discussion, and practice, he was also able to select what was important, though he still had trouble with summarizing for you. Another problem that you began to note was that Armando was still very text oriented. He now seemed to think of reading as getting the literal meaning from the page, and he was still having trouble understanding third-grade materials. By now, it was the end of the year, so it was time to write recommendations for the new teacher who would be coming in in the fall.

You recommended that Armando be encouraged to interact actively with the material, to use schema-related processes. He needed to work with easy materials on summarizing and elaborating, especially in terms of prior-knowledge elaborations and predictions. Moreover, he still needed to develop basic chunking fluency with more difficult materials, so you recommended that he be encouraged to read throughout the summer and the following year and that he be assigned someone with whom he could discuss these books. Finally, the comprehension remediation needed eventually to include content-area as well as narrative materials, because he needed to develop macrolevel skills for all types of materials to function effectively in the intermediate grades.

TEACHING COMPREHENSION IN THE CONTENT AREAS: EXAMPLES

What does all this mean to a content-area teacher? If you are currently teaching or plan to teach in a content-area classroom, you may be asking yourself this question. You may have understood the individual concepts as you read through this text, but now you may be feeling unclear about how it will all work in your day-to-day content-area activities. If you are planning to be a reading consultant for secondary teachers, you may be wondering how to translate all this information into readily accessible formats for the teachers in your school. So, let us visit a fictional high school to take a look at some content-area teachers who are beginning to teach comprehension. (Note that although these examples are from a fictional high school, they are applicable for all grades that have content-area lessons including, generally, grades 4 through 12.)

Mr. Brown teaches an elective auto mechanics course in George Washington High School. At his other school, the only students in his class were the ones who couldn't get into the regular college-preparatory curriculum, but here things are different. Many college-bound students who own their own cars sign up on the waiting list. Even intelligent girls who are trying to break stereotypical patterns have the courage to sign up for this class. When he took this job two years ago, he thought it was too good to be true. They even let him buy the shiny new auto repair manuals shelved neatly around the room.

But now Mr. Brown is feeling discouraged. Every semester, he has assigned readings in those shiny repair manuals, and every semester he has to go back and explain everything himself, just as in the old days. "It's really too bad," he thinks to himself. "There would be so much more they could learn if they could just read!"

Mr. Brown remembers having studied this text in college. At home that night, he turns to Part Two, "Recognizing Factors That Affect Basic Comprehension Processes." In reading Chapter Seven, Mr. Brown realizes that most of his students have little background in the industrial arts. They know very little about tools and nothing about engines. The vocabulary and the basic procedural knowledge being assumed in the manuals are unknown to them. In reading Chapter Eight, he realizes that although the text is at their level, it is poorly organized and provides little opportunity for review. The rest of that evening is spent listing basic vocabulary and mechanical processes that the students need in order to interpret the manuals.

Beginning the next day, Mr. Brown uses the advice given in Chapter Seven. He demonstrates basic procedures and lets the students practice them. He asks inferential and elaborative questions. He introduces basic vocabulary in meaningful groups and shows the students concrete examples and real engine parts. After he feels that the students are conversant in the basic terminology, he makes his first reading assignment. He remembers to preview, explain the purpose, and give them a reading method. While doing this, he shows them how the chapter is organized and how they should take notes for review using a hierarchical summary procedure. The students come to class the next day with their notes in hand. To his amazement, they are ready to work on their automobiles.

Ms. Garcia teaches down the hall from Mr. Brown. She fully understands his complaints: all of her students complain that their text is impossible to understand, too, and she is teaching the middle track only! For years she has tried to understand why. After all, it is a geometry text written at the ninth-grade level, according to the publisher. All of her students read at the ninth-grade level or above, according to the reading specialist. Moreover, they don't really seem to have trouble with the concepts when she explains them in class.

Mr. Brown shows Ms. Garcia the readability checklist. Perhaps it can give her some ideas. He also tells her that according to the ARCA structure, the first step in promoting comprehension is understanding the strategies required by the materials. Skeptically, she goes home to analyze the textbook one more time. The first thing she notices is that only one example is provided for each concept and that new concepts are introduced rapidly in succession. She also notices that the definitions are usually more abstract than they need to be and that they are written in needlessly long sentences. There are no main ideas, introductions, or summaries, and practice problems are saved for the very end of the chapter. She is beginning to understand why they are having trouble!

Ms. Garcia decides to try an experiment using ARCA. Before assigning the next chapter section, (she has decided to assign the chapters in small sections), she provides an introduction in which she reviews important prior knowledge. She points out why the section is important and what they should learn from it. They discuss the best strategy for reading for this purpose, which includes studying examples, paraphrasing definitions, and trying practice problems while they are reading. She models these strategies while they read the first part together, and she gives them a study guide that encourages them to complete these strategies while they read.

The next day, they discuss the new concepts, and she asks them to make up their own examples. She is amazed to find out that the majority of the students seem to have learned from reading the text. She asks them how the study guide worked, and they all say it was helpful. As a class, they design a study guide for the next section. Gradually, during the semester, the students become able to use the text as a learning tool. Ms. Garcia is very pleased that she has taught them how to comprehend math textbooks. She feels that this will make a real difference in their future performance in other classes.

Finally, Mr. Stoczek is the football coach at George Washington High School. He has a new freshman on his team this year who promises to be the best thing to happen since football was invented. But there is one big problem. This promising young star is failing all his classes, and his parents are thinking of taking him off the team.

Because Mr. Stoczek is taking a required reading methods course, he immediately suspects that maybe Johnny cannot read. He has Johnny do some oral reading and free and prompted recall on his assignments and finds that although Johnny identifies words very well, he does not seem to understand what he reads. A free recall analysis shows him that Johnny does not know how to select at either the microlevel or the macrolevel. Using the comprehension assessment checklist, Mr. Stoczek realizes that Johnny can't identify main ideas or summarize. He is motivated but extremely anxious and he doesn't expect to succeed. A reading comprehension interview reveals that Johnny has little awareness of study strategies or how to vary his reading methods to increase recall.

Mr. Stoczek requests a brief staff meeting with Johnny's other teachers. Two teachers and the school reading specialist (all of whom have read this book) are able to meet during lunch the next day. Mr. Stoczek shares his observations of Johnny's problems, and the teachers comment that they have many students who seem to have similar needs. After much discussion, the teachers decide to work with the reading consultant to integrate comprehension instruction into their curricula. In particular, they decide to experiment with teaching microselection and macroprocessing using cooperative groups working with the hierarchal summary procedure. The reading specialist agrees to teach these strategies in the content classes, and the content teachers begin to devise ways to reinforce the strategies throughout the year. Also, during supervised study periods, the teachers (including Mr. Stoczek) plan to work with students (including Johnny) who are having trouble with these processes.

At the end of the year, the teachers meet to discuss the results of their experiment. They are very pleased with their students' progress. They feel that all the students are studying more efficiently and remembering more. They have also found that they have incidentally taught many other processes like connective inference, prediction, and metacognitive processes even though they had not planned to do so. "One processing discussion just led to another!" They decide to continue the program the following year, and they feel that they are ready to teach the processes without the help of the reading specialist.

Oh, yes, Mr. Stoczek is happy, too. Johnny's grades have improved, and he has been able to stay on the team. Next week, they play for the championship.

YOUR TURN

If you found this chapter to be unnecessary, then you have probably already begun to teach comprehension strategies. If you found it helpful, then you are probably now ready to begin to apply the strategies suggested in this book. It is important that you not use the strategies described in this chapter as a template for your own decisions. Rather, you can use them to stimulate your own creativity and situation-specific responsiveness. In Figure 12-7 there is space for you to begin to write your own example. Pretend that you are describing your own classroom a year from now. In what ways are you teaching comprehension? What changes are still to be made? Skim this book (and others) for ideas. Have fun!

FIGURE 12-7   Final Example

Your name   _____

Date (one year from now)   _____

Comprehension Instruction Methods:

Results:

Changes yet to be made:

A FINAL NOTE: "OUTER CONTEXT"

Throughout my writing of this book, I have been aware of what Duffy (1982) has called the "outer context" affecting teacher effectiveness. By this he is referring to factors outside the classroom that affect the ways teachers can teach. This would include parental, administrative, and districtwide pressures to use specific materials in a lockstep manner. For instance, Shannon (1983) has gathered evidence to support the notion that because of the emphasis on using test scores and related scientific rationality to prove a district's effectiveness, classroom teachers feel pressure to apply basal programs stringently as if they were the only way to teach reading. He also found that this pressure to simply implement materials "alienates teachers from their reading instruction" (p. 71).

Thus, I have asked myself whether it is realistic to expect classroom teachers to use the active approach suggested in this book. I have asked teachers the same thing. The answer seems to be a resounding, "Yes." Teachers want to feel that they can use their own knowledge to increase the quality of instruction in their classrooms. It is my hope that this book will help teachers communicate new assessment and instructional ideas to parents and administrators in such a way that reading instruction becomes more than the mere management of commercial programs; content-area instruction is expanded to include content-area reading comprehension instruction; and comprehension is taught as an active, meaningful, constructive process. Perhaps the most appropriate way to end, then, is with a poem describing that active process—

> Unlock the shape of a letter, a word,
> Find a meaning that fits the shape.
> Engage the meaning into a train of several such,
> Link the train to others, to many.
> Carry a cargo of ideas along
> Link, unlink, and sort almost unaware.
> Check the cargo, validate the load.
> Come to a check point, check.
>
> Repeat the process, repeat.
> Arrive at a destination carrying the
> Necessary, the useful, the valued.
>
> And find the meaning rainbow wrapped in color,
> emotion, response, and inner knowledge.
> Find the cargo is no longer his, theirs;
> Now, it belongs to you.
> (Reba Estra, 1989. Reprinted by permission.)

REFERENCES

Duffy, G. (1982, December). *Context variables in reading teacher effectiveness*. Paper presented at the annual meeting of the National Reading Conference, Clearwater Beach, Florida.

Shannon, P. (1983). The use of commercial reading materials in American elementary schools. *Reading Research Quarterly, 19*, 68–85.

INDEX